Tho
Anita

Promoting Gender Equality Abroad

Gender-Diskussion
Gender Discussion

Band/Volume 24

LIT

Promoting Gender Equality Abroad

An Assessment of EU Action in the External Dimension

edited by

Thomas Kruessmann and Anita Ziegerhofer

LIT

Cover image: Dr.in Larissa Ogertschnig

Printed with the support of the University of Graz

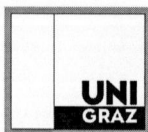

Bibliographic information published by the Deutsche Nationalbibliothek
The Deutsche Nationalbibliothek lists this publication in the Deutsche
Nationalbibliografie; detailed bibliographic data are available on the Internet at
http://dnb.d-nb.de.

ISBN 978-3-643-90616-8

A catalogue record for this book is available from the British Library

© LIT VERLAG GmbH & Co. KG Wien,
Zweigniederlassung Zürich 2017
Klosbachstr. 107
CH-8032 Zürich
Tel. +41 (0) 44-251 75 05
E-Mail: zuerich@lit-verlag.ch   http://www.lit-verlag.ch
Distribution:
In the UK: Global Book Marketing, e-mail: mo@centralbooks.com
In North America: International Specialized Book Services, e-mail: orders@isbs.com
In Germany: LIT Verlag Fresnostr. 2, D-48159 Münster
Tel. +49 (0) 2 51-620 32 22, Fax +49 (0) 2 51-922 60 99, e-mail: vertrieb@lit-verlag.de

In Austria: Medienlogistik Pichler-ÖBZ, e-mail: mlo@medien-logistik.at
e-books are available at www.litwebshop.de

ÜBERSICHT

Introduction and Theoretical Framework

CHAPTER 1:

INTRODUCTION

Thomas KRUESSMANN and Anita ZIEGERHOFER

The Treaty on European Union (TEU) explicitly stipulates that equality and the respect for human rights are foundational values of the European Union (EU) that shall not only be promoted within the EU, but also in the external context (Articles 2 and 3 TEU). This undisputably also comprises the promotion of gender equality and of the respect for human rights of women in third states. While first European efforts to address the disadvantaged situation of women abroad can be traced back to the 1950s, ever since the 1990s the EU has invested considerable efforts into the development of a policy of gender equality promotion in the external dimension. Today this policy is based on a whole range of detailed policy documents and instruments and is being implemented world-wide. It is both an independent policy, based on specific policy documents and instruments, as well as a cross-cutting policy objective pursued in the framework of other external policies, in particular development policy, the European Neighbourhood Policy (ENP), trade policy, and foreign policy. The EU promotes gender equality through three principal instruments: mainstreaming, specific targeted projects, and political dialogue.

A number of scholars of different disciplines have so far analysed individual aspects of EU gender equality promotion in the external dimension. Several thereof have focused on EU activities in specific regions, in particular Latin America, Africa, and Central Asia. A second strand of publications has targeted and assessed the use of individual instruments, in particular mainstreaming. Some publications have addressed the role of gender in individual EU external policies, like development and trade policy. Existing literature on the topic of EU gender equality promotion abroad is spread out over various journals and a few edited publications while the existing knowledge has not recently been comprehensively presented in a separate publication explicitly devoted to the topic.

It was against this background that in November 2013 a conference at the University of Graz (Austria) was held that brought together scholars of various academic backgrounds working on the topic of EU external gender equality promotion. The goal was to discuss and share their analysis and assessment of EU policy-making and implementation, both in terms of methodological questions and in terms of research results. Now, more than three years later and taking into account the lapse of time, the authors' contributions have been re-worked, their hypotheses re-tested and their results re-contextualised.

What finally emerged is a book that starts from the notion of the EU as a normative actor and asks how the EU conceptualises its mandate to promote gender equality in the various "abroads" that it faces. The EU is often seen as applying a double standard in what it asks of its own Member States to do and what it requires third countries, esp. accession candidates or countries in the neighbourhood, to do. The book's concept takes this idea one step further by exploring how the EU, despite its overall commitment to norm creation and diffusion, is acting under distinctly separate sets of logic in the various policy fields and vis-à-vis different stakeholders. The same normative commitment to gender equality, when filtered through the particular logic of the various policy fields, leads to different types of external action with rather different outcomes.

The book begins with a conceptual framework to contextualise the idea of interventions in third countries' domestic policy. Using the experience of the Western Balkans and Eastern European countries in EU association and accession, *Marina Blagojević Hughson* ("Conceptualisation of the Gender Policy Field") shows that policy interventions have different dynamics in the respective countries. There is variety in the impact that they have on civil society engagement and awareness, especially when it comes to promoting gender equality. And ultimately, there is no uniform result in terms of effectiveness and efficiency.

Building on this conceptual framework, the book then distinguishes three policy fields or "abroads" in which EU external action operates:
- the EU enlargement scenario vis-à-vis specific accession candidates where the "carrots and sticks" approach is most powerful;
- specific policy fields which appear to be driven by technology and / or economic rationales, but which seriously impact on the goal of gender equality;
- more distant, from the EU's point of view, regions of the world such as South Africa and Latin America where the EU, beyond the issue of trade, tries to realise its ambition as a global gender actor in inter-regional relations.

The first policy field devoted to situations of EU accession and enlargement begins with *Karolina Ristova-Aasterud*'s paper "The Gender Dimension of EU Enlargement: A Case Study of Macedonia as a Candidate Country" which gives an analytical overview of how the process of European integration has been affecting the advancement of gender equality in Macedonia as a candidate country, thus exemplifying the effectiveness of EU's gender equality policies in the enlargement process. The following article of *Aida Orgocka and Nikolina Kenig* ("The EU's Role in Combating Domestic Violence against Women in South Eastern Europe – Perspectives from Albania and Macedonia") discusses the EU's role in combating domestic violence against women within the larger field of gender-based violence. They argue that the EU is in a singular position to exert stronger influence with a heftier impact, if it clearly identifies how to capitalise on its exceptional significance as a policy-setter and pathmaker for these countries.

The second policy field takes the readers into trade and climate change. *Anna van der Vleuten* ("The Conflicting Logics of Regionalism and Gender Mainstreaming: EU Trade Agreements with Southern Africa") shows how the dominance of a non-interventionist market logic in economic integration and the conflicting logics of trade liberalisation and gender mainstreaming create actor constellations in which actors promoting gendermainstreaming are disempowered. *Sam Wong*'s paper ("Gendering Green Climate Finance: Potential and Limitations") shows us that the Green Climate Fund is not effective in achieving gender equality for a great number of reasons. He advocates a deeper understanding of the impact of climate change on vulnerable men in developing countries, thus shifting attention from 'women-specificity' to 'gender-sensitivity'.

The third policy field investigates the EU's approach to interregionalism. *Petra Debusscher* ("The Quality of Gender Equality Policies in EU Development Co-operation with South Africa") looks at the EU as a global gender actor. *Conny Roggeband* and *Andrea Ribeiro Hoffmann* ("Gendering EU-Latin American inter-regional relations") analyse to what extent and how gender has been addressed in EU-Latin America and Caribbean Inter-regional Relations in order to contribute to the discussion on the relevance of the (inter)regional level in the dynamics of norm diffusion and norm travelling in a multi-level-process of governance.

The major benefit of the approach of the book is that it breaks free from the Lisbon-inspired notion that the EU is a unitary (gender) actor and also from the self-reflective perspective on Member States. It enables the reader to look at the various strands of EU external action in its entirety. According to the policy fields and actors addressed, the goal of gender equality gets conceptualised and operationalised in different ways according to the logic of the respective policy field. The normative goal of promoting gender equality abroad thus gets absorbed and deformed by the different sets of logic in the respective policy fields (climate protection, trade promotion, EU accession, Neighbourhood policy).

At the stage of policy implementation, appropriate contextualisation is often an issue. Sometimes policy interventions simply fail to have an effect (for a variety of reasons), sometimes they produce a backlash and reinforce re-traditionalisation of the society in question. The effectiveness of policy interventions thus depends on a number of factors both inside the respective societies and between them, i.e. taking into account transnational and (sub-) regional initiatives. Ultimately, promotion of gender equality abroad cannot be achieved in a "once size fits all"-approach. It is an ambitious goal that is easily neglected and sometimes, due to lack of contextualisation, does not become effective.

As editors, we would like to express our gratitude for the financial support granted to the publication of these research findings by the Vice-Rector for Research of the University of Graz and the Dean of its Law Faculty.

CHAPTER 2:

CONCEPTUALISATION OF THE GENDER POLICY FIELD

Marina BLAGOJEVIĆ HUGHSON[1]

The EU's promotion of gender equality abroad is taking place in the complex and ever-changing contexts of the EU on the one hand, and the societies in question on the other. By engaging with these complexities my paper will bring new theoretical considerations to the issue, based on different insights from my multiple professional positions. The paper identifies, maps out and conceptualises contexts which are relevant for EU promotion of gender equality abroad, such as: 1. The transnational web of gender stakeholders where the EU is one, but not the exclusive agent in the field, 2. semiperipheral social contexts which bear the characteristics of specific gender regimes, and 3. the gender policy field itself, which has already been established in the "neighbouring countries" in a period of several decades. Instead of arguing for one specific approach or one specific perspective or one disciplinary angle, and instead of concentrating on one specific case study of one policy, this paper examines those interlinking complexities to conclude that contextualisation of policies is necessary as an on-going work in progress of 'translation and assemblage' (Clark, Bainton,Lendvai and Stubbs, 2015), but always with the critical edge on empirical data, facts and figures on the existing gender inequalities. Conceptualisation of the policy contexts as explained in this paper is seen as a necessary condition for adequate contextualisation, which clearly contributes to the effectiveness and impact of EU engagement in the field of gender equality.

"Over the past fifty years of development history, we have seen the repeated distortion of good ideas and innovative practices as they are lifted out of the political and historical context in which they evolved and rendered into formulas that are 'mainstreamed'. This usually involves divesting the idea of its cultural specificity, its political content, and generalizing it into a series of rituals and steps that simulate its original elements, but lacking the transformative power of the real thing. Thus good ideas, evolved to address specific development challenges, are altered into universally applicable panaceas. Transferring the correct rhetoric – buzzwords and catch phrases emptied of their original meaning – is a vital part of this legerdemain. This is not to question the transfer and replication of effective interventions

---

[1]   This paper is part of the project related to Social Inclusion, financed by the Ministry of Education, Science and Technological Development, Serbia (project No 47011).

for social justice and development, but the manner and motives for which it is done." (Srilatha Batliwala)

1. SELF POSITIONING: MULTIPLE PERSPECTIVES AND CROSS-SECTORAL APPROACH

This paper is largely based on my polyvalent professional / personal history which includes a combination of a number of different fields: 1. academic career 2. women's and peace activism in the 90-s in Serbia, 3. international expert engagements in the last 15 years (Balkans, Eastern Europe and Caucasus). During my professional career I experienced many different roles, and I was inhabiting different organisational settings (including universities in different countries, NGOs, governments in different countries, different international and transnational organisations, such as UN Women, UNDP, IFAD, EU Commission, EU Parliament etc.). As an academic, expert and activist who was moving between the sectors, subjects, disciplines, and moving from one country to another, I have been exposed to different experiences and diverse systems of thought. This permanent state of 'translation' between different fields and sectors is both challenging and heuristically rewarding. Cross-fertilisation of different types of knowledge allows for new insights and, hopefully, offers some kind of holistic understanding, in which different parts of the picture are not seen as antagonistic any more, but as a part of a larger circle of interconnected phenomena. This movement between the sectors and fields enables me to step out of the highly specialised technical discourses, academic and non-academic, and to move into the position of observation from the 'above and beyond', which allows for better understanding of long-run structural change. 'Translation' is thus becoming a key epistemic strategy for making critical policy studies (Clark, Bainton, Lendvai and Stubbs, 2015).

As a sociologist I am very much aware of the structural constraints, of slow societal transformations, of controversies over social and economic developments, limits of social engineering and risks coming from fast and imposed bureaucratic solutions. Therefore, I define beneficial public policies as those which are well contextualised, meaning that they find the right balance between what is desirable and what is possible in a certain society, and which can be both effective and efficient, while not producing profound counter-effects. Although all those terms might be challenged from different theoretical positions, this definition should be taken just as an effort to make further argumentation as clear as possible.

To clarify even more, I would define my own intellectual location as being a 'non-naïve idealist' and 'pro-active hyper-realist'. I refuse to see any collision between idealism and realism, and I believe in the possibility of intelligent, constructive and comprehensive intervention into social reality. However, it would be fair to say that in academia's immersion into the globalisation and Europeanisation narratives, it is becoming more and more difficult to express any 'outside' theoretical or political position without the serious threat of being misunderstood or being ascribed a certain ideological position (i.e. 'rightist, 'leftist', 'conservative', or 'Marxist') and ideologically confronted, or drawn into so-called 'academic debates' which often simply ignore very real differences in social contexts and different social locations of the authors.

As a feminist I fully accept the notion that knowledge is 'embedded' and 'embodied', meaning that it always comes from a certain context and is being made by those who occupy certain social locations and positions of power. This is why self-reflection, exposure and self-positioning are necessary practices in feminist knowledge production. Further on, knowledge which is produced about the semiperiphery of Europe (Eastern Europe, Southern Europe, 'neighbouring countries' or countries in the accession process)[2] is often lacking theoretical background which would allow better understanding of structural dispositions of societies in question. Societal contexts at the semiperiphery are being mostly ignored as givens, and instead they are approached as 'empty spaces' upon which a policy exercise could be performed, almost without limitations. When problems with this approach become evident, they are often addressed as 'problems of implementation', instead of problems emerging from the inadequate contextualisation. For an intellectual coming from the semiperiphery, I often find that the knowledge which is produced at the 'centre' is creating serious distortions and creating negative implications for public policies, including gender policies. Therefore, it is important to say that meanings and connotations, as well as discursive strategies, are always limited, even when they come from the centre, or, especially when they come from the centre (Blagojević and Yair, 2010)

The history of my own 'translations' between the sectors and, in fact, different contexts, is both inspiring and difficult, since institutions, organisations and groups function within their ghettoised discourses and practi-

---

[2] The naming of the specific regions is becoming increasingly difficult due to the fact that there is on-going process of classification in relation to the EU accession process. However, the very intention to name the 'semiperiphery' as a specific part of Europe is an effort to go beyond political classification, into the structural characteristics of different countries.

ces, and crossing borders is often a risky and self-marginalising strategy. But, for the sake of the argument which I want to develop here, it should be noted that I also have a history of very direct and concrete influences on public policies, locally, regionally and internationally. Just to mention a few cases, the European Parliament has brought a Resolution for the improvement of the position of women in South East Europe (Resolution, 2003)[3], relying on my study "Women's Situation in the Balkan Countries (Blagojević, 2003). Also, based on my research and expert projects a wave of activities related to the improvement of the position of rural women has started in the region of the Balkans (Hughson, 2015). Additionally, as an EU Commission expert on women in science (Enwise group expert), I have been included into a number of EU projects related to the improvement of the position of women in science at the EU level (i.e. Enwise Report, 2003). While being a leading expert on gender in Serbia for the Serbian National Plan to implement MDGs, I succeeded to include violence against women into the Millennium goals, which made Serbia the first country in the world to actually widen the scope of the Millennium Goals into that direction (2006). In 2014 I was engaged by the EU Commission to create the first Country Gender Profile Study for one accession country which was meant to be used as a background for IPA and EIDHR (Hughson, 2014). These are just a few of the examples which I bring forward only to be able to claim that strategic thinking about gender equality policies requires a cross-sectoral approach, which includes theory, research, as well as experiential knowledge (referring to both activism and expertise). Jeff Hearn defines this field as knowledges/policies/practices (Hearn, 1998). Academic knowledge can be very practical, and the other way around, experiential knowledge (from activism and expert work) can lead to deep and useful theoretical insights. There is a strong epistemic tradition in feminist theory related to knowledge production from 'below', such as 'stand point theory' (Harstock, 1983; Harding, 2004).

So, this text is bringing new theoretical considerations on the issue, combining all kinds of different insights and knowledge of the author. The text identifies, maps out and conceptualises contexts which are relevant for EU promotion of gender equality abroad, such as: 1. the transnational web of gender stakeholders where the EU is one, but not the exclusive agent in the field, 2. semiperipheral social contexts which bear the characteristics of specific gender regimes, and 3. the gender policy field itself, which has already been established in the 'neighbouring countries' in a period of se-

---

[3]   Women in South-East Europe, European Parliament Resolution on Women in South-East Europe (2003/2128(INI)).

veral decades. Instead of arguing for one specific approach, or one specific perspective, or one disciplinary angle, or concentrating on one specific case study of one policy, this text, on the contrary, examines those interlinking complexities, to conclude that contextualisation of policies is necessary as an on-going work in progress of 'translation and assemblage' (Clark, Bainton, Lendvai and Stubbs, 2015), but always with a critical edge on empirical data, facts and figures on the existing gender inequalities. Conceptualisation of the policy contexts exposed in this text is seen as a necessary condition for adequate contextualisation, which clearly contributes to effectiveness and impact of the EU engagement in the field of gender equality.

2. Transnational web of gender stakeholders

To understand how the policy interventions related to gender equality are actually being formulated and implemented, it is important to capture the complex transnational web of gender stakeholders, in which EU institutions and instruments represent only one, but not the exclusive actor or agent. The web of stakeholders is promoting gender equality, which as a policy object is being regulated by an ever-growing set of international and European conventions and documents, as well as national ones. As the scheme (graph 1) indicates, in a globalised world, gender equality is not a marginal issue of concern of a few women, but, instead, an overwhelming developmental issue, which involves all major players on national and international political and financial playgrounds.

Gender equality as a focus of policy intervention is both on the EU level and on the level of individual societies articulated through a comprehensive system of negotiations between many different stakeholders. Those stakeholders include the following: all major institutions in the EU and on the international and transnational level; women's transnational NGOs and women's and men's movements; international and transnational organisations; different international and transnational agencies which address women's issues; donor organisations with different foci; intermediate organisations / networks; different UN, EU and state machineries for 'gender mainstreaming'; political parties on national levels and associations of political parties on international level; women's organisations within the parties and their associations; women's unions and organisations within the unions; and finally, individual women and men leaders and politicians. In addition to those political and policy agents, the web is being exposed to and infused by new knowledge related to women's, gender and men's studies.

In the time of intense development of social media and Internet, this web is additionally being strengthened by dense communications and ex-

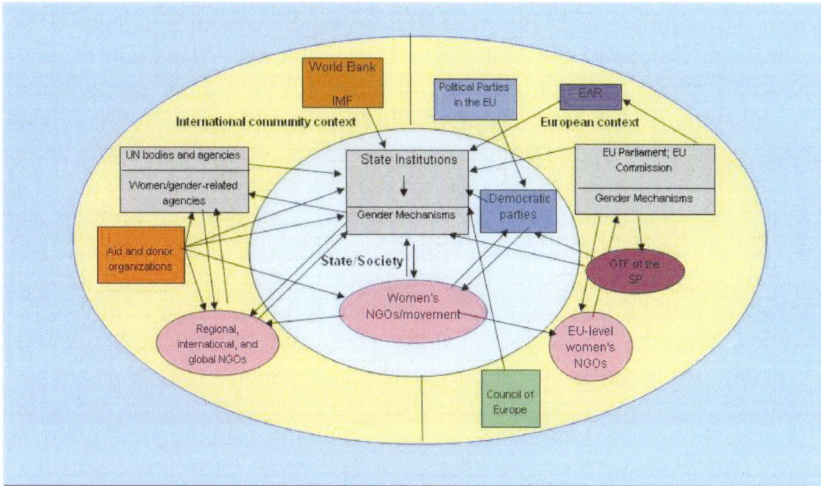

Graph 1: Transnational web of gender stakeholders

changes in which transnational, horizontal, less formal and more individualised ties often prevail over more institutionalised and hierarchical relationships. Moreover, the 'national' is embedded in the 'transnational' (Hearn and Blagojević, 2013) in a way which creates not only different power constellations, but also empowerment through resource sharing. At the same time, the dynamics of change in formulation and approach is defined by the growth of knowledge, expertise and 'know how' related to gender equality. While, on the one hand, an overall impression could be that there is increasing complexity which makes governability ever more difficult, on a another level, and from a different perspective, those speedy changes actually shape the whole field of perception of what gender equality is about and why it is relevant. If the focus is changed from the states and their institutions to societies and their institutions, then the issue is not as much on increased governability or purposeful social engineering, as much as it is on change of a value system in favour of gender equality and broader social consequences which emerge from that. The process of social learning is getting more enhanced and more advanced and new arguments, new policies, new measures (like the EU gender equality index[4]), as well as new milestones are being defined accordingly. The policy work on gender equality is 'work in progress'.

The communication and networks of different stakeholders are both wi-

---

[4] Available at http://eige.europa.eu/gender-statistics/gender-equality-index.

dening exponentially in real time (embracing more and more stakeholders) as they are 'deepening' in knowledge. Through connections and exchanges, joint projects and joint activities, a density of the web is also growing, getting crystallised in more institutionalised practices and discourses. This creates good ground for both advocacy and expertise development in the area. Also, new ideas and approaches develop from the web itself, from different encounters of different stakeholders, from different knots in the web of communication. The possibility for political mobilisation in favour of gender equality on the national, international and transnational level is growing as well (although not in a simple uni-linear mode). Because of the more horizontal nature of the exchange, the web is increasing the overall ownership of different stakeholders over gender issues, both in scope and in density. It is also creating the possibility of a 'backlash', since increased visibility through public policies and new media is bringing other political agents into a dialogue over gender equality issues. The web is both making effective different human rights instruments, by translating them into the national contexts, as defining new frontiers of a new consensus of what gender equality is about.

This approach, defined here as a 'web', brings considerable challenges for further conceptualisation and theoretisation, but in a real life it also brings to light many unresolved contradictions and undefined issues that are linked to gender policies on a transnational level, including the EU policies in the "neighbourhood". If the 'web' is being approached not as a structure, which it is not, but rather as a process, a flow of exchanges of resources (material, virtual, human, informational), then it is becoming even more evident how the old way of thinking through structures and institutions becomes difficult and inappropriate. This approach, then, is also affecting our understanding of what the 'implementation' of the laws and regulations actually means and what the limits of that concept are.

Further on, when it comes to the 'neighbourhood' of the EU, not only that the 'neighbourhood' is constantly changing, being redefined and repositioned in a relation to the EU, but it is often simultaneously exposed to both UN influences and EU influences when it comes to gender equality policies. This is being reflected in concepts and discourses related to gender equality. On the 'ground', individual countries' gender policies are being defined according to the set of prevailing influences of different organisations and donors. The confusion is often increased not only by different discourses which are being used by different stakeholders, but the real change in their position. For example, with the accession process the influence of the EU is growing while the influence of the UN is decreasing, which effectively shifts the discourses from 'women and development' to 'employ-ment' and 'work-life balance', or 'knowledge economy'. Also, even what is perceived as a strong organisation 'on the ground', such as UN agencies (e.g. UN Women) is often actually just an intermediary between the 'local' organisation and a donor. In an overall context of decreasing funds and in-creasing pressure for 'delivery', a growing number of gender stakeholders is competing for decreasing number and scope of resources. In that compe-tition the position is often being built on a shaky identity of the organisati-on, or preferential status of a few. The 'own territory' is being protected by highly specialised expert discourses, with the specific concepts used by a specific player in the field. The social learning process, however, demands a wide consensus which can be shared as a public discourse and a meta-narrative into which arguments in favour of gender equality can be built in.

The field itself, i.e. the gender policy equality field, is regulated by a set of international and European conventions and documents. In a globalised world, gender equality is not a marginal issue of concern of a few women, but, instead, an overwhelming developmental issue, which involves all ma-jor players on national and international political and financial playgrounds. The multiplicity and the variety of gender stakeholders contributes both to the internationalisation of women's issues and political pressures which move things forward, while at the same time bring new challenges related to consensus and effectiveness of gender equality policies.

3. SEMIPERIPHERAL SOCIAL CONTEXTS AND GENDER REGIMES

The EU, together with the UN, is one of the most important international actors in the field of gender equality. The influence of the EU in fostering gender equality and women's empowerment worldwide, and especially in countries which are in the process of EU integration, is both very relevant and very evident. Within the EU the principle of gender equality is being integrated into all Community policies and activities through the frame-work of gender mainstreaming. Over time, the EU also strengthened requi-rements related to the accession process. That was especially effective in the first decade of the 21st century, when it became obvious that there is a kind of close correlation between gender equality and EU accession. As I stated in the study commissioned by the European Parliament:

"There is an ongoing intense process of formulating and adopting legal provisions for gender equality and of establishing functional mechanisms ('gender machine-

*ries') for their implementation in most of the countries in the region. Between the
process of providing a formal framework for gender inclusion, and the process
of accession, or 'closeness' to EU, there is a clear connection. This means that
'harmonization' is absolutely beneficial for gender mainstreaming in the Balkan
countries. The position of the country in relation to EU correlates with the quality and scope of specific programs, action plans and institutional mechanisms.
However, at this point it would be important to compare the real effects of gender mainstreaming in the West, with the expectations in the Balkans related to the
establishment of gender machineries."* (Blagojević, 2003: 64)

It seemed for a while that a 'magical formula' had been invented: international conventions, gender mechanisms, and gender equality laws, copying
EU Member States' standards, followed by national strategies and plans of
action. Countries 'in transition', or at the semiperiphery of Europe, have
been seen as 'receivers' of the 'solutions' which have been already 'invented' in the EU. In the spirit of accession much hope has been invested into
the legal regulation and setting up of institutional mechanisms for gender
equality. However, it is becoming more and more obvious that there is a
growing problem with so-called 'implementation'. The emphasis on formal and legal provisions has led to a situation which has been described
best as 'more compliance than commitment' (Spehar, 2012). That is not the
case only with gender equality policies, but with many other public policies
as well. 'Implementation' is often understood as the simple establishment
of different institutional mechanisms, including control mechanisms with a
more or less defined chain of responsibility. It is usually not seen as an issue
of adequate contextualisation which would engage with societies in question on a deeper, structural level, and therefore enable better understanding of
possibilities and obstacles. It is habitually believed that the 'ownership' of
the local gender equality policies is ensured by the engagement of women's
organisations and local experts, without looking deeper and more analyti-
cally into the structural social, economic and cultural differences which,
consequently, shape diverse gender regimes (Hughson, 2015).

'More compliance than commitment' is not only a precise definition
of the state of art of public policies related to gender equality in countries which are at the semiperiphery of Europe, but it is also a description
of a very specific state of social vacuum which has been created, on the
one hand, by over-regulation, and, on the other hand, by social resistance
to change, or even social 'slipping away' from intentional action. However, that resistance, active or passive, is not simple 'traditionalism' or 're-
traditionalisation' as much as it is a result of survival strategiesof a large
majority of the citizens in the countries in question. 'Re-traditionalisation'
of gender-roles during times of 'transition' is not a straightforward con-

sequence of increased conservativism, but a consequence of what I have described and elaborated as the problem of 'de-development of the semiperiphery' (Blagojević, 2009; Hughson, 2015). It could be claimed that what appears as 'resistance' or 'lack of implementation' is actually a social survival strategy under unfavourable conditions of lasting economic crises, collapse of social protection, increasing inequalities, increase of precariat, lack of rule of law, growing anomy, institutional collapse, and the feeling of powerlessness of the great majority of citizens who see themselves as 'losers of transition'. Moreover, de-development of the semiperiphery has created profoundly different gender regimes, from the one existing at the core ('old Europe'), thus, also requiring a different approach to policy-making (Hughson, 2015). Differences in institutional set-ups should not be underestimated, either. The simple truth that socialism as a system had collapsed because its institutions have collapsed first, is often ignored when policy solutions are prescribed to copy institutions from the centre (Heinrich, 1999). Further on, austerity measures, although in many ways detrimental in the social contexts of the centre, are often a much more serious problem in 'transitional' countries where the 'losers of transition' make up the great majority of population.

At the same time, despite all the problems with 'implementation' there are some unquestionable gains related to gender equality which result from the accession process. According to Spehar (2012: 59) those gains are the following:

1. new gender legislation;
2. institutional mechanisms for advancement of gender equality;
3. women's movements strengthened and legitimacy gained. (2012: 59)

But, all of those gains should also be seen within the context of the semiperiphery, faced with the 'de-development' and 'surplus of humans',[5] two phenomena which in many ways are similar to the features of 'demodernisation' of previously industrial societies. However, even when there is similarity on the surface, there are still very deep structural differences between the countries at the core and those at the semiperiphery. So the gains of gender equality policies were and are strongly limited since the transitional social contexts have the power to de-construct them, and even to reverse them. In the end, it is the quality of the social context that enables policies to be successful or not, especially if the contextual differences have been ignored in the design of the policies. The gains, not surprisingly, inspired strong anti-feminism and provoked a strong backlash. In other words,

---

[5]   I have dealt with the concept of 'de-development' in more detail in a number of my publications (Blagojević, 2009; Hughson, 2015).

interventions with the aim of diminishing gender inequalities were experienced by the general public mainly as 'exaggerated', 'imposed', or 'anti-men' etc. Discursively, they were also mainly constructed as 'imposed' by the 'West', and as another part of a neo-colonial agenda which deeply interferes with privacy and intimacy, especially in terms of sexual identities (Antonić, 2011). Gender equality policies fell into the trap of being defined as 'alien', 'forced', and 'threatening', not only because of the 'natural backwardness' of the semiperiphery, but because resistance, as a matter of context, had been ignored. In other words, it is not enough to ideologically link anti-feminism, homophobia and misogyny to neo-conservativism and dismiss them. It is necessary to go a step further and connect them to the overall de-development process which is largely taking place in semiperipherial societies.

Usually there were no parallel measures to meet these resistances and to create a more favourable atmosphere for progressive societal change. Growing evidence is showing that in a longer run, the EU accession process has ambivalent and contradictory effects on gender equality in different countries. Stakeholders overall agree that there exists a profound gap between stated goals and their actual implementation. Country experiences from Central and Eastern Europe, as well as from Bulgaria and Romania, are already showing that the problem with 'implementation' of laws and policies on gender equality, and even the backlash that can be observed, is quite deep and deserves more attention. This resulted in a growing tendency to approach the EU accession process on gender equality as more complex and context-sensitive issue than previously was the case.

Research by Spehar (2012) who is using a comparison between Croatia and Macedonia demonstrates how the 'façade democracies' of the Western Balkans are immanently creating obstacles to reaching a higher level of gender equality. The weak impact of the EU strategy on 'de facto' gender inequality is due to a number of reasons: EU anti-discrimination policy has remained confined within the limits of liberal individualism, doing little to tackle the broader structural aspects of gender (in)equality; implementation of the adopted legislation in Croatia and Macedonia is slow and inconsistent due to poor governance (elite corruption and elite closure); lack of gender awareness affects the implementation of EU gender equality directives (Spehar, 2012).

The problem of 'implementation' is also deepened by the fact that 'gender policy fatigue' within the EU meets 'accession fatigue' in the Balkans. Spehar believes that a possible way out would be in shifting from *'equality of rights'* to *'equality of results'* (Spehar, 2012). Besides a growing understanding that women and men being equal in rights does not mean that they will achieve the same results, there is more consideration of the fact that the EU accession process itself has different effects in different countries, as well as in different phases of accession. For example, the EU accession process of Turkey has proved to be beneficial, especially since the position of women has been in some aspects very unfavourable (honour crimes, for example). In that case the normative power of the EU plays a very positive role. However, with the later weakening of the EU integration process the EU's normative power in Turkey has led to a weakening of civil society, and gender issues have been used as a tool to settle domestic political disputes (Tunkrova, 2010).

The real level and strength of EU commitment to gender equality in accession countries can be seen in the Enlargement Strategy and Main Challenges 2012-2013[6] and 2014-2015.[7] These documents hardly address any issues related to women and gender. When women are mentioned it is mostly in the context of human rights and in connection to violence. Specific countries and women's and gender issues are randomly connected, and only in a very general manner. Also, the framing of the problems is quite general and actually can be applied to more than one country. Both documents give a lot of attention to minority rights, and women are often addressed in the context of 'other minorities'. This kind of approach which often exists in UN documents as well, minimises the relevance of gender inequalities and their structural relevance. Even the intersectional approach (which includes ethnicity, sexuality, gender identity and religion) actually minimises gender inequalities and obscures their relevance. Hate speech, for example is addressed as an issue exclusively related to minorities, while gender-based stereotypes and prejudices are not being mentioned. Further on, gender mainstreaming, or gender budgeting, as major policy approaches and methods are not specifically mentioned although their implementation would gradually contribute to the elimination of gender-based inequalities in all spheres of social life. Gender inequalities are seen as a simple consequence of the 'lagging behind' of Western Balkans countries in terms of their economic and structural development, but not as a substantial social structure which is at the core of all other social inequalities, including the discrimination and exclusion of other vulnerable groups (such as those grounded in sexual orientation). While domestic violence as well as vio-

---

[6] Available at http://ec.europa.eu/enlargement/pdf/key_documents/2012/package/strategy_paper_2012_en.pdf.

[7] Available at http://ec.europa.eu/enlargement/pdf/key_documents/2014/20141008-strategy-paper_en.pdf.

lence against children and people with disabilities is addressed as an area of concern, violence as such is not perceived as a profoundly gendered phenomenon based on gender misbalances of power as well as gender-based hierarchies between men themselves. Although it is stated that "Homophobia, discrimination and hate crimes, including violence and intimidation on the basis of sexual orientation and gender identity are still widespread in the Western Balkans and Turkey" (Strategy 2014-2015, p. 15), hate speech against women and their objectification and commodification in media is not mentioned. Moreover, it seems that the 2014-15 Strategy as well as the 2012-2013 Strategy requires serious gender-mainstreaming itself, since connections are not made between gender and different sectors. This Strategy reflects very well the situation in the EU. However, on another level, the EU accession process has instruments which allow gender to be integrated, especially within some of the accession chapters.

The lessons from reading both Strategies are the following:
– Larger programmes are favoured over individual projects.
– All assistance for transition and institution-building is gender-relevant and could be gender-mainstreamed.
– For civil society and especially small women's organisations the problem of eligibility for EU funding support remains.
– Since accession countries are 'weak states' with a high level of corruption, lack of rule of law, elite seizure and elite closure, it is highly questionable whether a strategy which favours large programmes will actually favour democracy, or, on the contrary, deepen the democratic deficit including the gender equality deficit.

In conclusion, it is clear that effective policies need to be well contextualised into the specific country / national contexts to be able to address both historical, economic, social and culturally-based gender inequalities as well as the new realities created by economic crises, 'transition' and present political developments. But, apart from being situated within the country context, policies are also situated within the social context of gender policy development itself. So, the purpose of this text is to show how gender policies at the semiperiphery of Europe have developed, as a result of a complex set of movements which actively re-defined our understanding of what gender equality policies are about. Policies are being defined both from 'the above' and 'from below', both from the EU instruments applied during the accession process as well as from the women's movements, women's organisations and knowledge communities which exist in the accession countries. They have developed through the active communication with different gender stakeholders, as described earlier. In reality it is a process of social learning through a series of interactions, trials and errors, as well as through 'translation and assemblage' (Clark, Bainton,Lendvai and Stubbs, 2015).

4. UNDERSTANDING THE 'GENDER POLICY FIELD'(GPF)

4.1. SOURCES

In this chapter I share some of the insights which I gained while working as an external evaluator / international gender expert on a review of projects supported by the Swedish International Development Agency (Sida)[8] in Eastern Europe and the Western Balkans 2001 – 2012.[9] This expert work which was conducted from January to March 2013, enabled me to profoundly analyse the project documents. The purpose of the desk-review was to identify major lessons learned, to map out tendencies, patterns within the regions and in specific countries, related to the results of Sida-funded gender-related projects. The major question was to find out "where the 'success' of gender policy interventions comes from".

I applied content analysis of the projects, using also reports, evaluations, country and regional overviews which were available.[10] This expert exercise was a unique challenge since it created an opportunity to get an overview of projects in the course of more than ten years in a dozen of countries in the neighbourhood of the EU.

The task of mapping encountered some very important limitations related to the quality of sources. In fact, it was very difficult to see what had really been achieved and where the resources have been invested, especially when looking beyond individual projects.[11] On the other hand, the

---

[8]   See http://www.sida.se/English/.

[9]   There were two experts engaged for this assignment: myself in a role of team leader and Ms Kateryna Shalayeva. I would like to note that this paper is based on my own separate work related to that assignment, and that I am solely responsible for all the opinions expressed here.

[10] The desk review included pre-selected projects per country and region. Pre-selection was done by the focal points in Swedish embassies. Therefore, mapping did not imply full mapping of all existing Sida-funded projects in the period 2001-2012, but only those that were pre-selected, primarily on the basis of their innovative nature and relevant impact.

[11] Accessibility of information was a big challenge. Sida has no electronic database where experts could browse and search for necessary documents (applications, quality control, reports, evaluations, studies). In addition, not all documents were available in electronic format.

information provided was random in many ways and focused on 'good examples', with the rationale that those best practices would encourage faster learning.[12] In spite of all these limitations, it was still possible to see how some regularities and patterns emerge. Many gender-related projects have been shown to be very similar in their nature, which was the case especially with Kvinna Till Kvinna (KtK)[13] work in the region, due to its specific focus and methodology. This created the ground for the next important analytical step – conceptualisation of the Gender Policy Field (henceforth GPF).What this mapping revealed was the learning process which is a process of creation of knowledge in the field of gender policies. This process has been largely un-theorised and un-conceptualised. I also discovered that ownership of the knowledge and, in fact, the social innovations which have been created in many domains, stayed captured by power relations defined by funding schemes and relations of dependency between the donors on the one side, and other social agents on the other.

4.2. WHAT IS THE GPF?

If we move beyond individual projects and have a perspective on them as the sum of intentional interventions into society which is what public policy is about, then the GPF emerges. It is a dynamic field which is in constant process of transformation. The more this field is understood in its own logic and existence, the more we approach an understanding of how policy interventions work, both within and beyond the projects.

The GPF is defined here as the sum of policy interventions, through programmes and projects in the field of gender equality. Looking separately, each project is a tool of policy intervention. However, if they are in connection and together then the wider field of policy interventions emerges. This perspective on the whole field, being defined by the sum of individual projects and programmes, offers a comprehensive understanding of strategic and long run changes of the field and within the field of policy interventions beyond individual projects.

The key characteristic of the GPF is the movement that is visible within the field. The graph below shows how this movement, most convincingly expressed in a change of policy foci, took place. Although this scheme is provisional and not fully applicable to every country to the full extent, it discloses a phasing within the field, a gradual increasing, extension and

---

[12]   It is really hard to claim that 'best practices' are better learning sources than 'worst practices'. However, the choice of the first one became a prevailing practice.

[13]   Kvinna till Kvinna is a major Swedish organisation engaged in women's rights from the beginning of the 90-ies in the Balkans, see http://kvinnatillkvinna.se/en/.

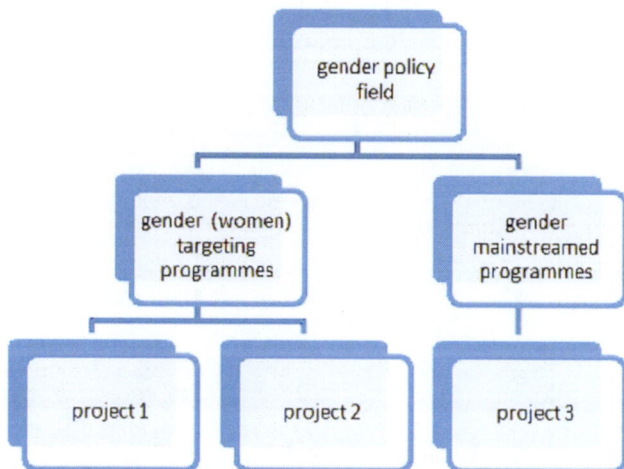

Graph 2: The GPF: network of projects and programmes

moving into new areas and methods of intervention, while the old ones, such as those at the core (women victims, gender-based violence (GBV), trafficking etc.) still stay in the core. This could be seen as positive, but it is also a considerable challenge to donors and other gender stakeholders, unless they understand the immanent logic of the change and act accordingly.

Looking at projects at large and in the period of a decade, the movements, or series of movements, are visible in the following directions:
- from women only to gender and to men;
- from women's NGOs to institutions;
- from random and scattered knowledge to more systematic research and statistics;
- from lack of regulation to legal provisions;
- from legal provisions to implementation;
- from violence to politics to economy;
- from scattered interventions to more holistic approaches;
- from random projects to overarching (national) mainstreaming;
- from competition between women's NGOs and institutions (gender mechanisms) to more collaborative approaches;
- from activism to professionalism;
- from women's movement (genuine, without donors) to donor-driven projects and interests;
- from lack of gender knowledge to a biased 'transmission' of knowled-

ge from the 'core' (especially US, much less from Europe) to the more creative approach to knowledge production with stronger regional and national ownership;
– from countries at war with each other to regional co-operation;
– from a chaotic situation on the 'gender market' to a more developed 'division of labour' between different gender stakeholders;
– from vague criteria of donors to a "result-based management" (RBM) design of projects, with a significant increase in specialised work and knowledge related to management, coordination, finances.

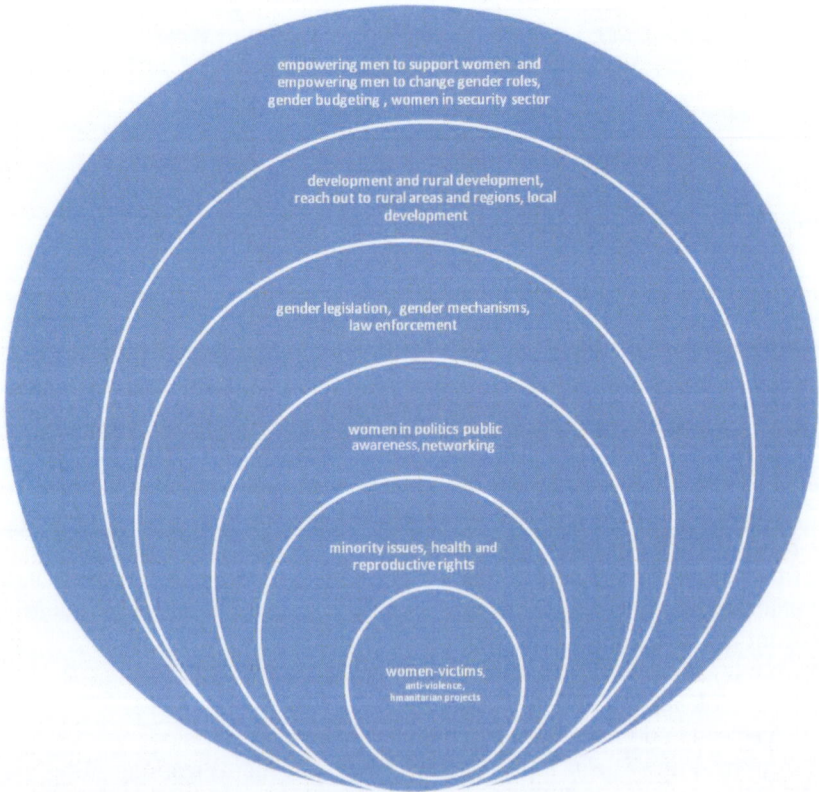

empowering men to support women and empowering men to change gender roles, gender budgeting , women in security sector

development and rural development, reach out to rural areas and regions, local development

gender legislation, gender mechanisms, law enforcement

women in politics public awareness, networking

minority issues, health and reproductive rights

women-victims, anti-violence, humanitarian projects

Graph 3: The GPF thematic expansion

This larger picture of 'movements' is relevant from the angle of policy because it enables a perspective which shows what is possible and what is a more advanced phase. From humanitarian projects (women as victims of war) and the 'discovery' of 'women's movements' in the Balkans (Croatia and Serbia), the circle has expanded to the level of holistic approaches of gender mainstreaming of institutions and society at large and men's integration; from women as victims of violence to women in the security sector, and gender mainstreaming of the sector. The expansion is huge and reflects the growing need for intervention into different spheres of social life. Also, the growth of the circle itself, caused by the introduction of new issues and new approaches, necessarily creates some setbacks. Things are being 'jumped over', there is no real 'saturation' of some issues (i.e. GBV), while others are 'oversaturated', like 'women in politics'.

The growth of the GPF happened in the last 10-15 years in parallel with the change of methodologies of policy interventions, rapid growth of new technologies, which creates different needs and possibilities, as well as in connection to fast changes in the international setting (economic and political crises, donors phasing out, availability of new funds, higher engagement of some multilateral bodies, higher regulation of the field with different resolutions, conventions, gender indicators etc.). There is also considerable growth of knowledge within women and gender studies, with Sweden being the leading country in Europe with regard to gender equality, and actually becoming recognised in international diplomacy as such, and defining its own national and political interest in that regard. All those changes are translated into the GPF accordingly. Projects reflect those changes and new possibilities, and also reflect the new, more sober, logic of saving within the donor's community.

4.3. CONTEXT OF THE GPF

Not only that the field is changing and developing, there are also changing international and national contexts of the field itself. There is a specific 'disillusionment' on the side of donors. There is also a gender and accession 'fatigue' which is the consequence of several factors: financial crises and the logic of saving; ambivalent political messages coming from different countries in Eastern Europe; realisation that neither can women stop the wars, nor can their NGOs play a major role in reconciliation (since they are not the major power brokers); realisation that 'transition' is in many ways a very vague and ambivalent process; and that cultural differences between societies can be huge, often influencing the projects in a profound, but, in fact, highly predictable way. In other words, there are structural constraints to change. This new 'context of disillusionment' requires new approaches which can be translated into more efficient policies and donors' strategies, if the possibilities are understood from a different level, i.e. from the level of managing social change.

While the set of projects creates the 'field of policy interventions', individual projects are also situated within the context of a certain society. However, the 'context' itself is a complex issue, and it also includes the timing, political momentum, and accumulation of previous steps made in this domain. Success of a project is, thus, a result of different factors:

1. adequate social contextualisation of the project which includes well contextualised objectives, adequate timing, favourable political climate and available and accessible means to achieve those objectives;
2. adequate policy contextualisation of the project, which includes understanding of the field of intervention, its phasing, its growth, its development;
3. adequate project design, RBM of the project, a set of adequate indicators for achieving results, and openness to the learning process during the project implementation;
4. success can be seen on the level of the project, through outcomes, but also through its wider impact within the social context.

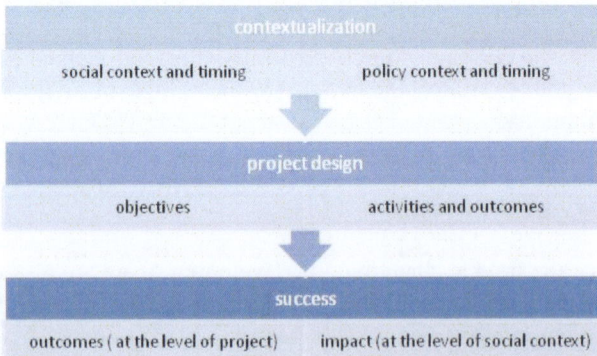

contextualization	
social context and timing	policy context and timing

project design	
objectives	activities and outcomes

success	
outcomes (at the level of project)	impact (at the level of social context)

Graph 4: Projects' success as contextualised policy intervention

Social contextual factors are of key relevance since they influence objectives and activities. However, policy interventions do have their own development logic which can speed up the process, through lessons learned and dissemination of best practices, even within contexts which are less favourable to those interventions. Further on, in the field of gender equality, policy interventions are often introduced 'from above', from the international community (UN, EU) and different international and multilateral gender stakeholders. Organisations such as UN Women disseminate 'best practices' via their knowledge products, which enable faster learning in the field of gender policies.

4.4.PROJECT SUCCESS AND RBM

Policy projects are increasingly facing the demands to apply the logic and tools of RBM. While this business-like approach has its benefits since the whole project cycle is better controlled and responsibility of the implementing partners is enhanced, it also has its limits. These come from both ends: deciding about the specific objects of the policy intervention and relating the project to the wider social context through impact analysis (graph No 3). So, there is a tendency with some projects to actually perform very well on the level objects-activities-outputs, while the bridge between outputs and outcomes is weak, and the impact, as the even larger and more abstract category, becomes quite vague. In other words, there is a danger that projects which offer considerable levels of expertise of RBM can be more successful in fundraising than projects which really have a larger impact in a concrete setting, although not sophisticated in RBM. The technical and managerial side of the project can prevail over the real benefits and impact, which in the long run creates a profound disillusionment in connection to public policy.

The answer to the question 'What works and what does not?' depends on the context and momentum, on the one hand, and project design and management, on the other. The best projects are not those which necessarily 'go smoothly' because that could very well be the result of the fact that there were no challenges in the first place, that the learning process was missing, or that they were designed to go 'smoothly' (like many of the trainings and workshops, or public awareness events). On the other hand, those projects which show how the problems on the ground were really solved, how the things were really changed, or how they paved the way for more sustainable changes (creating knowledge products, or gender mainstreaming of educational institutions, or large-scale employment possibilities, for example), could also be the ones which do not go 'smoothly' because they can encounter more obstacles. Ensuring these 'real life' changes often remains beyond the RBM logic since society is a very different entity from business corporations for which RBM was constructed. And although much of the 'business logic' is being applied in administration everywhere, the effects remain contradictory. RBM lenses often do not reveal 'who' the people involved are, how small the circle of professionals is which takes a 'part of the cake'. It does not reveal nepotism and cronyism, or how democratic or non-democratic decision-making within the applicant organisation is. It does not reveal strategies of inclusion or exclusion applied, narrowing down the circle of supporters. It also does not secure fair treatment of 'ownership' of knowledge 'from below', expertise, or women's movements themselves, since it over-emphasises the advantage of technical and managerial knowledge over other types of knowledge. It also does not reveal 'activity for activity sake' as a problem, because everything can be 'in place' while actually being like 'Potemkin's villages'. Therefore, it is very important that donors encourage projects which build on democratic internal structures with a democratic leadership,and which are widely inclusive and respectful to meritocracy and ownership of different stakeholders. Otherwise, negative images and real lack of co-operation and expertise (due to the negative selection) have a negative impact on the quality of the project, but also a quite negative effect on the general public and its understanding of civil sector or gender equality. Donors need to understand that creation of a so-called 'NGO elite' or 'gender elite' creates a favourable ground for anti-feminism in some, or even most, of the countries which are in the neighbourhood of Europe.

4.5. PROJECT SUCCESS AND MOMENTUM

Success of the project or some of its elements is often connected to the momentum of a certain policy or an issue within the concrete social context. The graph below represents three phases of policy development as changing momentum:

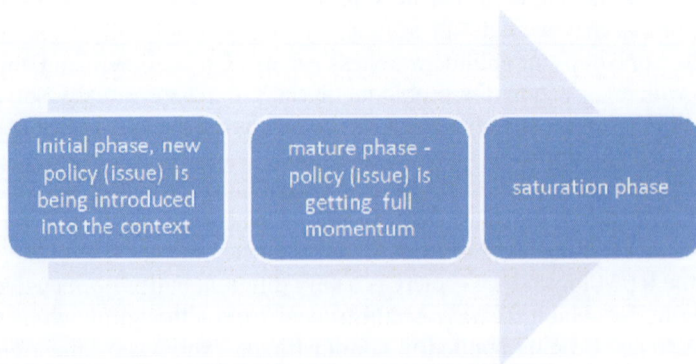

Initial phase, new policy (issue) is being introduced into the context

mature phase - policy (issue) is getting full momentum

saturation phase

Graph 5: Policy development as changing momentum

1. Initial phase – a new policy (issue) is being introduced into the context: the new policy is taking off, there is high motivation, a high quality selection of stakeholders, there is an attraction of the effect of 'discovery', intense raising of consciousness and an intense learning process, stakeholders take their positions, a constellation of formal and informal relations is being set up.
2. Mature phase – the policy (issue) is getting full momentum: repetition of the methods, reaching out for 'new territories' for the same issues, new stakeholders and beneficiaries are being included, higher level of institutionalisation and professionalisation.
3. Saturation phase – the policy (issue) is present for a longer time in a given context, limited or no evident movement forward, potential beneficiaries are being exhausted or donors lose interest, higher competition between the stakeholders, the issue has been institutionalised and professionalised, or marginalised, limited success (resistance of the context, backlash), necessity for new approaches, methods, issues and rationales emerges.

Moreover, momentum itself is a complex phenomenon, and it builds on many specific moments, as is shown below.

CONSCIOUSNESS-RAISING MOMENTUM

In gender issues there is often a moment of 'discovery' present when 'ordinary people', women and men, face for the first time the notion of 'gender' as a social and cultural construct. Especially women tend to have a pronounced feeling of satisfaction and even gratification because they get different perspectives on their lives and the problems they face. Often, the knowledge they receive has a very strong empowerment effect, as part of a consciousness-raising moment. As stated in the project report related to Women in Governance, in Albania:

"The beneficiaries in Shkodra and Vlora expressed an extraordinary enthusiasm and commitment to be part of the organized activities and forums. They were highly motivated by the concrete aspect of gathering together, beyond party cleavages and regionalism, sharing and gathering experiences gained cross generation. Forums were a place of importance where women felt equal."

The success factor here could be related to the first phase of consciousness-raising activities, when women are discovering for the first time that there are other women in similar situations, when they actually discover their own genderness. However, as it has been the case with other countries, this is only one phase, and an adequate response is to try to keep the momentum and to move more to institutionalised modalities of women's empowerment (women's clubs, resource centers, networks).

POLITICAL MOMENTUM

Political momentum, when analysing the Balkans, was very relevant for the high-level mobilisation of women and the creation of a women's movement through the opposition to wars and nationalisms. That later contributed to building partnership with KtK and enhancing different gender-related policies and laws, including the creation of gender machineries. Political pressure produced by wars led to a high mobilisation of women. The other example goes in a different direction. The accession process is highly favourable to legal changes and a normative approach to gender equality, based on the human right's approach. However, because of the political momentum, it is often easier to introduce legislation then to enable implementation, as already explained. In a certain phase of the EU accession process, while it is highy acceptable to introduce new laws, their later implementation stays as a problem ('compliance rather than commitment'). So, political momentum which seems positive in fact can produce saturation with norms, and there can be a considerable gap between those norms and the changes in reality. This, in turn, can feed 'gender fatigue' and frustration on behalf of the activists and movements, resulting in passivity and disappointment, with the overall feeling that 'nothing can be done'. The gap between norms and reality, when it is so wide as it is the case with 'transition countries', instead of 'pulling reality forward' it can contribute to an overall anomie, lack of orientation, and the overall feeling of helplessness.

OVERSATURATION OF THE ISSUE

It is critical for the success of the project to have a good judgment whether positive movements might be reached with old approaches and methods. An issue might be overly exhausted in a certain context or becoming increasingly irrelevant. For example, the "Women in Government" project in Albania failed to increase the number of women in politics on the local level, although that was one of the important goals. The failure is often not a simple result of the project's immanent failure, but a consequence of unfavourable circumstances which are related to structural constraints beyond the project's reach. However, this could also be an issue of how to define the right strategy for the given context. For example, instead of targeting women in politics as potential leaders, the more effective approach to gender equality might be targeting a wide circle of women professionals and leaders who in post-socialist countries represent large numbers and who create an excellent pool for the recruitment of new leaders, including political leaders.

ABANDONING THE ISSUE BEFORE THE PROFOUND POSITIVE EFFECT HAS BEEN ACHIEVED.

Another problem might be related to the fact that donors often, as it is observed by the NGO community, 'change the fashion', move their interest from one issue to another, even before some more profound effects have been achieved in one area, before the phase of 'saturation' has been completed. What often happens is that discursively some problems get 'exhausted', while in reality they stay the same. Public campaigns can contribute to the discursive 'oversaturation', especially if there are no real movements in that specific field of reality (for that reason, for example, indicators on media coverage can have limited value, although they are one of the most favoured indicators of the policy / project 'success'). These factors contribute to 'gender fatigue' in the long run. Also, changes of donor's focuses, looking for some 'new territories', often produce change of foci for NGOs which can lead to the loss of their previously gained knowledge and expertise. This has an overall negative impact on the general sustainability of the projects, but also on gender policies at large. Many projects related to GBV run the risk that public awareness campaigns do not match the low real positive effects in this domain.[14]

LOSS OF MOMENTUM BECAUSE OF INERTIA

Sometimes simple inertia and lack of innovativeness keep issues and methods unchanged even when the context has changed and requires new approaches. Educating politicians and administrators about gender issues, over and over again, with each new election, becomes a never-ending task. Instead, those resources might have been invested in introducing gender issues in regular educational institutions and processes, and by now a new generation with new knowledge would have been gender-sensitised. The whole approach of presenting gender issues to politicians who themselves have not shown any interest to learn those things earlier, bears a high risk of lack of sustainability and effectiveness, especially at the present historical moment. A realistic understanding of the political elites in the regions is necessary. It is also very important to introduce gender into the understanding of the functioning of those political elites, from the perspectives of critical

---

[14] Example from Serbia: the construction of one or two safe houses has taken a lot of attention of media for a long time, and although that could be seen as relevant for consciousraising, the real scope of intervention was very limited. In the long run this leads to 'discursive saturation', while in reality change does not happen.

studies of men and masculinities (Hearn, 2004), since these elites persist to be male elites, and even when a few women get elected to high positions that does not change their overall 'male', meaning patriarchal, way of functioning.

The major conclusion linked to the connection between success and momentum is that serious analysis related to context and gender has to precede over project design. However, that analysis should be both structural and dynamic, taking into account the change of context and the dynamic of the GPF (level of development of gender equality issue, as shown in graph 2, 3 and 4, as well as the previously discussed problem of 'implementation' within the EU accession framework). This means that it is necessary to 'bring into the open' the issues of process, timing, momentum and change, so that it becomes clear how the project corresponds to the timing within both contexts: the one of the concrete society, and the one of GPF.

5.INSTEAD OF A CONCLUSION

The further development of gender policies in the post-socialist context of the Balkans and Eastern Europe could take two directions. The first one would engage with the theoretical critique of policy-making and deconstruct the whole field, its discourses as well as practices. This approach, inspired by anthropology, ethnology, philology, and cultural studies in general, could be very inspirational and heuristically rewarding. An excellent example of this kind of approach is the new book *Making Policy Move: Towards Politics of Translation and Assemblage* (Clark, Bainton, Lendvai and Stubbs, 2015). In this book the authors explain their own epistemic and theoretical position as a "sense of deep dissatisfaction with a policy studies orthodoxy that treats policy movement in terms of policy transfer, policy diffusion and policy learning." Further on, they work on 'policy as meaning'. They also "explore concepts of space, scale and time and their usefulness in a critique of both 'methodological nationalism' and 'methodological globalism' in policy studies". This is how they explain their interest in 'translation and assemblage' (p. 18). In the very broad perspective which they take, the authors explore various 'turns' in theory with their epistemological consequences (the argumentative turn, the interpretive turn, the linguistic turn, the discursive, and even the cultural turn).

The second one, which has been offered here as the small piece of analysis, is in line with what I would name the 'ontological turn', the one which takes materiality of both contexts and gender into account. This is not to be understood as a movement towards essentialism, but rather a movement towards materiality which cannot be denied and which cannot be captured by sociological and social science analysis and apparatus. That materiality is also shaping gender equality policies in the countries of Eastern Europe and the Western Balkans. It is expressed through tangible social phenomena and processes and established patterns, as described above. This more structural, rational, and in fact sociological approach to gender equality policies is affirming the relevance of social contexts and their immanent dynamics of change, as well as their given constraints and possibilities.

Within this approach, our analysis based on careful reading of documents and reports opened up new insights into the patterning of gender equality policies in the post-socialist countries of the Balkans and Eastern Europe. Thanks to the analysis of a large pool of projects, an entire field, the GPF, was revealed which exhibits its own internal logic in its development towards a holistic and comprehensive set of gender equality policies. The GPF is also intrinsically connected with the process of social learning, diffusion, and ownership of different actors, most importantly genuine women's movements in the Balkans. The very idea of gender equality intervention has grown and developed in the neighbourhood of Europe as a reaction to the wars in the Balkans and the immanent need for (humanitarian) intervention. Further steps, however, have led to the gradual expansion of the whole field, thus creating very different and more complex challenges. At the same time, donor organisations such as Sida, mainly through KtK, became learning organisations and disseminators of ideas and methods once developed in the Balkans (Blagojević, 1998). The ownership of social innovation brought up by women's spontaneous self-organising in the Balkans, got re-appropriated and re-constructed by donors, thus enhancing the process of social learning while at the same time de-contextualising gender policies. This constant movement between contextualisation and wider generalisation and implementation in other contexts creates a tension which is resolved only through re-contextualisation and re-appropriation. The analysis has shown that contextualisation is not only about time and space of policy intervention, but that it also includes proper contextualisation within the policy field itself.

REFERENCES

Antonić, Slobodan (2011). *Iskušenja radikalnog feminizma, moć i granice društvenog inžinjeringa (Challenges of Radical Feminism: Power and Limits of Social Engeneering)*, Beograd: Službeni glasnik.
Batliwala, Srilatha. *When Rights go Wrong*, available at http://www.india-seminar. com/2007/569/569_srilatha_batliwala.htm.

Blagojević, Marina (ed.) (1998). *Ka vidljivoj ženskoj istoriji: Ženski pokret u Beogradu 90-tih (Towards Visible Womens History: Women's Movement in Belgrade in the 90-ties)* Beograd: Centar za ženske studije.

Blagojević, Marina (2003). Report for the EU Parliament (No. IV/2002/16/03), presented at the EU Parliament, Committee on Women's Rights and Equal Opportunities. Brussels: 10-6-2003.

Blagojević, Marina (2003). *Women's Situation in the Balkan Countries.* Report for the EU Parliament (No. IV/2002/16/03), presented at the EU Parliament, Committee on Women's Rights and Equal Opportunities. Brussels: 10-6-2003.

Blagojević, Marina (2009). *Knowledge Production at the Semiperiphery: A Gender Perspective.* Beograd: IKSI.

Blagojević, Marina and Yair, Gad (2010). *The Catch 22 Syndrome of Social Scientists in the Semiperiphery: Exploratory Sociological Observations*, Sociologija, Beograd, No 4, 2010 (pp. 337-358).

Blagojević, Marina (2010). *Feminist Knowledge and Women's Movement in Serbia: Strategic Alliance*, Aspasia 2010/ Volume 4.

Clark / John, Bainton / Dave, Lendvai / Noémi and Stubbs / Paul (2015). *Making Policy Move: Towards Politics of Translation and Assemblage*, Bristol: Policy Press at the University of Bristol.

Communication from the Commission to the European Parliament, The Council, The European Economic and Social Parliament, The Council, The European Economic and Social Committee and the Committee of the Regions: Enlargement Strategy and Main Challenges 2014-15.

Enwise Report: *Waste of Talents: Turning Private Issues into a Public Debate* (2003), European Commission, available at https://ec.europa.eu/research/swafs/pdf/pub_gender_equality/enwise-report_en.pdf.

Harding, Sandra (ed.) (1987). *Feminism and Methodology: Social Science Issues.* Bloomington: Indiana University Press.

Harding, Sandra (ed.) (2004). *The Feminist Theory Standpoint Reader: Intellectual and Political Controversies.* New York: Routledge.

Hartsock, Nancy C.M. (1983). *The Feminist Standpoint: Developing the Ground for a Specifically Feminist Historical Materialism,* in Sandra Harding and Merrill B. Hintikka (eds.), *Discovering Reality, Feminist Perspectives on Epistemology, Metaphysics, Methodology, and Philosophy of Science,* Boston: Ridel 283–310

Hearn, Jeff (1998). *Theorizing Men and Men's Theorizing: Men's Discursive Practices in Theorizing Men,* Theory and Society 27(6): 781–816.

Hearn, Jeff (2004). *From Hegemonic Masculinity to the Hegemony of Men*, Feminist Theory 5 (1): 49–72.

Hearn, Jeff and Blagojević, Marina (2013). *Introducing and Rethinking Transnational Men* in: Hearn Jeff, Blagojević Marina and Harrison Katherine (eds.):

Transnational Men: Beyond, Between and Within the Nations, New York: Routledge.

Heinrich, Hans Georg (ed.) (1999). *Institution Building in the New Democracies: Studies in Post-Communism*. Budapest: Collegium Budapest.

Hughson, Marina (2013). *Review of Gender Equality Review of Gender Equality Support in Eastern Europe and the Western Balkans (2001 – 2012)* Swedish International Development Cooperation Agency – Sida- Desk Study, March 2013 (manuscript).

Hughson, Marina (2014). *Gender Country Profile: Final Report*, European Commission, Sarajevo.

Resolution (2003) Women in South-East Europe, European Parliament Resolution on Women in South-East Europe (2003/2128(INI)).

Hughson, Marina (2015). *Poluperiferija i rod: pobuna konteksta (The Semiperiphery and Gender: The Rebellion of the Context)*, Beograd:IKSI.

Spehar, Andrea (2012). *European Union and Western Balkans: What Prospect for Gender Equality?* in: Kersten-Pejanić Roswitha, Rajilić Simone and Voss Christian (eds.): *Doing Gender – Doing Balkans*, Berlin: Kubon and Sagner GmbH (pp. 53-64).

Tunkrova, Lucie (2010). *Democratization and EU Conditionality: A Barking Dog that Does (not) Bite*, in: Tunkrova, Lucie and Šaradin, Pavel (eds.) *The Politics of EU Accession: Turkish Challenges and Central European Experiences*, London and New York: Routledge.

Promoting Gender Equality in EU Enlargement

Chapter 3:

The Gender Dimension of EU Enlargement:

A Case Study of Macedonia as a Candidate Country

Karolina RISTOVA-AASTERUD

This chapter gives an analytical overview of how the process of European integration is affecting the advancement of gender equality in Macedonia as a candidate country, thus exemplifying the effectiveness of EU's gender equality policies in the enlargement process. The focus is placed on two main levels of the issue. The first is the national level, i.e. what are the key achievements and the key problem areas of gender equality in the country's overall efforts for EU membership? The second is the EU level and the EU' policies and projects regarding gender equality in Macedonia as a candidate country. The main criticism I put forward is that gender equality is treated as a secondary issue in the EU's membership criteria, and in the overall enlargement process, which enables the political elites of candidate countries such as Macedonia to disregard, even to de-construct gender equality in a patriarchal direction, particularly in areas that are not within the scope of the EU's supranational competences.

1. Introduction

In the first years after Macedonia declared its independence from the Yugoslav federation in 1991 gender equality was a non-issue in the political, legal and public discourse. No gender-equality debate had been initiated, not even by the mere fact that the first democratic and multi-party elections held in 1990 ended up with only 4.2% of female representation (five female MPs in the national *Sobranie* out of 120), a significant decrease compared to former communist times of 1970s and 1980s when it had varied between 12-17%.[1]

For most of the 1990s, the country's political and overall societal agenda had been burdened with the devastating effects of the violent dissolution of Yugoslavia, and later with its own six-month inter-ethnic conflict of 2001. In the early 1990s the country also had to struggle for international recognition of its statehood due to the "name dispute" with Greece, a dispute that is on-going to this day. In such overall circumstances, peace, stabilisation and international recognition were the highest priorities, including for female voters and women's organisations.[2]

In addition, in that period the domestic transition to a democratic political system and market economy had just started to take shape, dominated by systemic legal reforms and an on-going process of privatisation of socially-owned companies. Those legal reforms did not dismantle any of the advancements concerning gender equality that had come as a legacy of the socialist ideology embedded in the legislation of the previous political regime, such as equal political rights, educational equality, equal work pay, nine months maternity leave, protection against discrimination on the basis of pregnancy and motherhood in employment, and a very liberal abortion law. In fact, that legacy has entrenched a widely-held view that gender equality had been an achieved goal.

This myth had started to be called into question only in the mid-1990s, mainly for three reasons. First, the creation of the private sector in the economy has started to create novel problems, such as gender discrimination in employment based on pregnancy and motherhood and sexual harassment at the workplace.[3]

---

[1] Data taken from Ristova (2003: 197). *Establishing a Machocracy: Women and Elections in Macedonia (1990-8)* in R. E. Matland and K.A. Montgomery, eds. (2003), *Women's Access to Political Power in Post-communist Europe.* Oxford: Oxford University Press, 196-216, 197.

[2] For example, according to a survey conducted for the period of 1990-1994, the value system of women in Macedonia was as follows: 1. Peace; 2. Honesty; 3. Just financial compensation for one's work; 4. Solidarity; 5. Gender equality; 6. Living standard; 7. Political pluralism. Data taken from Mojanovski (1996: 226). *Socijalniot i politickiot profil na politickite partii vo Makedonija.* Skopje: Liber, at p. 226 (In Macedonian).

[3] For more, see Takeva Grigorievik, Veskovc Vangeli and Petroska (1994). *The women's position in contemporary societal tendencies.* Skopje: Organization of Women of Macedonia (in Macedonian).

Second, the preparation of the first report on gender equality for the UN's Fourth World Conference on Women in Beijing in 1995 had provided a pretext for a new focus of women's organisations on the state of gender equality. A third stimulus was Macedonia becoming a member of the Council of Europe in 1995, which had opened up a debate about implementation of all key human rights conventions of this European human rights regime, including with respect to gender equality. This was quite a different situation from the one with the UN human rights regime, which Macedonia as a successor state of the former Yugoslav federation had succeeded with hardly any debate. Eventually, all this had led to the country's first national action plan for gender equality that was adopted by the Macedonian government in 1999. In 2003 Macedonia has also ratified the Facultative Protocol to the UN's Convention for Elimination of All Forms of Discrimination Against Women (CEDAW) that obliges the country to regularly report under the Convention's regime, which in recent times regularly mobilizes wide-ranging debates on the state of gender equality in the country. Although all these forms of international integration have much contributed to placing the issues of gender equality in the public's awareness and domestic political agenda, they did not bring any significant legal, policy or institutional changes. Such changes came only after Macedonia had applied for EU membership in 2004, and especially after being granted a candidate country status in 2005.

This article explores how the process of European integration is affecting the advancement of gender equality in the country, at the same time exemplifying the gender dimension of the EU enlargement process, especially the effectiveness of EU's gender equality legislation and policies. First, the national level is explored, i.e. what are the key achievements and the key problem areas of gender equality in Macedonia's overall efforts for EU membership. The main argument that I put forward is that although some notable advancements in gender equality have been made in legal and institutional terms, there is a worrisome trend of weakening women's socio-economic and cultural position that makes the achievements declaratory and hollow. There are indications that much room is left for prospective EU member states to deconstruct EU's values and policies regarding gender equality. Next, the gender dimension of EU enlargement is addressed from the EU perspective, again by using Macedonia as a case study. The main criticism I make is that the EU itself treats gender equality as a secondary issue in the membership criteria and in the overall enlargement policies and instruments.

2. MACEDONIA ON ITS WAY TO EU MEMBERSHIP: GENDERING THE INTEGRATION AGENDA

2.1. OVERVIEW OF EU-MACEDONIA RELATIONS: FROM STABILISATION TO ASSOCIATION

Macedonia's relations with the EC/EU had started to evolve in the context of the violent dissolution of Yugoslavia in 1991, and in a framework of a peace conference and an arbitration procedure.[4] Although Macedonia had received a positive opinion for state recognition of the Arbitration Commission ("Badinter Commission") established by the EC,[5] in January 1992 the European Council decided to recognise only the independence of Slovenia and Croatia, but not of Macedonia. This was due to the resistance of Greece as a member state, asserting that the constitutional name of the country cannot contain the name "Macedonia" as it indicates territorial claims towards its own territory.[6] The relations between the EU and Macedonia began to improve only after the dispute was transferred to the UN system in 1993, followed by an admittance of the country into UN membership under a provisional name,[7] and by conclusion of an Interim Agreement with Greece in September 1995 that stipulated that both countries agree that the dispute

---

[4]   After the declaration of independence of Slovenia on 26 June 1991, under the umbrella of the European Political Co-operation, EC foreign ministers decided to convene a peace conference that would bring together all (former) Yugoslav republics with representatives of the EU Council, the Commission and member states in order to deal with the dissolution of Yugoslavia in a peaceful manner. For more, see Karolina Ristova-Aasterud (2002), The Political and Legal Aspects of EU-Macedonia Relations: An Ever Closer Union? *Macedonian Affairs* Vol IV, No. 1.Skopje: Macedonian Information Centre, 29-61.

[5]   The Arbitration Commission composed of five judges-presidents of constitutional courts of EU member states. See Conference on Yugoslavia Arbitration Commission: Opinion on Questions arising from the dissolution of Yugoslavia, 31, I.L.M 1488 (1992).

[6]   Bull EC 12 (1991).

[7]   Macedonia was admitted as UN member on 8 April 1993 under the provisional name "former Yugoslav Republic of Macedonia," pending "settlement of differences which have arisen regarding its denomination."

would not hinder Macedonia's international integration, including integration into the EU.[8]

The first step of advancing EU- Macedonia relations was the establishment of diplomatic relations in December 1995.[9] This was followed by Macedonia being admitted to the PHARE Programme in 1996[10] and by concluding a Co-operation Agreement in 1997 which had entered into force in 1998.[11] However, the declared goal of all these forms of co-operation was mere economic and political stabilisation of the country. The EU membership perspective opened up only after the war in Kosovo in 1999, and only after the promotion of the EU-led Stability Pact for South Eastern Europe in Cologne, Germany on 10 June 1999.[12] The EU's approach in the Pact was to include a clear EU membership perspective for the "Western Balkans" (Albania, Bosnia and Herzegovina, Croatia, FR Yugoslavia and Macedonia) based on two main pillars: Community Assistance for Reconstruction, Development and Stabilization (CARDS), introduced in 2000,[13] and conclusion of Stabilisation and Association Agreements (SAA).

Macedonia was the first country from the Western Balkans to conclude such an agreement with the EU on 9 April 2001, in the midst of a civil conflict that had begun in the country one month before, and threatening to turn into an inter-ethnic war. In effect, the conclusion of the SAA had demonstrated the EU's support for the Macedonian state. For that purpose, the EU, together with the USA and NATO, further facilitated negotiations between the main political parties in the country, resulting in the "Ohrid Framework Agreement" of August 2001 that ended the conflict. Two years later, encouraged by the conclusions of the Thessaloniki European Council and EU-Western Balkans Summit of June 2003 that clearly offered EU membership perspective to the countries of the Western Balkans,[14] as well as from the EU's high evaluation of the implementation of the Ohrid Frame-

---

8   Official Gazette of Republic of Macedonia no. 48 /1995.
9   Official Gazette of Republic of Macedonia no. 61 /1995.
10 O.J. L 65 (1996).
11 O.J. L 348 (1997).
12 In 2008, The Stability Pact was replaced with the Regional Co-operation Council, available at http://www.rcc.int.
13 Council Regulation (EC) No. 2666/2000, (2000) O.J. L 206.
14 Council of the European Union, *Presidency Conclusions, Thessaloniki European Council, 19-20 June 2003*, 20 June 2003, available at http://www.refworld.org/docid/3f532b584.html.

work Agreement, Macedonia had applied for EU membership on 22 March 2004. On 1 April 2004, the SAA entered into force.[15] After the European Commission had given its positive opinion on Macedonia's EU membership application on 9 November 2005,[16] the Council granted the country candidate status on 16 December 2005. In 2009 the Commission recommended the opening of membership negotiations, repeated in all its subsequent annual progress reports ever since. The Council, however, has not decided to open the negotiations with Macedonia so far, primarily because of the opposition of Greece over the "name issue."[17] Moreover, in recent years Macedonia has also been receiving EU criticism on the deteriorating situation with respect to the political membership criteria. For this reason, and in the absence of accession negotiations, a High Level Accession Dialogue with the EU was established in 2012, especially focused on protection of freedom of expression in the media, rule of law and fundamental rights, reforms in the public administration, electoral reform and developing the market economy.[18] Still, the most recent Commission's progress reports of 2013 and 2014 mark no significant progress on the issues. The situation has taken a turn to worse when the opposition parties refused to enter Parliament after the parliamentary elections held in April 2014, claiming grave election violations. All these contributing factors leave Macedonia with no EU membership negotiations opened-up and with no such perspective in the near future.

---

[15] (2004) O.J. L 84, Vol. 47.
[16] Communication from the Commission – Commission Opinion on the application from the former Yugoslav Republic of Macedonia for membership of the European Union, COM (2005) 562 final, available at http://eur-lex.europa.eu/legal-content/EN/TXT/?uri=CELEX:52005DC0562.
[17] The formulation used in the Commission's 2014 Progress Report is usual restatement of this obstacle: "It remains essential that decisive steps are taken towards resolving the 'name issue' with Greece. The failure of the parties to this dispute to reach a compromise after 19 years of UN-mediated talks is having a direct and adverse impact on the country's European aspirations. Available at http://ec.europa.eu/enlargement/pdf/key_documents/2014/20141008-the-former-yugoslav-republic-of-macedonia-progress-report_en.pdf.
[18] High Level Accession Dialogue Conclusions, Skopje, 15 March 2012. Available at http://ec.europa.eu/commission_2010-2014/fule/docs/news/20120315_conclusions.pdf.

2.2. THE GENDER EQUALITY *acquis* IN EU ENLARGEMENT AND MACEDONIA

The 'enlargement article' – Article 49 of TEU stipulates "any European state which respects the values referred to in Article 2 and is committed to promoting them" may apply for EU membership, while Article 2 of TEU explicitly mentions "equality between women and men" as such value. In addition to these general provisions, there are the Copenhagen membership criteria adopted by the European Council in 1993[19] that require the applicant states to meet certain political criteria (stable institutions guaranteeing democracy, the rule of law, human rights and respect for and protection of minorities), certain economic criteria (functioning market economy and the capacity to cope with competition and market forces in the EU) and to embark on the adoption of the EU's *acquis communautaire* (ability to take on and implement effectively the obligations of membership). In this context, ever since the first EC/EU enlargement in 1973 gender equality has also begun to accompany the accession of each new member state as a membership issue, gradually transforming into an explicit part of each of the above-mentioned membership criteria.[20] As a membership criterion, gender equality addresses the adoption and the subsequent implementation of the gender equality *acquis* that is commonly defined as "all the relevant Treaty provisions, legislation and the case law of the Court of Justice of the European Union (CJEU) in relation to gender equality."[21] In addition to this legally binding *acquis,* gender equality may also be addressed and promoted through forms of "soft law" of the EU institutions that are most directly involved in the enlargement process: the annual resolutions by the European Parliament regarding the Commission's yearly progress reports on candidate countries, or its special resolutions targeting gender

---

[19] European Council in Copenhagen, Conclusions of the Presidency (21-22 June 1993, SN180/1/93) 12.

[20] For more on this development see Y. Galligan and S. Clavero. Gendering Enlargement of the EU in G. Abels and J.M. Mushaben (eds.). (2012) Gendering the European Union. New Approaches to Old Democratic Deficits. Basingstoke: Palgrave Macmillan, 104-123.

[21] S. Burri and S. Prechal. (2013) EU Gender Equality Law. Update 2013. European Network of Legal Experts in the Field of Gender Equality. European Commission, Directorate-General for Justice. Available at http://ec.europa.eu/justice/gender-equality/files/your_rights/eu_gender_equality_law_update2013_en.pdf, p. 1.

equality in the enlargement process, the most recent with respect to the Western Balkans being the *European Parliament Resolution on Women's Rights in the Balkan Accession Countries* of 2013;[22] certain policy documents of the Commission, such as the annual *Enlargement Strategy and Main Challenges* or the *Strategy for Equality between Women and Men 2010-2015;*[23] and, certain key documents of the Council of the European Union, such as the *European Pact for Gender Equality (2011-2020).*[24] Furthermore, the EU has designed a specific legal and policy framework, as well as certain financial instruments to help the reforms in the candidate countries and potential candidate countries towards meeting the membership criteria. With respect to the Western Balkan countries[25] the framework has four main components:

– *Stabilisation and Association Agreement (SAA)* as a main form of contractual relationship between the EU and a candidate country from the Western Balkans;
– *Accession Partnership* aimed at providing additionally tailored support to the candidate country in meeting the EU's membership criteria by identifying priority areas for reforms and financial assistance;
– *Instrument for Pre-Accession Assistance (IPA)* which is an umbrella instrument for EU's financial and technical help for fulfilling EU's membership criteria;
– *Progress Reports by the EU Commission* that serve as an annual evaluation of the progress made in meeting the EU's membership criteria, and which are also used as a basis in deciding whether to move a candidate country towards the next phase of the accession procedure.

If we analyse the gender equality dimension of these components in the case of Macedonia as a candidate country, the situation is as follows:
– The *SAA* has no specific provisions targeting gender equality, apart from one article that concerns social co-operation area and the adjustment of

---

[22] 2012/2255(INI)) of 4 April 2013, rapporteur MEP Marije Cornelissen.
[23] COM(2010) 491 final, Brussels, 21.9.2010, p. 9.
[24] Council conclusions of 7 March 2011 on European Pact for Gender Equality (2011-2020). (2011) O.J.C 155/10.
[25] As of June 2015, candidate status has been granted to Macedonia (2005), Montenegro (2010), Serbia (2012) and Albania (2014), while Bosnia and Herzegovina and Kosovo are still considered as potential candidate countries. Membership negotiations have been opened only with Montenegro (2012) and Serbia (2014).

the legislation on "working conditions and equality between men and women" (Article 90.3). Moreover, there is only a general reference to "human rights" in Title 1 of SAA (General Principles) and in Article 2 which stipulates that "the respect for democratic principles and human rights" is an essential element of the SAA.[26] In effect, this means that everything that has been subsequently done in terms of adopting the EU's gender equality *acquis* in Macedonia is legally covered only indirectly under Title VI of the SAA. This title refers to the "approximation of laws and enforcement," and legally binds Macedonia to approximate all domestic legislation with all of EU's *acquis*, both in terms of "hard law" (EU regulations, directives) and "soft law" (EU resolutions, recommendations, policy documents, best practices in the member states, etc.);

– The *Accession Partnership of 2008* in the short and mid-term priorities mentions "women's and children's rights," but its text neither mentions nor contextualises gender equality or women's rights.[27]

– The *High Level Accession Dialogue EU- Macedonia* established specifically for the country in 2012 also has no explicit mentioning of gender equality in its agenda, despite the fact that all the issues it focuses on (freedom of expression in the media, rule of law, fundamental rights, reforms in the public administration, electoral reform, developing the market economy) do involve problems concerning women's rights and gender equality, as it is analysed in more detail in part 2. The (non)presence of gender equality in IPA and in the Commission's Progress Reports on Macedonia is analysed in part 4.

---

[26] (2004) O.J. L 84, Vol. 47. The SAA that were later concluded with other Western Balkan countries in the period 2007-2009 contain more provisions regarding gender equality, not only in the area of social co-operation, but also in the area of education and training. The subsequent accession partnerships also prioritise labour market integration of women. See Ivana Petričević (2012). Women's Rights in the Western Balkans in the Context of EU Integration: Institutional Mechanisms for Gender Equality, p. 7-8. Available at http://www.ured-ravnopravnost.hr/site/images/pdf/report\%20womens\%20rights\%20in\%20the\%20western\%20balkans.pdf.

[27] Council Decision 2008/212/EC of 18 February 2008 on the principles, priorities and conditions contained in the Accession Partnership with the former Yugoslav Republic of Macedonia and repealing Decision 2006/57/EC.

2.3. Gender mainstreaming of Macedonia's EU-integration agenda

2.3.1. The legislative framework for gender equality

Macedonia's aspirations for EU membership have provided an additional impetus for further development of its gender equality legislation, especially in tackling some novel problems that have occurred due to the transition to market economy.[28] The Constitution of 1991 contains both a gender equality clause (Article 9) and a gender anti-discrimination clause (Article 54). It also guarantees reproductive rights and free reproductive choices (Article 41). All the systemic and key laws explicitly restate the gender equality and gender anti-discrimination clauses.

Macedonia was a pioneering country in the Western Balkans with a gender quota of a "minimum 30% of each sex" on candidate lists in its election legislation in 2002,[29] upgrading it to a "quota of 30% both on the first and the second half of the submitted candidate lists" in 2004[30], and finally to a "minimum 30% of the less represented sex on candidate lists for both parliamentary and local elections" in 2006. It also added the requirement that in each three positions on the lists, one is given to a candidate of the less represented sex.[31] However, the quotas do not apply to mayors elections or to the composition of the national government. Furthermore, the Law on Political Parties of 2004 explicitly obliges the political parties to promote the principle of gender equality in their activities, as well as to enable gender-equal access to party functions.[32]

After the entry into force of the SAA in 2004, the Labour Law of 2005 was the first systemic law adopted through a procedure of approximation with EU law, incorporating the EU directives concerning gender equality in labour relations. It introduced the EU's concepts of direct and indirect discrimination, sexual harassment at work, burden of proof in cases of dis-

---

28 For a comprehensive presentation and analysis of Macedonia's gender equality legislation, especially in the context of the transposition of EU's legislation, see K. Ristova-Aasterud (2012: 101-134). Country Report on Legal Perspectives of Gender Equality in Macedonia *in* Legal Perspectives of Gender Equality in South East Europe, SEELS Network Lawyers for Europe. Skopje: Center for SEELS, 101-134.
29 Official Gazette of Republic of Macedonia no. 42/2002.
30 Official Gazette of Republic of Macedonia no. 35/2004.
31 Official Gazette of Republic of Macedonia no. 40/2006.
32 Official Gazette of Republic of Macedonia no. 76/2004.

crimination based on sex, protection of breastfeeding workers and parental leave[33] – all of which were novel concepts in the Macedonian legal order.

Legislative projects that are *lex specialis* regarding the transposition of the EU's gender equality *acquis* in the Macedonian legal order are the Law on Prevention and Protection against Discrimination of 2011[34] and the Law on Equal Opportunities for Women and Men of 2012.[35] The anti-discrimination law was the first law adopted with corresponding tables of compliance with EU law, and prohibits all forms of discrimination on grounds of gender. It applies to all state bodies, units of local self- government and legal entities with public authority, as well as to all individuals and legal entities in the area of employment relations and working conditions, education, culture, science, sports, social security and social protection, health insurance and health services, housing, information of the public and media, access to goods and services, membership and activity in unions, political parties and the NGO sector. It also enumerates acts of discriminatory behaviour that are sanctioned as misdemeanors, with monetary sanctions ranging between 400-1000 Euro, as well as provides judicial protection against certain acts of discrimination in a competent civil court. As for the Law on Equal Opportunities for Women and Men, the initial version had been adopted in 2006, amended in 2008, but because it did not meet all EU's standards,[36] it was completely revised in 2012. The declared subject matter of the law is equal treatment and equal opportunities of women and men in Macedonia. It regulates the general and the special measures for achieving that goal, the rights and duties of all responsible subjects, and

---

[33] The prior labour laws of Macedonia had only recognised the paid maternity leave of nine months, while the fathers had the right to parental leave for a newly born baby only if the mother was dead, sick or abandoned the baby. Also, there were no legislative provisions on breastfeeding (female) workers. Official Gazette of Republic of Macedonia no. 60/2005.

[34] Official Gazette of Republic of Macedonia no. 50/2010.

[35] Official Gazette of Republic of Macedonia no. 6/2012.

[36] In June 2011 the Ministry of Labour and Social Policy had issued a comprehensive *Analysis on the Level of Implementation of the Law on Equal Opportunities for Women and Men,* and it was concluded that some of the legal definitions regarding gender equality and gender discrimination, the competences of implementing institutions and the sanctions provided in the law were not in compliance with the EU standards. This was also part of the criticism and the recommendations of the NGO sector, the EU/European Commission and OSCE/ODIHR, which initiated a change in one third of the law's text.

the procedure for establishing and protection from an unequal treatment. The law gives precise definitions of equal treatment, equal opportunities, discrimination based on sex and its forms as direct and indirect discrimination, harassment and sexual harassment based on sex. It introduces the concept of gender mainstreaming in accordance with CEDAW and EU legal standards and definitions. This represents a significant novelty in the Macedonian legal order, especially in the forms of gender-sensitive budgeting and statistical gender mainstreaming. Just as the anti-discrimination law, this law also equally applies to both the public and the private sector. There is an extensive list of measures for establishing equal gender opportunities with accompanying designation of the concrete subjects responsible for their adoption and implementation. Curiously, the measure of 40% political gender representation as a targeted threshold, initially introduced in the law's version of 2006, is no longer included in the list. The law also obliges the national parliament to adopt a "Strategy for gender equality" every eight years, which is to be prepared by the Government, followed by a "National plan for action on gender equality" every four years and annual operative plans.

2.3.2. GENDER EQUALITY POLICY FRAMEWORK

The Macedonian government adopted its *National Strategy for European Integration of the Republic of Macedonia* in September 2004, but with no explicit referral to gender equality in meeting the EU's membership criteria.[37] The subsequent governmental *National Programme for the Adoption of the EU Law,* first adopted in 2006, and its later revisions (nine as of 2015) do mention the gender equality *acquis* in the context of meeting the membership criteria. As this programme follows the formulation of the Copenhagen membership criteria, it is apparent that the EU's gender equality *acquis* is covered only in limited terms in the sections dedicated to the political criteria ("Human rights and protection of minorities"). For the most part, it is covered in the sections dedicated to the "Ability to take on the EU membership obligations," more precisely, in the section "Social policy and Employment," subsection "Anti-discrimination and Equal Opportunities", as well as in the section "Justice and Fundamental Rights."[38] In other

---

[37] National Strategy for European Integration of the Republic of Macedonia. Government of the Republic of Macedonia, Sector for European Integration, Skopje, 2005.

[38] The (revisions) of the NPAA are available at http://www.sep.gov.mk/en.

words, the EU's gender equality *acquis* is not covered throughout the EU membership criteria, least of all in the part covering the economic criteria.

In addition, there are several other national policy documents that target gender equality specifically, the most important being the *Strategy for Gender Equality 2012-2020*[39] and the *Strategy for the Introduction of Gender Sensitive Budgeting 2012-2015*,[40] both drawing as their legal basis on the above-mentioned Law on equal opportunities between women and men. The latter strategy is a novel approach for the country, incorporating the experiences with gender-sensitive budgeting in the EU and its member states. In 2013 the Ministry of Labour and Social Policy, in co-operation with the Ministry of Finance and UN Women, have also prepared a *Manual for gender- sensitive budgeting for the administration of Republic of Macedonia.*[41]

Other strategies that explicitly or implicitly concern women and gender equality in Macedonia are as follows:
- *Strategy on Equality and Non-Discrimination based on Ethnicity, Age, Mental and Physical Disability and Gender 2012-2015* (aimed at implementation on the EU-standardised anti-discrimination law),
- *National Strategy on Prevention and Protection Against Family Violence 2012 – 2015* (provides for gender-sensitive measures and procedures for female victims as main victims of family violence),
- *National Strategy and Action Plan for Employment* (targets female unemployment as a separate category, provides for special measures for female (self)employment, especially of rural women and women belonging to ethnic minority groups),
- *National Strategy and Action Plan for Combating Human Trafficking and Illegal Migration 2013-2016* (with special measures and procedures targeting women and girls as victims),
- *Strategy for Demographic Development 2008-2015* (includes special provisions on equal opportunities for women and men, and special measures for combating female poverty and social exclusion),

---

[39]   Official Gazette of Republic of Macedonia no. 27/2013.
[40]   The strategy is available on the official web site of the Ministry of Labour and Social Policy at http://www.mtsp.gov.mk (in Macedonian, accessed 20.01.2015).
[41]   Available at http://www.mtsp.gov.mk/wbstorage/files/priracnik_rodovo_mkd.pdf (in Macedonian).

– *National Action Plan on the Implementation of the UN Resolution 1325 on Women, Peace and Security 2012-2015* (it targets female inclusion in the decision-making and implementation of policies concerning peace and security issues, strengthening female participation in military and civil missions in preventive and post-conflict activities, and prevention of violence against women in pre-conflict and post-conflict situations).[42]

2.3.3. INSTITUTIONAL FRAMEWORK AND REMEDIES FOR THE PROMOTION AND PROTECTION OF GENDER EQUALITY

Subsequent to the equal opportunities law of 2012, the country has developed a variety of institutional and procedural forms for promotion and protection of gender equality. The main institutional forms are: a) Permanent parliamentary commission for equal opportunities for women and men – it was first established in 2006, and it oversees the implementation of the law, the strategies and the action plans concerning gender equality, it reviews all legislative initiatives and policy documents concerning gender equality that are to be adopted by the parliament, and fosters co-operation with all relevant institutions and the NGO sector; b) Governmental coordinators for equal gender opportunities for each ministry, governmental institution or agency, as well as an inter-sectoral advisory group on equal opportunities that is composed of representatives of the government, employers, workers, local self–government and experts – they all have certain competences to follow the implementation of gender equality legislation and policy documents in and across the ministries. The overall supervision on the governmental side is coordinated by the Ministry for Labour and Social Policy, more concretely, by its special department for equal gender opportunities headed by an appointed state adviser for equal opportunities; c) Equal opportunity commissions in the local assemblies of each unit of local self-government and coordinators for equal opportunities in the executive offices of the mayors; d) The Broadcasting Council of Macedonia supervises the implementation of the equal gender opportunities law with respect to the media, which, on their part, are under obligation to raise public awareness about gender equality, as well as to refrain from gender offensive and depreciating images or speech. The Council is obliged to prepare an annual analysis on these issues and submit annual reports to the national

---

[42] For more on these strategies see at the official web site of the Ministry of Labour and Social Policy of the Republic of Macedonia at http://www.mtsp.gov.mk.

parliament. It also has the competence to issue recommendations and warnings to the media, as well as to impose monetary sanctions if the law is violated.

The procedural and (legal) remedies for protection of gender equality consist of: a) Petition against unequal gender treatment before the legal representative of the Ministry of Labour and Social Policy – the petitions may be submitted by individuals or legal entities directly or by their legal representatives, under no financial charge, upon which, if violation is established, a recommendation by the minister is addressed to the subject against which the petition was submitted, and under the obligation to remedy the situation within 90 days; b) Petition against gender discrimination before the Office of the Ombudsman – these petitions refer to cases of gender equality violations or gender discrimination committed by the state administration or any other legal entity and physical person with public authority. On the merits of the case, the Ombudsman may issue opinions, recommendations, proposals, initiate disciplinary procedures, procedures before the office of the state prosecutor or request temporary suspension of administrative acts; c) Petition against gender discrimination before the Commission for protection against discrimination, which is an independent body of seven human rights' experts, established by the national parliament, and with competences defined in the anti-discrimination law of 2011. On the merits of the case, the Commission may issue recommendations to the perpetrators to remedy the situation within 30 days, and if that is not the case, initiate procedures before competent organs or institutions; d) Judicial protection of the right for equal gender treatment and against gender discrimination – the equal gender opportunities law and the anti-discrimination law both provide avenues for court protection of gender equality and against gender discrimination, namely, lawsuit for violation of the right for equal treatment based on sex, and lawsuit against discrimination. In both cases, it is a civil type of lawsuit and treated as urgent. The burden of proof as it is regulated in these two laws is in compliance with the EU Council Directive 97/80/EC of 15 December 1997 on the burden of proof in cases of discrimination based on sex.

3.MACEDONIA ON ITS WAY TO EU MEMBERSHIP:
COUNTER-GENDERING THE INTEGRATION AGENDA

3.1.REALITY CHECK OF THE COUNTRY'S GENDER EQUALITY INDICATORS

In the aftermath of gaining the EU candidate status in 2005 the country's focus has been placed solely on the adoption of the EU's gender equality *acquis*. This, of course, is an important advancement in itself. But, if we put into the equation different statistical and other indicators, a more complex picture of the actual advancements in gender equality emerges. It must be duly noted that this sobering process can also be credited to the introduction of the EU's statistical standards in the work of the State Statistical Office, which, as of 2008, has begun to generate gendered statistics and publish them in a special edition titled *Women and Men in Macedonia*.

3.1.1.GENDER (IN)EQUALITY IN POLITICS AND PUBLIC SECTOR

Even before Macedonia's status as a candidate for EU membership, the EU had a key influence in advancing female political representation in the country through the Gender Task Force of the Stability Pact of 1999, especially by actively supporting the introduction of election gender quotas.[43] As a result, women's representation in the national parliament and in the local councils has significantly increased. From less than 8% prior to the introduction of the quotas in 2002,[44] the female parliamentary representation first jumped to 18.3% in 2002 elections, then reaching to 34.1% in the last 2014 elections, which is above the current average of 27% in the EU. In the local councils, women's representation from 6.1% in 1996 had initially jumped to 22.7% in 2005, and then to 30% in local elections of 2013. However, there are no quotas for the executive power on national and local level. Since 1991 there is an unwritten "two women rule" in the government, "broken" only in 1998 when the government included four female ministers out of 24 (16.6%). For the most part, women's representation in

---

[43] (2013) Commission for Equal Opportunities for Women and Men of the Assembly of the Republic of Macedonia (formation, activities, results 2006 – 2013). Skopje: UN Women (in Macedonian). Available at http://www.sobranie.mk/WBStorage/Files/KEMBroshura.pdf.

[44] The female parliamentary representation was 4.2% (1990-1994), 3.3% (1994-1998) and 7.5% (1998-2002). Source: Reports on Electoral Results of the State Electoral Commission. Available at http://www.sec.mk.

the national government has never reached above 10%, with the current number being two female ministers out of 26 (7.6%), significantly below the EU's current average of 27%. In the last local elections of 2013, out of 339 candidates for mayors, 26 were women (7.6%), and only 4 out of total 81 elected mayors are women (4.9%), which is an improvement compared to the local elections of 2009 when no woman was elected mayor, or compared to only three women mayors after 2005 local elections (3.5%).

With respect to state and local administration, a 2011 study of the Ombudsman established that only 29.4% of the state servants are women.[45] In sectors that are considered "masculine" (military and police forces, public prosecutors, prisons, economy, agriculture), men are overrepresented (60-80%) both in employment and in management positions, while women's representation is stronger (40-60%) in sectors such as education, health, labour and social welfare. The only curiosity is the "feminisation of the legal professions", including the positions of judges, where women are represented with above 50%, in some courts reaching 80%.[46]

When it comes to political parties, a 2010 gender study on 17 parliamentary parties[47] found out that female party membership had ranged between 25-40%, with only four parties where it had reached towards 50% (in two major and two minor parties). Ten parties have statutory gender quotas, in most cases of 30%, although one party has a 20% quota (the opposition ethnic Albanian party DPA) and one 40% (Liberal Democrats). However, even in those parties which do not have gender quotas (including the ruling VMRO-DPMNE), women's participation in party organs has reached up to 30%. Only two minor parties have female presidents, but the social-democratic SDSM as one of the two biggest parties in the country had been led by a woman in the recent past (2006-2008). As for the party programmes, the study of 12 party programmes indicated the following: the issue of women's position in society was addressed mainly in terms of human rights, (reproductive) health, demographic and social policy, econo-

---

[45] Available at http://www.ombudsman.mk/upload/documents/Informacija\ %20-Ednakvi\%20moznosti-mk.pdf.

[46] Ristova-Aasterud (2012: 124-129). Country Report on Legal Perspectives of Gender Equality in Macedonia, *supra* note 33, at. 124-129.

[47] (2010) Women in Politics. Gender Analysis of the Programmes of the Political Parties. Skopje: Women Civic Intiative Antico. Available at http://www.antiko.org.mk/eng/ publikacii.asp.

mic empowerment and family violence, but with no specific mentioning in the context of EU enlargement or EU's gender equality *acquis*; these issues were addressed either in special sections or throughout the programme. Only seven party programmes specifically addressed gender equality and gender discrimination.

3.1.2. SOCIO-ECONOMIC AND CULTURAL GENDER (IN)EQUALITY

The EU Commission 2012 Gender Equality Country Profile of Macedonia[48] presented gender (in)equality in the country through five indicators, including comparison to the EU's average: 1.) General participation rate of women in the labour market was 35.3% (58.5% in EU). However, the share of women actively looking for work (31%) exceeded the EU average (9.8%); 2.) The rate of women working part-time (6.7%) was significantly below EU-average (31.6%); 3.) University education attainment of women equaled 15%, well below the EU-average of 24.8%, and was marked with gender-specific choices in the fields of study and with corresponding under/overrepresentation in occupations and sectors (as illustrated in 3.1.1 with respect to state and local administration). Thus, the existence of "typically male" and "typically female" fields of study is predominant; 4.) The under/overrepresentation of women and men in hierarchical positions in companies was ambivalent, being 15% (14% in EU) in corporate boards and 29% in management positions (33% in EU). A more recent EU review of the progress for 2013 indicated that women take 20.3% of the boards of large companies (16.6% in EU).[49] 5.) No official data exist for the gender pay gap in Macedonia, but different studies indicate that the gap is 15-25% in favour of men (16% in EU). On the last point, a 2013 comprehensive study on the gender pay gap in the Western Balkans[50] indicated that the Macedonian average gender pay gap was 13.4%. The gap was biggest in

---

[48] The Current Situation of Gender Equality in Republic of Macedonia – Country Profile 2012. European Commission, Directorate–General Justice. Available at http://ec.europa.eu/justice/gender-equality/files/epo_campaign/country-profile_fyrom_en.pdf.

[49] Women and men in leadership positions in the European Union 2013. A review of the situation and recent progress. European Commission. Justice. Available at http://ec.europa.eu/justice/gender-equality/files/gender_balance_decision_making/131011_women_men_leadership_en.pdf.

[50] Avlijas, Ivanovic, Vladisavljevic and Vujic (2013). Gender Pay Gap in the Western Balkans: Evidence from Serbia, Montenegro and Macedonia. Belgrade: FREN – Foundation for the Advancement of Economics.

the middle wage distribution (19.5%), but it shrank when going towards the lowest wage distribution (11.5%) and towards the highest wage distribution (10.3%). The gender wage gap also tends to shrink with the education levels, i.e. it is 10.4% for university-educated women, compared to 20.1% for those with secondary education, and 22.3% for those with primary. The gender gap also increases with the tenure with the employers, whereas lesser gap exists for women employed in "socialist times" (2.1%), but it increases for younger women who experience greater wage discrimination in the newly formed private sector (between 14-17%).

The Macedonian gendered statistics for 2014[51] indicate that women make 40% both in the employment and unemployment rates. In the urban areas, only 34.8% of the employed are women, while in the rural areas the rate is even lower, only 29.3%. Women make 63.2% of the population inactive in the labour market, which is due to the correlation between employment and education in favour of men. The data show 60% of the employed with elementary and high school education are men, while women with lower levels of education are discouraged to seek employment, especially in older age groups (55-64) in urban areas, as well as in the rural areas where 65.3% of the unpaid family workers are female. In contrast, 74.1 % of the employers and 80.9% of the self-employed in the rural areas are men. A recent study has also shown that due to the strong patriarchal traditions, and in spite of the equal inheritance rights, in 89% of rural families, it is the men who own the family house, and that only 6% of the women own farmland.[52] In urban areas, women have better chances for employment if they possess university diplomas, and they represent 51.2% of the university-educated employees. But, women also make up 62.2% of the university-educated who are unemployed. This significant gap is indicative of gender discrimination at the point of employment. Indeed, a 2012 survey of the Ministry of Labour and Social Policy reported that 22% of the women applying for jobs in the private sector had experienced discrimination during job interviews by being asked about their marital status and

---

[51] Women and Men in Macedonia. (2014). Skopje: State Statistical Office, Republic of Macedonia.

[52] Centre for Research and Policy. (2012) Perspectives of the women in the rural areas. Skopje: UN Women. Available at http://www.crpm.org.mk/wpcontent/uploads/AboutUS/Perspectives\%20of\%20women\%20in\%20rural\%20areas_ENG.pdf.

plans to have children.[53] Another study on discrimination in job announcements published in media, which was conducted by the Anti-discrimination
commission in 2013, established that in 55% of the cases the job announcements are discriminatory on the basis of gender (explicit preference for
male/female employees), while in 21% of the cases the announcements are
discriminatory on the basis of personal (marital) status (explicit preference
for married/unmarried employees), mostly in the private sector job pool
(93%).[54] These findings, together with the growing number of reported cases of women losing jobs due to pregnancy or maternity leave, had promp-
ted changes in the Labour law in 2013 to explicitly prohibit such practices.[55]
Finally, the 2014 statistics show that only 28.4% of employers are women
and only 20.4% of women are self-employed. In the highest paid jobs, women participate with only 19.2%.

Overall, the statistical indicators of women's socio-economic disempowerment can be attributed to a great extent to the persistent patriarchal traditions and cultural patterns which continue to coexist with the perceptions
of gender equality inherited from the previous system. As pointed out in the
2012 EU Commission's country gender profile on Macedonia, one of the
main reasons for the low women's participation in the labour market is that
the family duties and care for children and elderly are traditionally considered female domain. For example, the last official statistical survey of time
use from 2009[56] shows that on average men spend 3 hours of their time
on employment, and only 1.17 hours on domestic activities, while women
spend 1.37 hours on employment and 3.58 hours on domestic activities. In
families with small children (0-6) these disparities are greater, men spend
4.08 hours on employment and 1.32 hours on domestic activities, while women 1.33 hours on employment and 5.50 hours on domestic activities. The
pattern is the same for both employed and unemployed men and women.

A subsequent EU-funded study of 2010 on women's perceptions on

---

[53]   The survey and the data are referred to in the 2012 amendment package on the Labour
       Law. Available at http://www.mtsp.gov.mk (in Macedonian).
[54]   Discrimination in the job announcements (investigative report). Commission for protec-
       tion against discrimination. Skopje, 2013 (In Macedonian). At http://www.kzd.mk/mk/
       dokumenti.
[55]   Official Gazette of Republic of Macedonia no. 13/2013.
[56]   Time Use Survey, 2009, Statistical Office of Macedonia. Available at http://www.stat.
       gov.mk/Publikacii/2.4.11.01.pdf.

gender in the economy indicated that 62% of women agree that domestic obligations, especially childcare, represent an obstacle to women's freedom to participate in the labour market, employments and promotions to higher managerial positions.[57] According to official data of the Ministry of Labour and Social Policy cited in the study, only 23% of the children aged 0-6 are placed in childcare facilities.[58] However, in terms of balancing work and family life, the study also revealed that women are divided on the position that "it is not cost-effective for a woman to work if there are children or elderly in the household who are in need of care" (42% disagreed, 31% agreed and 27% have no opinion) and that women in great numbers believe that "a mother should put the care for her children ahead of her career" (54.1% fully agreed, 20.1% partially agreed), although when the same position is applied to fathers, the percentage of women's answer drop to 45% of full agreement and 19.6% partial agreement. As the study also indicated, while there is a high female confidence in equal gender job qualifications and high female support for equal gender treatment at employment and work, a significant number of women seems not to detect the correlation between gender equality at work and at home, as there is a significant number of women who believe that it is normal for men to be less involved in domestic activities (31.2% agreed and 17.5% had no opinion). In terms of the measures for increasing women's employment, women prioritised as follows: 1.) increasing the number of affordable care facilities for children and elderly (26.8%); 2.) introducing more flexible working hours (21.1%); 3.) improving access to better paid jobs (19.9%); 4.) improving access to sectors in which women are under-represented (16.7%); 5.) reducing the gender pay gap (1.4%). Placing the gender pay gap at the bottom indicates that most women are not aware of the existing gap, and continue to believe in the myth of equal gender pay from "socialist times." Pointing in the same direction are also the findings of the study that, apart from the equal rights to education and pay and the protection of pregnant women, half of the surveyed women did not have a clear understanding of the new legislation adopted in accordance with the EU' gender equality *acquis.*

---

[57] Reactor – Research in Action. (2010) Women in the Macedonian Economy. Available at http://www.reactor.org.mk/CMS/Files/Publications/Documents/women\%20in\ %20the\%20macedonian\%20economy\%202010\%20eng.pdf.

[58] *Ibidem,* at p. 25.

Finally, we must add into the equation some of the findings from the most comprehensive study on domestic violence in Macedonia[59] that had been conducted in 2012.[60] It reaffirms not only that the conservative patriarchal values are still embedded in the family life in Macedonia, but that their vitality is very much in correlation with the economic disempowerment of women: 60% of the victims of domestic violence are women, while 62% of the perpetrators are male; in terms of physical domestic violence, 80% of victims are women that are unemployed or inactive; 67% of the domestic violence happens in rural areas; in terms of economic domestic violence, 76.6% of the victims are female, with the highest prevalence among unemployed (36.6%) and homemakers (22.3%) who are mostly victimized by refusal of money for household expenses (42.7%), prevention from seeking or getting employment (35.17%) and taking away the money earned (16.5%).

IMPLEMENTATION OF THE EU GENDER *acquis*
For the most part, the institutional machinery and legal remedies that had been introduced with the new legislation as presented in 2.3.1, have been formally established. The negative exception is the Ministry of Labour and Social Policy, the very institution that is in charge of the overall supervision of the new legislation. The Ministry is obliged to appoint a legal representative for gender equality to deal with petitions ever since the first equal gender opportunity law of 2006, but it had employed such representative only in December 2009. After the transfer of the legal representative to another ministerial job in 2012, the Ministry has not appointed a replacement, and all petitions are now forwarded to the anti-discrimination commission, in clear violation of the equal gender opportunity law of 2012.

As for the anti-discrimination commission, the data published on its official website are also very discouraging. In the period 2011-2014, it had dealt with only six petitions on grounds of gender discrimination, out of 183 (3.2%), and in four of those cases no discrimination was found. In

---

[59] Macedonia has signed the Council of Europe Convention on preventing and combating violence against women and domestic violence (Istanbul Convention) on 8 July 2011 with no reservations. The ratification is pending. Data taken from http://conventions. coe.int/Treaty/Commun/ChercheSig.asp?NT=210\&CM=\&DF=\&CL=ENG.

[60] See Popovska, Rikalovski and Vilagomez (2012). Study Report on the National Survey of Domestic Violence. Skopje: Ministry of Labour and Social Policy of the Republic of Macedonia.

terms of multiple grounds of discrimination, out of 53 petitions, only 12 included gender (22.6%). It seems that women prefer this type of petitions because out of 12 such petitions, ten were submitted by women, usually accusing gender discrimination in combination with age (two cases), health / maternity leave / employment (five cases) and family and marital status (five cases). In only one of the 12 cases, discrimination had been established (gender/age/employment). In the other cases, no discrimination was found, citing lack of evidence or procedural grounds (late petitions or incompetence). As of June 2015, there is not a single court case initiated on the grounds of gender discrimination.

Furthermore, a 2014 NGO analytical study on the two-year implementation of the equal gender opportunity law has concluded that the obligations stemming from the law and the subsequent strategies are hardly being implemented. Much of the by-laws and institutional adjustments in different state institutions and agencies have not been made (only in 16.7%), and in most of the local councils only 36% of the equal opportunity commissions have been activated. Apart from the positive changes in collection of gendered statistical data, the concept of gender mainstreaming and gender-sensitive budgeting are not functional. The commission on equal gender opportunities in the national parliament also has a modest activity, limiting itself to minor changes in legislative and policy proposals.[61]

3.2.*Facta non verba*: GOVERNMENTAL DECONSTRUCTION OF EU'S GENDER EQUALITY VALUES

On 23 October 2012 which is a national holiday "The Day of VMRO" (a historical organisation which fought for an independent Macedonian state in the times of the Ottoman Empire), the President of the Macedonian government since 2006, Nikola Gruevski, made a speech in which he addressed the issue of negative demographic trends in the country, i.e. the fact that there is no simple demographic reproduction on the part of the ethnic Macedonians. Then he continued by pointing out that despite the fact that the country was facing such a grave problem "we have this twisted debate in the country about gay marriage, adoption of children by gay couples, about rights of women and rights of men, who was more represented in politics and business." The statement promptly caused unusually strong

---

[61] Akcija Zdruzenska (2014).

protest reactions from women's organisations. The very next day he had a meeting with the president of the parliamentary equal opportunity commission, who is also president of a minor coalition party in the government, on her request. After the meeting she made a statement to the media that Mr. Gruevski had clarified to her that his speech had been misinterpreted, that he was a supporter of gender equality, and that there was no need for apology for his speech. In any case, this statement of the President of the Macedonian government is paradigmatic for the double talk and mixed messages of his Government's policies with respect to gender equality. On the one hand, as presented under 2.3, his Government obediently transposes the EU's gender equality *acquis* into the domestic legislature, adopts different national strategies and action plans, and formally establishes an institutional machinery for its promotion and protection. On the other hand, there is the Government's extensive and intrusive political and policy narrative of "family values" and "multi-children families" in a very patriarchal and "demochristian" mode that has never been seen in Macedonian politics before.

Here I would point out the five key indicators of the governmental deconstruction of gender equality. First, as a starting point, gender equality is not included in the declared governmental "strategic priorities and goals" for 2011-2015, not even in the part on human rights.[62] Moreover, in the ruling party's election programme 2014-2018, gender mainstreaming and gender budgeting are mentioned almost in a reporting manner, and only when referring to the Government's obligations to the EU. In terms of concrete measures, the programme is dominated by measures on protecting women's motherhood role, such as building day-care centers for children.[63]

Second, ever since Gruevski's Government adopted its national strategy on demographic development 2008-2015, there is an on-going and visibly expensive media campaign promoting "family values" and "benefits of having multi-children families." A study of the governmental PR campaigns published in January 2015 had pointed out these campaigns did not aim at informing the citizens of governmental policies, but at imposing a system of values on the private lives of citizens, especially by reinforcing the traditio-

---

[62] See official site of the Government of the Republic of Macedonia at http://vlada.mk/node/331?language=en-gb.

[63] Official web site of the party VMRO-DPMNE. Available at http://vmro-dpmne.org.mk/?p=23038 (in Macedonian).

nal, religious-inspired and patriarchal gender roles, completely against the commitment towards gender emancipation and equality.[64] The campaign messages openly attack individuals, especially women, for "being selfish" if they pursue careers or if they resort to abortions. Instead of creating sustainable demographic policies and quality living standard, the Government's "demographic policy" reverses the pressure towards brainwashing the citizens to accept a bipolar model of "family or career," to the extent of open promotion of a "return" to the traditional extended family in which young couples live with their parents "who would take care of their children".[65] The "family values" campaign even went on the ridiculous side in 2013 when a new law supporting domestic music production was adopted, and it stipulated that governmental subventions would be given to domestic musical compositions dedicated to, among other topics, "family values" and " multi-children" families (10 compositions annually!), but, of course, none to gender equality.[66]

The third deconstruction happened in 2008 with the changes in the law on protection of children by introducing a new right to a "parental financial supplement" of 150 euro monthly over a period of ten years, but to which only mothers who decide to have their third or fourth child are entitled, unlike the regular parental supplements for the first and second child to which either of the parents are entitled.[67] The new version of the law of

---

[64] For example, in one of these campaign adds, the vocal slogan is that "children are our treasure, they make us closer to God," while in another a girlfriend tells her boyfriend that she is pregnant and that "the baby is a boy, and he will look like you" and "our parents will help us out with raising him."

[65] The PR of the Government: Monitoring the Government's Media Campaigns. Skopje: NGO Infocentre (2015). Available at http://nvoinfocentar.mk/en/monitoring-na-vladinite-mediumski-kampanji.

[66] Official Gazette of Republic of Macedonia no. 119/2013.

[67] In 2014, there was a petition on grounds of gender discrimination before the Commission for the protection against discrimination submitted by a father who had been denied such supplement for his third child because the mother of the child is a foreign citizen, and the right is only for the mothers who are Macedonian citizens. The Commission's opinion stated that this was not a case of discrimination because the "state has promoted this affirmative measures for its female citizens as birth-givers. Unlike the other parental supplements tied to the child, this one is tied to the mother who is responsible to nurture the child.". See, Opinion on petition no. 07/1130-1 from 10.09.2014, available at http://www.kzd.mk/mk/pretstavki/2014/category/67-Повеќе основи (in Macedonian).

2013 has reaffirmed this same right.[68] Ever since its introduction, this legislation raises many controversies, especially among experts and women's organisations. They worry that with the current unemployment rates such measure would cause more women to withdraw from actively seeking jobs, revising an achievement which even surpasses the EU average. Moreover, considering the fact that the sum for the third and fourth child combined is higher than the average salary in the country, it is very likely that in more traditional or poorer regions it will increase the (family) pressure on (unemployed) women to give up on pursuing education, jobs or careers and focus solely on having more children.

The fourth deconstruction is the Ministry of Education's decision to suspend gender studies at the biggest state university SS. Cyril and Methodius in Skopje, beginning from the academic year 2014/15, and replace them with "family studies." This decision goes against the need for educating qualified professionals who will attain gender equality expertise and who will prospectively fill in the positions in the institutional machinery established with the recent gender equality legislation, as presented in 2.3.3. The Ministry is also facing frequent media exposure for approving more and more study books for elementary and high school education in which the children are served with patriarchal gender stereotypes in family lives and jobs, completely opposite to its legal obligation for gender mainstreaming in education.

The fifth and most intrusive and controversial deconstruction came in the form of the new Law on termination of pregnancy adopted in June 2013.[69] The Law was adopted in less than a month after its announcement and without opportunity for substantial debate in the national parliament and the public. The regular three-phased legislative procedure was avoided, and the so-called "shortened legislative procedure" was used, accompanied by a governmental explanation that the new Law would make only language interventions in the concept of the previous liberal abortion law of 1972 that was from the previous socialist regime and "outdated" in that respect. Moreover, the Government publicly insisted that all changes in the law are for "stronger protection of women's health." Although the new Law in de-

---

[68]   Official Gazette of Republic of Macedonia no. 23/2013.
[69]   Official Gazette of Republic of Macedonia no. 87/2013.

finitional terms does not challenge the constitutionally guaranteed right to abortion, it introduced many novelties, primarily of procedural nature, that are aimed at obstructing its realisation in practice. Such are the unjustified number of documents from different institutions that a woman must collect to realise the right in the timeframe of ten weeks after the conception when she can freely abort, mandatory medical counsel on the "health benefits of carrying on the pregnancy and harmful health effects of abortion", a mandatory waiting period of three days after the mandatory counsel and the prohibition of more than one abortion per year. Violations of these provisions of the law are subject to severe monetary penalties, and, in certain instances, prison terms for the doctors. Subsequently, in September 2013 the Law was challenged before the Constitutional Court by the author of this article and a group of NGOs, but with no success. After one year of deliberate ignorance, in October 2014 the Constitutional Court announced that it had refused to perform constitutional review of the Law "as the law is not unconstitutional, it does not ban abortion, and it only regulates the right for the protection of women's health," with only one judge submitting a separate opinion in favour of the petition. This came as no surprise to the petitioners or the public, as the composition of the Constitutional Court had been completely and deliberately reconstructed in 2012 by parliamentary and presidential appointments of judges that are known political supporters of the current Government, causing doubts in its independence, as it has been also observed in the 2014 progress report of the EU Commission. Moreover, the Government's attack on the constitutional right to abortion did not come as a complete surprise. As early as 2009, this Government had commissioned a campaign for "informing the public on the purported consequences of abortion," mostly through billboards and TV videos, and in one of those videos there was even an explicit labeling of abortion as murder.[70]

---

[70] In the video a doctor approaches an expecting man in a hospital corridor and tells him: "Congratulations, you have just murdered a baby."

4.THE EU BETWEEN DECLARATION AND DEDICATION TO GENDER EQUALITY IN MACEDONIA

4.1.GENDER EQUALITY IN THE EU'S ENLARGEMENT POLICY AND POLITICAL RHETORIC

As pointed out in 2.2, gender equality is part of the legal framework of the EU's enlargement process. As of 2015, it is reinforced by three key policy documents. The first one is the Council's *European Pact for Gender Equality for the Period 2011-2020* in which it "reaffirms its commitment to reinforce governance through gender mainstreaming by integrating the gender perspective into all policy areas including external action."[71] The second one is the Commission's *Strategy for Equality between Women and Men 2010-2015* in which there is a special part dedicated to gender equality in external action, including EU enlargement: "Candidate countries must fully embrace the fundamental principle of equality between women and men. Monitoring the transposition, implementation and enforcement of EU legislation in this area remains priority of the enlargement process, which the EU supports financially."[72] Finally, there is the Commission's *Enlargement Strategy and Main Challenges* that accompanies the annual progress reports on candidate countries. In its most recent version of 2014-2015[73] "women's rights" and "ensuring gender equality" are placed in the part "fundamentals first," and accompanied with declared dedication that both in membership negotiations (especially on chapter 23 – judiciary and fundamental rights) and in the pre-accession assistance (IPA II) these issues would get more attention and in a more structured manner (early opening, closing at the end to allow for maximum time for solid track record and irreversibility of the reforms, substantial guidance, interim and closing benchmarks, safeguards and corrective measures, including stopping negotiations on other chapters if progress on chapter 23 lags behind). The Commission further points out that "more needs to be done to support women's rights and to ensure gender equality" and outlines the most serious problems, such as discrimination in

---

[71] *Supra note* 24, p. 5.
[72] COM(2010) 491 final, Brussels, 21.9.2010, p. 28.
[73] Available   at   http://ec.europa.eu/enlargement/pdf/key_documents/2014/ 20141008-strategy-paper_en.pdf, p. 10-16.

employment, low women's participation in the workforce, and persistence of stereotypes and traditional gender roles that in some cases are "to such an extent that they seriously limit the ability of women to assert their rights."[74] If this Commission's enlargement strategy is compared to the first one prepared for the Western Balkan countries for the 2006-2007 period[75], a significant progress can be observed in the Commission's language and declared dedication to gender equality in the enlargement context. In the first strategy, gender equality had not been mentioned in the "main challenges" at all, and it had been marginalised to incidental comments in the context of reviewing the situation with membership criteria in some of the countries included in the process. But then, if we look again at the current enlargement strategy 2014-2015, especially the part referring to Macedonia, the general outline of the problems regarding gender stereotypes is not put forward as a priority problem for the country, in spite of all the Government's de-constructing policies outlined in 3.2 of this article.

Moreover, as mentioned in 2.2, gender equality issues are not part of the agenda of the High Level Accession Dialogue EU-Macedonia, nor mentioned in the public statement of the EU Enlargement Commissioner at the time, Stefan Fule.[76] In fact, in all the years of Macedonia being a candidate country (2005-2015) there is not a single political statement of the highest EU representatives involved in the EU's enlargement process that addresses gender equality in the country, not even in the addresses before the Macedonian national parliament made by the President of the EU Commission (Romano Prodi in 2003 and 2004 and of Jose Manuel Barroso in 2006), or by the EU Enlargement Commissioner (Olli Rehn in 2005).[77] The current EU Enlargement Commissioner (2014-2019) Johannes Hahn, in his answers to the European Parliament's questionnaire as commissioner-designate, also did not address explicitly the issue of gender equality in the context of EU enlargement, apart from stating: "Fundamental rights need to be fully respected in practice not just in law. It is particularly import-

---

[74] *Ibidem,* p. 17.
[75] Available at http://ec.europa.eu/enlargement/pdf/key_documents/2006/Nov/com_649_strategy_paper_en.pdf.
[76] Available at http://ec.europa.eu/commission_2010-2014/fule/headlines/news/2012/03/20120315_en.htm.
[77] Data taken from annual reports of the Assembly of Republic of Macedonia at http://www.sobranie.mk/godishen-izveshtaj.nspx.

ant to ensure integration of minority groups and prevent discrimination on any grounds. These issues will be our priority with all countries and in our annual progress reports."[78]

4.2. MONITORING THE ADOPTION AND IMPLEMENTATION OF THE EU GENDER *acquis*

The main instrument for monitoring the fulfillment of EU membership criteria, including the EU's gender *acquis*, is the Commission's annual progress report.[79] The first such report for Macedonia was published in 2005 in the form of an analytical report for the Commission's opinion on the country's EU membership application. In the structure of the report, the EU's gender *acquis* was treated only in the part dedicated to "adoption of the *acquis*" as a membership criterion, more concretely, in negotiating chapters 19 (Social policy and employment) and 23 (Judiciary and fundamental rights). This approach has been kept in all subsequent progress reports, nine in total so far (2006-2014).

In terms of the political criteria, women's rights and gender equality are only occasionally mentioned in the context of "democracy and rule of law" and "human rights and protection of minorities." For example, election gender quotas and female political representation do get mentioned in terms of the criterion "democracy and rule of law" in some progress reports (2006, 2011), but not in a regular manner after each elections, and never with respect to reviewing the other branches of state power (government, judiciary, public administration, etc.). When it comes to the political criterion "human rights and protection of minorities," women's rights and gender equality are always treated in the section of "economic and social rights," in a very brief manner, and always referring to the "adoption of *the acquis*" criterion i.e. to chapters 19 and 23, and occasionally to chapter 24 (Justice, Freedom and Security – the problem of trafficking of women and girls). Gender equality and women's rights are never explicitly covered in the progress reports' parts that are reviewing the economic membership criteria.

---

[78] Available at http://ec.europa.eu/commission/2014-2019/hahn_en.

[79] Available at http://ec.europa.eu/enlargement/countries/strategy-and-progress-report/index_en.htm.

In the 2006-2010 period, the emphasis has primarily been put on the adoption of the gender *acquis,* while in the following years the Commission's review and criticism has moved more towards the lack of institutional capacity for its implementation. Beginning with the 2009 report, the Commission has begun to also include criticism of widespread discriminatory customs and traditions, as well as of gender stereotypes, pointing them out as serious obstacles that undermine women's basic rights. In the 2011 report, for the first time, the Commission has begun to openly criticise that "the equal opportunity issue is not a political priority of the government," and only in the 2014 report it has begun to openly put the blame for fuelling discriminatory practices and gender stereotypes on "some national policies and initiatives," but with no further elaboration, which is contrary to the Commission's usual approach regarding some of the other fundamental human rights (rights of ethnic minorities, for example). Moreover, neither the 2013 nor the 2014 progress report mention the new abortion law and the challenge to its constitutionality, not even in the sections dedicated to the "human rights" or "rule of law" criteria. If we compare the criticism expressed in the 2014 progress report with the subsequent governmental *National Programme for the Adoption of the EU Law (Revision 2015-2017)*, we can conclude that the Macedonian government largely ignores EU's criticism, and that it intends to address it only in terms of short-term priorities regarding education and media.[80]

In addition to the progress reports, there are two other mechanisms that can prospectively assist the Commission in the monitoring process, as well as in shaping better gender equality policies in the enlargement context of Macedonia. The first such mechanism is the gender equality country fiche for each candidate country, which is prepared by the European Network of Experts on Gender Equality (ENEGE). Although these fiches are produced for the needs of DG Justice of the Commission, they are growing into annual gender equality country profiles, promoted at the same time with the overall progress reports, as was the case with Macedonia's gender equality profile in the framework of the EU's initiative "Equality Pays Off."[81]

---

[80]   *Supra* note 38.
[81]   See Equality Pays Off. A Europe 2020 Initiative. European Commission, Justice. Available at http://ec.europa.eu/justice/gender-equality/files/epo_campaign/epo_leaflet_en.pdf.

The second such mechanism is the Commission's Database on women and men in decision-making. This database was created in 2003, and it covers 34 countries (EU members states, EEA countries and candidate countries), and is focused on regular collection of data on gender representation in political decision-making on national and local levels and in the European corporate world.[82]

4.3. GENDER (NON) SENSITIVE BUDGETING OF EU'S PRE-ACCESSION FINANCIAL ASSISTANCE

4.3.1. THE INSTRUMENT FOR PRE-ACCESSION ASSISTANCE (IPA)

The main financial assistance that Macedonia receives from the EU for meeting the membership criteria is through IPA. In the framework of IPA I (2007-2013) Macedonia had been allocated 622.5 million Euro. However, as it is stated in the 2014 progress report, the country has had trouble with its absorption capacity under the decentralised managing system that makes the national authorities responsible for managing most of the IPA money (470 million Euro under IPA I). As it was indicated, this was mostly due to the lack of adequate qualification and commitment on the part of the state administration, causing the country to lose 21 million Euro by the end of 2013 (out of the 113.2 million Euro). The overall absorption capacity was 37.3 % of the allocated IPA I funds i.e. only about 232.6 million Euro used.[83]

In the context of spending IPA funds on project that concern women's rights and gender equality, the only data available are those on the official website of the EU Delegation in Macedonia. These data are not gender mainstreamed, and we had to extract them for the purposes of this article from the plain enumeration list of the IPA projects. Out of 400 IPA-financed projects, only eight concern gender equality, women's rights and women's empowerment in some form, as presented in the table below:[84]

---

[82] http://ec.europa.eu/justice/gender-equality/gender-decision-making/database/index_en.htm.

[83] http://www.sep.gov.mk/en/content/?id=361.

[84] http://eeas.europa.eu/delegations/the_former_yugoslav_republic_of_macedonia/projects/overview/index_en.htm.

Table: IPA I 2007 – 2013 Gender Equality Projects in Macedonia

IPA Component	Title/Period/Aim of IPA Project	Sums for the project in Euro
IPA Component I (Institution Building)	*Strengthening linkages for gender-aware and inclusive policy making processes* (2011)	53.500
IPA Component II (Cross Border Co-operation)	*Promoting woman's business enterprises in cross-border area* (2011)	21.980.18
	Women crossing borders for change (2011)	25.406.66
	Women in network for innovation and entrepreneurship (2012)	73.717.33
	Equality and gender mainstreaming across borders (2014)	129.820.46
IPA Component IV (Human Resource Development	*Support to the employment of young people, long-term unemployed and women* („multi-annual 2007-2013, grand scheme)	1.300.000 (the indicators from the project reports do not segregate the data according to gender, so one cannot deduct how many women benefitted from the measure)
	Strengthening capacities for integration of marginalised women at the labour market, focus on ethnic minority women (multi-annual 2007-2013, grant schemes) – Grants were provided to NGOs, agencies, economic chambers	1.500.000
	Support to the implementation of gender equality (begins second half of 2015, 18 months, IPA Twinning Project) – main objective is to identify bottlenecks for the country's equal opportunities law and gender equality strategies, and to develop G-markers for implementation and for the EU-funded projects	855.000
Total:		2.659.424, 63 (gender) + 1.300.000 (cross-cutting) = 3.959.424,63

If we add all these projects together, from IPA I funds allocated to Macedonia just above 2.5 million Euro had been spent on gender equality projects. In a generous estimation, if we add the 1.3 million Euro for the cross-cutting projects targeting employment of women with some other target groups, the sum raises to almost 4 million Euro, which makes only 0.6% of the allocated and only 1.7% of the used IPA I funds. In addition to these national IPA projects, Macedonia had also been included in one regional IPA-funded project (176.339.87 Euro) regarding gender equality titled "Preparatory measures for the participation of candidate countries and potential candidate countries in EIGE's work" obtained by the European Institute for Gender Equality (EIGE) for the period of 18 months (2013-May 2014). The main project objective was to strengthen the capacity of candidate countries and potential candidates to comply with the EU policies in the field of gender equality. It was a pilot project to establish contacts, assess the needs and expectations of candidate countries and potential candidates, and explore ways of co-operation with EIGE in the future.[85]

Under IPA II (2014-2020), the promotion of gender equality is selected as one of the policy areas that will be specially targeted. Out of the 664.2 million Euro planned, 53.2 are indicated for allocation on gender equality projects, yet again jointly with employment, social policies, education and human resource development.[86]

4.3.2. EUROPEAN INSTRUMENT FOR DEMOCRACY AND HUMAN RIGHTS (EIDHR)

Although EIDHR does not target the EU's enlargement process specifically, Macedonia has also received financial funding for gender equality projects through this EU instrument. Since 2007, the following EIDHR's projects have been procured and financed through the EU Delegation in Skopje, in total worth of 280.720,53 Euro: *Introduction of Gender Sensitive Approach in Macedonian Policy Making* (2008 – 36.000 Euro); *A Step towards Gender Equality* (2008-41. 997.15 Euro); *Woman in Economy* (2009 – 41.232,67 Euro); *Achieving Gender Equality in Rural Communi-*

---

[85] http://eige.europa.eu/content/ipa-project.
[86] Instrument for Pre-Accession Assistance (IPA II). Indicative Strategy Paper for the Republic of Macedonia (2014-2020). At http://www.sep.gov.mk/data/file/Pred\ %20Pristapna\%20podrska/IPA\%202/CSP\%202014-2020_adopted.pdf

ties (2011 – 63.259,18 Euro); and, *Which Gender is the Ohrid Framework Agreement* (2011-72.231,53 Euro).

5. CONCLUDING REMARKS

Macedonia represents a case study that clearly indicates both the strong and the weak points of the gender dimension of EU enlargement. In positive terms, the country's path from gaining independence to stabilisation in the aftermath of the violent dissolution of former Yugoslavia, and from stabilisation to association with the EU as a candidate country for EU membership, exemplifies the overall constructive and positive role of the EU in the process, including with respect to the issues of women's rights and gender equality. Indeed, the EU's gender *acquis* and gender equality policy documents do create pressure on the candidate countries to make progress, especially in terms of the "adoption of the *acquis*" as a membership criterion. In this article I have extensively elaborated that only after the SAA of 2001 had entered into force in 2004, and only after the subsequent gaining of a candidate status for EU membership in 2005, Macedonia started to develop a solid legislative and institutional framework for the advancement and protection of gender equality, and against gender discrimination in all areas of social life. On the positive side, it can also be observed that the EU itself has developed solid methods and instruments for gathering relevant information and statistical data in order to detect and identify candidate countries' progress regarding the membership criteria, gender equality *acquis* included. This is best illustrated through the allocation of EU's financial aid (IPA), i.e. by what types of projects are financed. In Macedonia's case, the financial aid is aimed primarily towards building the institutional capacity for the EU's gender equality *acquis* implementation and towards the problems of women's unemployment and socio-economic empowerment, which, as presented indicators do show, are indeed major problems.

But, apart from these positive aspects, Macedonia's case unfortunately gives more arguments to conclude that women's rights and gender equality are still treated as secondary issues in the context of EU enlargement by the EU itself. There are several major weaknesses that need to be overcome, as well as more steps to be taken to turn the EU's declaratory dedication into an effective commitment. First, gender equality must receive a more prominent and explicit place not only in EU's general policy documents regarding enlargement, but also in the concrete pre-accession instruments such as the association agreements and accession partnerships, which currently deal with the issue only implicitly. Second, gender equality should not be covered almost exclusively through the criterion "adoption of the *acquis*," but throughout all the membership criteria (political and economic). This especially refers to the monitoring instruments such as the Commission's annual progress reports on candidate countries, which, as of now, deal with the EU's gender equality *acquis* prominently only in the negotiation chapters 19 (social policy and employment) and 23 (judiciary and fundamental rights). Moreover, the progress reports should also start to take more critical positions regarding cases whereupon gender equality is de-constructed as an EU's treaty value, even when such violations are committed implicitly and in areas that formally come under national jurisdiction, as it is very clearly the case with some of the patriarchal (legislative) policies and projects of the Macedonian government. Third, the Commission should develop additional and more focused pressure mechanisms, such as annual gender equality country profiles on the candidate countries, drawing upon the Commission's database that, on its part, needs to be extended beyond the data collection on women and men in decision-making. Fourth, as the EU insists on developing gendered statistics and gender-sensitive budgeting by the candidate countries, it is only appropriate to lead by example by introducing the same approach with respect to the EU's financial instruments used in the enlargement, especially IPA. This will also provide a stimulus for better planning and targeting gender equality projects, and for building greater pressure to allocate more substantial funds on such projects, which currently are quite minimal and symbolic, as it is obviously the case with IPA I's allocations in Macedonia. And finally, in order for candidate countries to take seriously the EU's commitment to gender equality, the political figureheads and representatives of the highest EU's institutional level should also include the issue in their political rhetoric. As Macedonia's case clearly exemplifies, when a candidate country has issues with its international recognition, security and political stability, the EU tends to ignore gender equality as part of the "fundamental firsts" political rhetoric and policy approach. This is quite a wrong approach as it weakens the overall candidate country's dedication to meet the membership criteria, and eventually to become a stable and prosperous EU member state.

REFERENCES

Abels, Gabriele and Mushaben, Joyce Marie (eds.) (2012). *Gendering the European Union. New Approaches to Old Democratic Deficits.* Basingstoke: Palgrave Macmillan.

Akcija Zdruzenska (2014). *Two Years After: Monitoring the Advancement in the Implementation of the Law on Equal Opportunities of Women and Men.* Available at http://www.zdruzenska.org.mk.

Avlijas / Sonja, Ivanovic / Nevena, Vladisavljevic / Marko and Vujic / Suncica (2013). *Gender Pay Gap in the Western Balkans: Evidence from Serbia, Montenegro and Macedonia.* Belgrade: FREN – Foundation for the Advancement of Economics.

Burri, Susanne and Prechal, Sacha (2013). *EU Gender Equality Law. Update 2013.* European Network of Legal Experts in the Field of Gender Equality. European Commission, Directorate-General for Justice. Available at http://ec.europa.eu/justice/gender-equality/files/your_rights/eu_gender_equality_law_update2013_en.pdf.

Centre for Research and Policy (2012). *Perspectives of the Women in the Rural Areas.* Skopje: UN Women. Avaliable at http://www.crpm.org.mk/wpcontent/uploads/AboutUS/Perspectives\%20of\%20women\%20in\%20rural\%20areas_ENG.pdf.

Commission for Protection Against Discrimination. Discrimination in Job Announcements (Investigative Report). Skopje, 2013 (in Macedonian). Avaliable at http://www.kzd.mk/mk/dokumenti.

Commission for Equal Opportunities for Women and Men of the Assembly of the Republic of Macedonia (Formation, Activities, Results 2006 – 2013). Skopje: UN Women (in Macedonian), 2013. Available at http://www.sobranie.mk/WBStorage/Files/KEMBroshura.pdf.

Equality Pays Off. A Europe 2020 Initiative. European Commission, Justice. At http://ec.europa.eu/justice/gender-equality/files/epo_campaign/epo_leaflet_en.pdf.

Informacija od istrazuvanjeto za zastapenosta na polovite, Skopje: Office of the Ombudsman, 2011. Available at http://www.ombudsman.mk/upload/documents/Informacija\%20-Ednakvi\%20moznosti-mk.pdf.

Matland, Richard E. and Montgomery, Kathleen A. (2003). *Women's Access to Political Power in Post-Communist Europe.* Oxford: Oxford University Press.

Mojanovski, Cane (1996). *Socijalniot i politickiot profil na politickite partii vo Makedonija.* Skopje: Liber.

National Strategy for European Integration of the Republic of Macedonia. Government of the Republic of Macedonia, Sector for European Integration, Skopje, 2005.

Petričević, Ivana (2012). *Women's Rights in the Western Balkans in the Context of EU Integration: Institutional Mechanisms for Gender Equality*. Available at http://www.ured-ravnopravnost.hr/site/images/pdf/report\%20womens\ %20rights\%20in\%20the\%20western\%20balkans.pdf.

Popovska, Ljubinka, Rikalovski, Vlado, and Vilagomez, Elizabeth (2012). *Study Report on the National Survey of Domestic Violence*. Skopje: Ministry of Labour and Social Policy of the Republic of Macedonia.

Reactor – Research in Action. (2010) Women in the Macedonian Economy. Available at http://www.reactor.org.mk/CMS/Files/Publications/Documents/ women\%20in\%20the\%20macedonian\%20economy\%202010\%20eng. pdf.

Ristova, Karolina, *Establishing a Machocracy: Women and Elections in Macedonia* (1990-8) in R. E. Matland and K.A. Montgomery, eds. (2003). *Women's Access to Political Power in Post-communist Europe*. Oxford: Oxford University Press, 196-216.

Ristova-Aasterud, Karolina (2002). *The Political and Legal Aspects of EU-Macedonia Relations: An Ever Closer Union?* Macedonian Affairs Vol. IV, No. 1.Skopje: Macedonian Information Centre, 29-61.

Ristova-Aasterud, Karolina (2012). Country Report on Legal Perspectives of Gender Equality in Macedonia, *in* Legal Perspectives of Gender Equality in South East Europe, SEELS Network Lawyers for Europe. Skopje: Center for SEELS, 101-134.

Takeva-Grigorievik / Milka, Veskovc Vangeli / Vera and Petroska / Blaga (eds.) (1994). The Women's Position in Contemporary Societal Tendencies. Skopje: Organization of Women of Macedonia (In Macedonian).

The PR of the Government: Monitoring the Government's Media Campaigns. Skopje: NGO Infocentre, 2015. Available at http://nvoinfocentar.mk/en/ monitoring-na-vladinite-mediumski-kampanji (in Macedonian).

The Current Situation of Gender Equality in the Republic of Macedonia – Country Profile 2012. European Commission, Directorate –General Justice. Available at http://ec.europa.eu/justice/gender-equality/files/epo_campaign/ country-profile_fyrom_en.pdf.

Women in Politics. Gender Analysis of the Programmes of the Political Parties. Skopje: Women Civic Intiative Antico, 2010 (in Macedonian). Available at http://www.antiko.org.mk/eng/publikacii.asp.

Women and Men in Leadership Positions in the European Union 2013. A Review of the Ssituation and Recent Progress. European Commission – Directorate General Justice. Available at http://ec.europa.eu/justice/gender-equality/files/ gender_balance_decision_making/131011_women_men_leadership_en.pdf.

Women and Men in Macedonia. Skopje: State Statistical Office, Republic of Macedonia, 2014.

CHAPTER 4:

THE EU'S ROLE IN COMBATING DOMESTIC VIOLENCE AGAINST WOMEN

IN SOUTH EAST EUROPE – PERSPECTIVES FROM

ALBANIA AND MACEDONIA[1]

Aida ORGOCKA and Nikolina KENIG

This chapter discusses EU's role in combating domestic violence against women within the larger field of gender-based violence in Albania and Macedonia. Both countries aspire towards EU membership; they have already been granted candidate status. They have signed the 2011 Council of Europe Convention on Preventing and Combating Violence against Women and Domestic Violence; Albania has ratified it. There is evidence that a sound legal framework is in place and efforts have been made to improve institutional capacity to respond to domestic violence against women. Yet, its prevalence and incidence are high in both countries. This phenomenon remains largely under-reported, not sufficiently investigated and pro-secuted despite significant assistance from various donors including the EU. This chapter finds that the EU has adopted an approach of "soft integration" via pro-gress reports, communications and recommendations, to name a few. Recognising that the efforts of the international community through technical assistance and funding have contributed significantly to breaking the silence on domestic violence against women in both countries, the paper argues that the EU is in a singular po-sition to exert stronger influence with a heftier impact, if it clearly identifies how

---

[1] The contextual analysis and data used for this chapter relate primarily to a five year period from 2010 to 2015. However reference to earlier developments is also made. Changes in the country specific policy framework and related action on combating domestic violence after this period is subject to future work. Our thanks go to experts in Albania and the Republic of Macedonia consulted in the preparation of the initial draft of this chapter, Wenona Giles, Heather MacRae, Stojanka Mircheva and Emira Shkurti who reviewed the subsequent draft as well as Thomas Kruessman for editorial rigor and leadership.

to capitalise on its exceptional significance as a policy-setter and pathmaker for these countries.

1.INTRODUCTION

This chapter provides an expose to the role of EU assistance in combating gender based violence in EU candidate countries of South East Europe by focusing on Albania and Macedonia. While elsewhere EU assistance has been provided to address violence against women (VAW), in South East Europe the approach has been to initiate action at the level of *domestic* violence against women. Past research has been critical of EU's role in combating domestic violence and gender based violence elsewhere by positing that EU's limited competence in this field conditions its effectiveness as a social actor, thereby recommending that the EU partner with other actors for more significant change (e.g., Lamont, 2013). How has this trend been reflected in the countries of South East Europe? Answering this question is particularly important in view of the fact that combating domestic violence against women as part of ensuring implementation of conditionality clauses on implementation of human rights is dependent also on EU's assistance for these countries.

Domestic violence is one of the most widespread forms of violence throughout South East Europe,[2] and women are its primary victims.[3] Women-led civil society organisations (CSO) that bear the brunt of work done to address domestic violence suggest a high level of unreported cases of domestic violence, due to existing gender prejudices that discourage women from reporting domestic violence, and the lack of safe and prompt access to justice and protection. Furthermore, research shows that victims of domestic violence usually seek help only after being exposed to violence for several years, and after receiving physical injuries (e.g., Fugate *et al.*, 2005; Barrett and Pierre, 2011). While domestic violence, in this chapter, refers to "assaultive and coercive behaviours that adults use against their intimate partners" (Holden, 2003: 155), population-based studies of dome-

---

[2]   For the purposes of this article, the countries referred to within the region are those that have signalled their desire to join the EU and are working towards this goal: Albania, Bosnia and Herzegovina, Kosovo, Macedonia and Montenegro.

[3]   For case studies and work done at country level see for example, Oneworld – Platform for South East Europe (owpsee) Foundation, available at http://oneworldsee.org/.

stic violence suggest that women in heterosexual relationships are disproportionately affected (for recent research around the world see, for example,
Yount *et al* 2011). Overwhelmingly, measures to counter domestic violence
are directed toward supporting women, victims and survivors of domestic
violence.[4] Thus, in this chapter we refer to domestic violence perpetrated
on women by men in such relationships, and measures taken at the state
level to counter this phenomenon.

Whereas domestic violence against women has always existed, it is only in the last two decades that the region has begun to highlight and systematically define the problem and seek solutions toward combating it. This
coincides with worldwide action of organisations such as the United Nations (UN) which recognise the need to work towards the elimination of
violence against women (VAW) (including domestic violence) as a means
to achieve development. International aid has been instrumental in deter-
mining and shaping the action taken at the level of prevention, protection
and prosecution. Tackling VAW to achieve gender equality and women's
empowerment and to improve women's welfare is being addressed from
different entry points, including defining violence as a violation of human
rights. The EU, as a normative actor in promoting gender equality worldwide, has had a role to play in addressing domestic violence against women
in the region.

Pursuant to the EU Strategy for Equality between Women and Men
2010–2015, combating gender-based violence (GBV) within the EU is a
priority (see also EIGE report 2012). The same is true, in principle for candidate countries. EU's influence on improving state level responses to domestic violence against women in candidate countries is secured through
two main mechanisms: strengthening legislative frameworks in the areas
of criminal and civil justice as well as targeted policy initiatives (including
awareness-raising, the exchange of good practices, and appropriate measures for the empowerment of women). EU financial assistance to candidate
countries is key to both mechanisms. Whereas a specific policy response
to domestic violence is not a formal criterion for EU membership, since
the late 1990s responding to the issue has become part of the fundamental

---

[4]   The authors recognise that there is significant work done on prevention and protection
of children, victims of domestic violence but a discussion on this is out of scope of the
chapter.

norms and beliefs that shape the collective identity of the EU (Kriszan and Popa 2010). Referring to earlier processes of accession to the EU, research shows that former candidate countries were urged to show legal and practical measures to combat violence against women (Kriszan and Popa, 2010) suggesting that combating this phenomenon has been considered a core condition of EU accession relating to human rights and gender equality.

However, there are limits to this influence. Summarising past research, Krizsan and Popa (2010: 380) maintain that the EU has no strong competence with respect to domestic violence and that policy responses to domestic violence, while increasing in the last decade, remain restricted to soft law and capacity building measures. Other research regarding this influence in post-communist countries suggests that the EU has generally refrained from engaging significantly in becoming a norm setter (for an in-depth analysis, see Avdeyeva, Hrycak, Fabian, and Montoya, 2010). Montoya and Augustin (2013) point to the culturalisation/"other-ing" of violence against women at the expense of addressing situational context and intersecting forms of oppression. This has in turn led to policy aimed not at member states (where violence remains prevalent), but toward dealing with the violence in "other" cultures including distant candidate states such as those in South East Europe.

Following these conclusions, the chapter offers an exposé on two countries in South East Europe: Albania and Macedonia. Significant changes have happened in policy framework and action related to combating domestic violence in both countries and foreign assistance has been crucial in the dynamic changes observed in the last decade. Both countries have been accorded candidate status for EU membership. Albania received its candidate status in 2014 after going through a tumultuous process of gains and set-backs starting with the first membership application in 2009. While Macedonia received its candidate status in 2005, the country has been "in the waiting room" for a long time. As EU candidate countries, both continue to face long-term obstacles in the implementation of democracy, much greater than those encountered by other post-communist countries that have already become EU members (see Spehar, 2012 for a general description of challenges countries in South East Europe face as they prepare for accession to the EU, and Noutcheva, 2009 on the limits of EU's normative powers in South East Europe). By analysing EU involvement in these two South

East European countries, this chapter aims to broaden our knowledge about the EU's possibilities and limitations in tackling domestic violence in candidate countries. The authors have limited their observations to domestic violence against women, fully aware that the scope of action by national and international actors in both Albania and Macedonia is broader; legislative frameworks and policy responses cover a larger action field defined as family violence where domestic violence against women and girls is located. Beyond project reports, little research on domestic violence and EU aid, exists in these candidate countries. The chapter thus provides a foray into the task of drawing conclusions regarding the utility of the approach followed by the EU in candidate countries in South East Europe.

This chapter is organised as follows: We start by exploring the manifestation of domestic violence in Albania and Macedonia. Following a presentation of EU's general policy framework on violence against women, we then consider how the EU contributes to shaping the general trend on policy formulation processes and responses that set out strategies for action on domestic violence. Also of interest are the similarities between the processes in both countries and a specific understanding about the role of the EU in combating domestic violence. While it is not within the scope of this chapter to consider the extent to which the policies are enacted "on the ground", we do juxtapose these policies to the current state of affairs in Albania and Macedonia. We argue that the very process of building policies that can support the prevention of domestic violence and protection of women against such violence is, in its own right, a means of actually combating domestic violence in both countries. However, while there is a general perception that the EU has the resources to be a powerful actor and to use its power to its fullest capacity to promote violence-free countries, the chapter offers evidence that the EU's involvement to date remains lukewarm, thus questioning its ability to lead as a gender actor.

2. Brief overview of domestic violence and relevant responses in Albania and Macedonia

The women's movement in South East Europe, through awareness campaigns and protection centres (shelters), has successfully framed the issue of domestic violence against women so that it has become an issue worthy of state intervention. Although it is very important to find out how much funding has been allocated to programmes that tackle domestic violence against women by international and national agencies in both Albania and Macedonia, the current reality is that many entities do not disaggregate their budget by gender-related programmes let alone gender equality, women's projects or programmes combating VAW and domestic violence. Thus linking impact to concrete contributions by international funding remains, at best, challenging. However, there is no denial of the fact that without external support, action to combat domestic violence against women in both countries would have taken a longer time to materialise.

2.1. PREVALENCE AND INCIDENCE OF DOMESTIC VIOLENCE AGAINST WOMEN

In both countries, domestic violence against women is highly prevalent. Well above half of women surveyed in national studies experience various types of violence. Thus, the most recent national study on domestic violence in Albania (Haarr, 2013) indicates that domestic violence is on the rise in general. It is expressed mainly in psychological violence, while there is a slight decrease in physical and sexual violence from an earlier national survey of 2007. Nevertheless, State Police reports of 2013 indicate an increase of approximately 46% in the number of women killed as a result of domestic violence from 2010 to 2012. In most cases, the killer is a spouse. Only in 2012, of the 28 victims of family crime, 16 were women. Table 1 provides data on the number of reported cases of family violence in 2010-2015 and the number of orders of protection and immediate orders of protection[5] issued thereafter in the six years.

---

[5]   According to the Albanian Law on Family Violence, an order of protection is a court decision that defines a series of protective measures for a victim of family violence. This order is issued if the court finds sufficient evidence that the abuser may exert acts of family violence again, or when protection is necessary for the safety, health and well-being of the victim or other family members. An immediate order of protection is issued if the abuser presents a direct and immediate danger to the safety, health or well-being of the victim or other family members. This order is usually issued within 48 hours. Both orders are executed as soon as they are issued irrespective of whether the abuser has been notified.

Table 1: Albania: Number of evidenced cases of violence and orders of protection issued

Action	2010	2011	2012	2013	2014	2015
Reported Cases	1,998	2,181	2,526	3,020	4,121	3,866
Order of Protection	1,234	1,345	1,562	1,851	2,422	2,174

Note: Data extracted from a data summary produced by the State Police of Albania

This table shows an increase of reported cases and issuance of orders of protection and immediate orders of protection issued by year during 2010-2013.[6] While the numbers are not disaggregated by sex (suggesting a serious limitation in the methodology of data collection and analysis), conversations with advocates against domestic violence emphasise that most family violence is exercised against women, and most orders of protection are issued to women.

The first national study on experiences with domestic violence in Macedonia (Chacheva, Friscik, and Mishev, 2007) showed that over half of the 1,432 female respondents faced some violent act within the family at least once. A study by Popovska, Rikalovski and Villagomez (2012) indicated that prevalence of domestic violence for females was 39.4%.[7] Younger women, those that were unemployed, less educated and lived in rural areas were especially vulnerable. In most cases (over 50%), the perpetrators were intimate partners. According to the National Strategy for Prevention and Protection of Domestic Violence 2012-2015, domestic violence remains largely under-reported and not sufficiently investigated and prosecuted, in spite of significant increases in the numbers of domestic violence incidents recorded by the police (Table 2).

---

[6] The last two years, 2014 and 2015 were excluded from the analysis given that we do not have data for the full year.

[7] An unpublished review of the data collection methodology by Kenig, indicates that this figure may be biased. The researchers could not provide privacy of all respondents when these were interviewed. The interviewers were not well-trained to deal with situations in which privacy had to be ensured. For example, some spouses were present when women answered the interview questionnaire. Some questions also seemed to be biased and did not reflect well the context of domestic violence against women.

Table 2: Macedonia: Number of women reporting instances of violence against them (Macedonia)

Action	2008	2009	2010	2011
Criminal offences	378	404	481	593
Misdemeanours[8]	730	676	724	655
Complaints	3671	4034	3737	4609

The analysis of data from the Ministry of Interior in Macedonia shows that a large proportion (90% or more) of domestic violence victims are women and overwhelmingly, they were victimised by their spouses. An analysis of protection interventions against domestic violence shows that as many as 50% of women who had filed for court protection withdrew their petitions subsequently. Furthermore, court decisions continue to show evidence of a gender bias (Mircheva, Chacheva and Kenig, 2014).

Policy makers / implementers, practitioners and advocates in both countries commonly attribute the rise in numbers to the fact that more women come forward to denounce cases of violence due to an increased awareness of domestic violence as a crime. However, whether the system is able to offer the necessary protection needed remains an issue in both countries.

2.2. POLICY RESPONSES

Over the past five years, community and government recognition, understanding, and responses to domestic violence in Albania and Macedonia have shifted considerably. Influenced by strong activism and grassroots movement to "break the silence" of domestic violence in the 1990s, both countries' policies have gone through various iterations, and presently have explicit direction in addressing domestic violence, whether as part of a broader violence against women strategy and/or as a dedicated "action plan." Both countries include some form of a "whole-of-government" strategy at the levels of criminal justice and crisis support responses, as well as prevention strategies and community education campaigns. A review of the policy framework in both countries shows that while gender based violence (GBV) (of which domestic violence against women is a form) is well addressed in the Albanian legislation, Macedonia has yet to do so. Furthermo-

---

[8] Note that in this table domestic violence is classified as a misdemeanour indicating that the understanding of the phenomenon among staff at the Ministry of the Interior who collect and report data remains limited.

re, while resistance to addressing GBV in Albania is found among certain lobbies with religious undertones, in general the possibilities of combating GBV are located in human rights discourse. In contrast, state actors in Macedonia have made the first steps towards situating domestic violence in the frame of GBV one decade after it was recognised, addressed and explicitly criminalised. Gender-neutral definitions of domestic violence have also been encouraged. The same applies to the majority of professionals who work in the area of domestic violence protection. Changes are expected with the adoption of the Law on Prevention and Protection against Domestic Violence. As of January 1, 2015, the law recognises and defines GBV as a violation of human rights and makes provisions for a gendered understanding of violence in providing protection and support to victims.

Implementation of policies to prevent domestic violence, to protect women against all forms of violence and to prosecute perpetrators share similarities. In both countries, general goals of social development rarely incorporate the special concerns of women that are victims of domestic violence, despite the fact that domestic violence has an adverse impact not only on women's economic success and overall well-being, but also on society at large. Combating domestic violence and VAW in general is commonly seen as detached from general reforms on good governance, democracy and rule of law. In fact, overwhelmingly domestic violence as an agenda topic is introduced and sustained through external actors such as the UN as well as other bilateral and multilateral donors including the EU. Policy responses happen against the backdrop of obligations arising for each country from the international treaties on women's rights and the prevention of violence against women, and the influence of national and international actors working on improving implementation of women's rights. Policy responses are also shaped by contextual-based definitions as well as state involvement in preventing and / or prosecuting violence against women.

2.2.1. Ability to adhere to international obligations

The Convention on the Elimination of All Forms of Discrimination against Women (CEDAW), the Beijing Platform for Action (BPfA), and the Council of Europe's (CoE) Convention on Preventing and Combating Violence against Women and Domestic Violence (aka Istanbul Convention) are some of the international instruments that inform the drafting of national strategies on domestic violence, GBV and gender equality. "National gender machinery" with contact points at the parliamentary and government level is in place in both countries. However, its efficacy is uneven. The activity of gender machinery in Albania has recognized setbacks in the past three years. Since the last elections in June 2013 and the resulting downsizing (by 30%) and restructuring of the administration, Albania's gender machinery is in place but weak (Wittberger, 2014). Where state institutions are concerned, the implementation of gender policy in Macedonia is described as being little active, especially in the area of gender mainstreaming; women's NGOs are more active but they depend on foreign aid (e.g., Koteska, 2011; ESE and Akcija Zdruzenska, 2012; Petričević, 2012). Additionally, the strategies remain under-resourced. Common and persistent challenges include lack of awareness of gender issues at the decision-making level, scarcity of human and budgetary resources and lack of gender expertise. Due to insufficient human, technical and financial resources and capacities at national and local level necessary to support the implementation of the ratified laws and policies, a considerable number of actions (if not all) in this area depend on donor contributions and non-state actors.

2.2.2. CONTEXT-BASED DEFINITIONS FOR STATE ACTION

While the legal framework on domestic violence is relatively complete in Albania, in Macedonia it is still not fully harmonised with EU law on gender equality. There is no provision in the Criminal Code that criminalises GBV specifically; sexual harassment is addressed within the Law on Labour. Domestic violence is fairly broadly defined (encompassing various forms of inter–personal violence) in the Criminal Law, under the term *family violence* which frequently introduces confusion even among the professionals in the field (they believe that domestic violence is situated only within the family).[9] There is a gap between the existing legal framework and practice. Access to the justice system is not without barriers;[10] victims of domestic violence show high levels of distrust in institutions and feel helpless (Mircheva, Chacheva and Kenig, 2014). Finally, a serious challen-

---

[9]   At the beginning of 2015, a new Law on Prevention, Protection and Combating Domestic Violence has been introduced. For the first time, this Law defines GBV per terms stated in the Istanbul Convention. It further defines the obligations of the state in protecting victims.

[10] Barriers are higher when victims come from rural areas and particular regions in the country, as most institutions are concentrated in the cities.

ge comes from the growing conflict between the values that lie behind the EU policy on gender and the values promoted by the Government of Macedonia in various public discourses and through several changes in law, such as the recent amendments to the Law on Termination of Pregnancy.

2.2.3. STATE INVOLVEMENT

As shown earlier in the chapter, the reporting of cases of domestic violence and need for protection in both countries is on the rise. However, there is a huge gap between the needs and the existing resources. Both countries provide state shelter services and the government ministries allocate funds to these shelters as well as to the National SOS line linked to these shelters. In Albania, the referral mechanism for domestic violence needs further consolidation, co-ordination between central and local institutions needs to be improved, and the missing structures need to be established, namely public shelters and relevant social services for victims. A national toll-free line for victims and a system of victim compensation need to be established. The national shelter for victims of domestic violence applies unnecessarily restrictive criteria for admission and provides few facilities for emergency needs. Neither Civil Society Organisations (CSO) run shelters nor victims receive financial aid from the state. The re-integration programme for victims is minimal. In Macedonia, there are 6 shelters (4 of them state-operated) with a total capacity of 35 places[11] (predominantly funded by foreign donors), and service providers there face lack of all kinds of resources. In addition, there are other SOS lines and crisis centres run by NGOs, but typically, they provide service for only a maximum of 72 hours and can accommodate only very small number of victims. Although there are public provisions (e.g., a small percentage from the national lottery games), their services are completely dependent on sporadic donor funding. The system heavily relies on their assistance in providing physical, legal and psychological protection to victims of domestic violence. Government departments designated to address issues of domestic violence are financed both through the state budget and by donors, but the largest amount comes from the latter source.

---

[11]   The number of places in the different shelters varies, because not all shelters are functional at all times. According to the CoE's Minimum Standards for Support Services for Combating VAW, the country needs nearly 200 shelter places in order to meet the needs of victims of domestic violence (Kelly and Dubois, 2008).

3. THE ROLE OF THE EU IN COMBATING DOMESTIC VIOLENCE AGAINST WOMEN

3.1. THE EU'S APPROACH IN GENERAL

Despite its origins as an entity organised around economic issues, the EU has increasingly become an important alternative policy venue that promotes gender equality broadly. Equality between women and men is a key principle of European integration, enshrined in the Lisbon Treaty and the EU Charter of Fundamental Rights. The 2005 'European Consensus on Development', a joint statement of principles shared by the Member States and EU institutions, requires the EU to include a strong gender component in all its policies and practices in its relations with developing countries. EU development policy has been assessed by some as positive in terms of its formal commitment to gender equality and gender mainstreaming (see e.g. Kantola, 2010).

In relation to Gender Based Violence, the EU has not adopted its own definition of violence against women, nor has it enacted specific legislation encompassing the full range of women's experiences of violence. Instead, the EU makes reference to definitions developed by the UN and the CoE. The basis of EU external assistance to women victims of violence are the 2008 EU Guidelines on Violence and Discrimination against Women and Girls. These Guidelines suggest that the EU has shown a clear political will to treat the subject of women's rights as a priority and to take long-term action to address GBV worldwide.[12]

---

[12]   The guidelines are based on a solid multilateral *acquis*, the milestones of which are the UN Secretary-General's in-depth study on all forms of violence against women (2006), the work on indicators on violence carried out by Ms. Yakin Ertük, UN Special Rapporteur on Violence against Women (2008) (but see also 15 Years of the United Nations Special Rapporteur on Violence Against Women, Its Causes and Consequences (2009)), the 1995 Beijing Platform for Action, the 1979 Convention on the Elimination of all Forms of Discrimination against Women, UN resolution 61/143 on intensification of efforts to eliminate all forms of violence against women (2006) and UN Security Council Resolutions 1325 (2000) and 1820 (2008) on Women, Peace and Security, as well as Resolution 2005/2215 of the European Parliament on the situation of women in armed conflicts and their role in the reconstruction and the democratic process in countries after a conflict, the relevant articles of the Conventions on human rights and international humanitarian law and the Rome Statute establishing the International Criminal Court. The "EU Plan of Action on Gender Equality and Women Empowerment in Development 2010-2015" pays particular attention to addressing GBV. Other mechanisms

The guidelines and ensuing documents are also intended to encourage the implementation of a greater number of specific projects aimed at women and girls, financed by, *inter alia*, the European Instrument for Democracy and Human Rights (EIDHR), but also by any other appropriate financial instrument of the EU and the Member States. These funding mechanisms purport to improve prevention, enhance protection of victims and ensure prosecution of perpetrators. In this regard, the EU's approach is well-aligned with the practices and action planning of other actors such as the UN and EU Member States, which have been targeting GBV long before the EU formally issued these guidelines. Thus, the issue is whether the EU plays a distinctive role or aligns this role to other international actors in addressing GBV worldwide.

A critical review of action in different contexts has shown that although the EU is a major player in the international aid system, accounting for more than half of worldwide official development assistance, this position generally has not translated into effective leadership on issues around gender equality and has resulted in unintended consequences and impact (see for example, Women's Studies International Forum, 2013: 39). The 2013 and 2014 Reports on the implementation of the Gender Action Plan (GAP), covering the period from July 2012 to June 2014, indicated that the pace of progress in implementing the GAP was extremely slow. In particular, most projects lagged behind in achieving a satisfactory OECD/DAC gender marker score, and the gender-sensitivity aspects of projects were often neglected. Moreover, there is room for improvement with respect to the allocation of gender-focused aid, gender-related training and regular and comprehensive monitoring and evaluation of programmes and projects.

In relation to GBV, the 2012 Report on the implementation of the "EU Plan of Action on Gender Equality and Women Empowerment in Development 2010-2015" indicates that combating violence against women also remains a high priority for the Commission, Member States, the European External Action Services (EEAS), including EU Delegations. The involvement is likely to increase in activities moving beyond advocacy and

---

such as the 2011 Council of Europe Convention on preventing and combating violence against women and domestic violence (Istanbul Convention) reinforce commitment expressed through the guidelines and the Plan of Action (for action prior to 2008, see Montoya, 2010; see Altan (2014) for an in-depth analysis of recent EU action).

statements to specific actions in the field. While the aforementioned report outlines many achievements in addressing GBV worldwide, the Republic of Macedonia is not mentioned as a country where any successful action has been undertaken. Albania is mentioned only in the case of donor co-ordination meetings and drafting Local Guidelines to Combat GBV. Given that both countries aspire to membership in the EU and the fact that conditionality of the accession process requires that these countries behave as if they already were members, it is puzzling that few data are to be found that suggest that GBV is hardly high on the agenda of the EEAS including EU Delegations in these countries.

3.2. MAINSTREAMING NORMS THROUGH POLITICAL DIALOGUE

The main instrument through which the EU exerts its influence on national policies and action, including those on gender equality in both countries, is the Annual Progress Report. In the case of Albania the role of the reports has been significant in that it has pushed the government to take action on pressing issues regarding domestic violence. For example, the standards for shelter services, drafted by the UN, were approved by the Government because the 2012 Progress Report had evidenced the approval of these standards as "homework" for the Albanian government. However, the reports remain prescriptive and hardly encourage the Government of Albania to budget action against domestic violence using its own programmatic action. Instead, Albania continues to look to international donors for some of the most important work related to domestic violence against women. For example, the National Strategy of Gender Equality, Gender Based Violence and Domestic Violence 2011-2015 was poorly funded by the Albanian Government. The most recent Annual Progress Report of 2014 addresses concerns regarding combating domestic violence against women in rather soft terms.

"*Further work is needed* (authors' emphasis) to remove the remaining gender-discriminatory provisions in legislative acts, and to tackle gender bias in court decisions and law enforcement institutions (page 47); the protection of women against all forms of violence *needs* (authors' emphasis) to be considerably strengthened (page 57)."

In the estimation of gender advocates, the EU has "the carrot and the stick; it needs to resort to the stick" to help in combating domestic violence against women. In Macedonia, there is a perception among scholars and policy specialists that, in general, the EU reports are written in a "diplomatic" language not suitable for the political culture of the country (Ordanoski, 2012: 99; MCET& FOSIM, 2009: 6). Moreover, in a series which monitors media coverage on EU reports it has been documented that the majority of media in the country often play an important role in mitigating the reports' negative findings by manipulating them with the emotionally loaded name dispute and / or the lack of the adjective "Macedonian" in the reports (MCET & FOSIM, 2013: 17. For instance, the analysis of media coverage on the EU Progress report of 2011 showed that the public had been faced with contradictory messages that made it unclear "whether the remarks on the progress achieved by Macedonia were 'the best ever' or if the Progress Report's criticism was overemphasized and tendentious" (MCET, 2011: 24). While we do not have data on the impact of the progress reports in the past few years on Albania, a comparative analysis of the reports for 2010 to 2013 conducted by MCET for Macedonia shows that progress in the area of gender equality is quite slow. In comparing the three reports, it becomes evident that in the area of equal opportunities (and the impact of their absence following from a prevalence of GBV) either nothing changes, or the change is very slow and dependent on the financial aid from foreign donors. In fact, according to other actors active in the field of domestic violence, the EU has to send stronger messages to the state. On the one hand, the assessments are never or rarely positive enough when important changes have been achieved and on the other, they are equally "pale" when they address negative developments. In the absence of publicly shared figures regarding the extent of funding disbursed in this area, another indicator of the importance given to addressing GE and GBV is where the issue is located in progress reports. While these should be regularly featured as a cross-cutting issue, they are typically found only in Chapter 19 (Social policy and employment) or "somewhere in the footnotes" (according to one observer).

3.3. Targeted action

The main instruments of financing domestic violence action in both countries are EIDHR and the Instrument for Pre-Accession Assistance (IPA). Although there are no focused programmes on gender, every so often the calls for proposals for NGOs to include either an objective on gender equality and combating domestic violence, or assigning a funding lot for action related to these issues. While a more complete analysis of EIDHR-funded projects is in order, a brief analysis shows that interventions are at best fragmentary. In Albania, challenges include the capacity of non-state actors and insufficient support to implement proposed action. In Macedonia, actors interviewed maintain that the funds that the EU provides cannot make a significant difference - a proportion of this support is not used due to lack of capacities / knowledge (sometimes bureaucratic obstacles) or absence of political will and lack of an integrated national strategy. Furthermore, it is rather hard to evidence impact in both countries, given that the EU itself does not evaluate funding programmes that focus on promoting gender equality specifically, neither do they provide sufficient funding for NGOs to engage in such exercise internally. In fact, the EU country delegations do not include a Gender Officer – responsibilities regarding gender are included under those of a Human Rights Officer (usually junior level, as our observations reveal).

3.4. EU VIS-À-VIS OTHER ACTORS

Co-operation with international and local partners is a pillar of EU assistance in the field of domestic violence and, more generally, GBV. In 2012 a Memorandum of Understanding was signed between the EU and UN Women; other partnership agreements between some Member States and UN Women are now also signed. The EU also increased its financial support by almost 80% from 2010 to 2011 and remains a significant contributor to UN Women. However, this co-operation has its limitations. Interviews in Albania reveal that the EU participates in donor co-ordination meetings, but they "take the back seat and seem to tag along, not lead". Under the EU Action Plan on Gender Equality and Women's Empowerment in Development for the period 2010-2015 (GAP), the EU Delegations in both countries have introduced specific measures on the role of external assistance and development co-operation in their local strategies for the implementation of the EU Guidelines on Violence against Women and Girls and Combating All Forms of Discrimination against them. However, the authors could not find evidence on how actively these local strategies are implemented. In Albania, the 2010 EU local strategy on violence against women was completed with the assistance of UN staff, but there are no other reports to show progress. In Macedonia, the EU sent a note of attention for joint action in regards to implementing the recommendations for ending violence against women (set of measures until 2016) which suggests that the EU is seeking ways to co-operate with the other relevant partners in the country. However, its effects have not been assessed. At the time of writing this chapter, this was a new development and the authors did not have the means to verify the effects of such action.

4.CONCLUSION

This chapter has provided a general overview of the situation of domestic violence and related interventions as well as commented on the role of the EU in combating domestic violence against women in Albania and Macedonia. The overview confirms a trend exemplified by other research cited in this chapter in which the EU has yet to show a leadership role in addressing this phenomenon and, more broadly, engage significantly by ensuring implementation of gender equality. This conclusion is not far off from a critical assessment of the EU's role in promoting gender equality in other contexts as shown above.

The EU has contributed largely to raising the awareness that VAW is a serious violation of human rights. It has contributed to bringing the problem from the private to the public realm and supported various interventions related to prevention of domestic violence and protection of women victims of such violence. Soft law measures are still a means of raising public awareness, legitimising issues, and placing them on the political agenda. But our expose suggests that despite the fact that domestic violence is one of the areas addressed through external assistance, EU's practical engagement remains lukewarm. The EU could be in a position to exert its influence including changing the way domestic institutions think, use the instrument of assistance to dedicate funding to capacity building to combat domestic violence and other forms of GBV, and tie accession to results on GBV and gender equality. The lukewarm engagement means that the EU does not capitalise on its unique position to effect change in both countries. Although both countries aspire EU membership, the backseat approach EU has taken on addressing domestic violence by relegating this responsibility to other actors as well as the selective engagement give the impression that sketchy and fragmentary response to „homework" of progress reports is sufficient. In turn, this sends a negative message that working to address GBV is a lesser a priority than strengthening governance and democracy. Our analysis shows that the EU is missing an opportunity to exploit its true potential for influence and show its capacity as a key actor in promoting societies free of gender based violence.

REFERENCES

Altan, Levent (2014). Dignity, Integrity and the Elimination of Violence against Women. In *A new Strategy for Gender Equality post 2015*. Brussels, Belgium: Directorate General for Internal Policies. Available at http://www.europarl.europa.eu/RegData/etudes/STUD/2014/509984/IPOL_STU(2014)509984_EN.pdf.

Barrett, Betty Jo and St Pierre, Melissa (2011). Variations in Women's Help-Seeking in Response to Intimate Partner Violence: Findings from a Canadian Population-based Study. *Violence against Women 17*(1), 47–70.

Chacheva, Violeta, Friscik, Jasminka and Mishev, Stojan (2007). *Life in Shadow*, Skopje: Association for emancipation, solidarity and equality of women of RM – ESE, available at http://www.domesticviolence.org.mk/Root/_docs/Life\%20in\%20a\%20Shadow.pdf.

European Institute for Gender Equality (EIGE) (2012). Review of the Implementation of the Beijing Platform for Action in the EU Member States: Violence against Women – Victim Support.Luxembourg: Publications Office of the European Union.

ESE and Akcija Združenska (2012). *Republic of Macedonia, Shadow Report on the Implementation of CEDAW*. Skopje: Association for Emancipation, Solidarity and Equality of Women of Republic of Macedonia, and Akcija Združenska.

European Union. (2008). EU guidelines on violence against women and girls and combating all forms of discrimination against them. Available at http://euromed-justice.eu/document/eu-2008-eu-guidelines-violence-against-women-and-girls-and-combating-all-forms.

Fugate, Michelle, Landis, Leslie, Riordan, Kim, Naureckas, Sara and Engel, Barbara (2005). Barriers to Domestic Violence Help Seeking. *Violence against Women, 11 (3)*, 290-310.

Haar, Robin (2013). Domestic Violence in Albania: National Population-based Survey 2013.

Holden, George W. (2003). Children exposed to domestic violence and child abuse: terminology and taxonomy. *Clinical Child and Family Psychology Review, 6*(3), 151–160.

Lamont, Ruth. (2013) Beating Domestic Violence? Assessing the EU's Contribution to tackling Violence against Women. *Common Market Law Review 50,* 1787–1808

Kantola, Johanna. (2010). *Gender and the European Union.* Basingstoke and New York: Palgrave Macmillan.

Kelly, Liz and Dubois, Lorna (2008) *Combating Violence against Women: Minimum Standards for Support Services,* Strasbourg: Council of Europe.

Koteska, Jasna (2011). Implementation on Gender Mainstreaming, Comments Paper for the Republic of Macedonia,,. Text presented at the Conference: *Good Practice in Gender Mainstreaming,* European Commission of Justice (Brussels) and ÖSB Consulting GmbH (Wien), in Brussels. Published: *Europa, European Commission, Justice,* available at http://ec.europa.eu/justice/gender-equality/files/exchange_of_good_practice_be/mk_comments_paper_en.pdf.

Kriszan, Andrea and Popa, Raluca (2010). Europeanization in Making Policies against Domestic Violence in Central and Eastern Europe.*Social Politics,* 17(3). 379–406.

Mircheva, Stojanka, Chacheva, Violeta and Kenig, Nikolina (2014). *Voice for Justice: Assessment of Court proceedings in Domestic Violence Cases, with specific Focus on Assessing the Case Management from a Gender perspective.* Skopje: Center for Human Rights and Conflict Resolution and UN Women.

Macedonian Center for European Training (MCET) and Foundation Open Society Macedonia (FOSIM) (2009). *The Government Should Work 24/7 on the EU Agenda: First Quarterly Accession Watch Report.* Skopje: Foundation Open Society – Macedonia.

MCET and FOSIM (2011). *The Adjective More Important than the Progress Report: Monitoring of Media August 22nd– December 10th*2011.Skopje: Foundation Open Society – Macedonia.

MCET and FOSIM (2013). *Forgotten Agenda 2014: Sixteenth Quarterly Accession Watch Report.* Skopje: Foundation Open Society – Macedonia.

Montoya, Celeste (2010). The European Union, Transnational Advocacy, and Violence Against Women in Postcommunist States. In Katalin Fabian (ed), *Domestic Violence in Postcommunist States: Local Activism, National Policies, and Global Forces,* pp. 293-307. Bloomington, Indiana: Indiana University Press.

Montoya, Celeste and Agustín, Lise Rolandsen. (2013) The Othering of Domestic Violence: The EU and Cultural Framings of Violence against Women. *Social Politics, 20*(4), 534-557.

Noutcheva, Gergana. (2009). Fake, Partial and Imposed Compliance: the Limits of the EU's Normative Power in the Western Balkans. *Journal of European Public Policy, 16*(7), 1065-1084.

Ordanoski, Sašo. (2011). The Story of Macedonian Populism: Äll We Want is

Everything". In: Jacques Rupnik (ed), *The Western Balkans and the EU: The Hour of Europe,* pp.95-109. Paris: Challiot Papers.

Petričević, Ivana. (2012). *Women's Rights in the Western Balkans in the Context of EU Integration: Institutional Mechanisms for Gender Mainstreaming.*"The European Parliament.

Spehar, Andrea. (2012). This Far, but No Further? Benefits and Limitations of EU Gender Equality Policy Making in the Western Balkans. *East European Politics and Societies, 26(2),* 362-379.

Wittberger, Dolly. (2014). Gender Scorecard: UNCT Performance Indicators for Gender Equality and Women's Empowerment. Report of One UN Programme in Albania.

Women Studies International Forum. (2013). Unintended consequences of EU policies: Reintegrating gender in European studies. Special issue.

Yount, Kathryn M., Halim, Nafisa, Hynes, Michelle and Hillman, Emily R. (2011). Response effects to attitudinal questions about domestic violence against women: A comparative perspective. *Social Science Research, 40(3),* 873–884.

Promoting Gender Equality in Specific Policy Fields: Trade and Climate Change

Chapter 5:

The Conflicting Logics of Regionalism and Gender Mainstreaming: EU Trade Agreements with Southern Africa

Anna VAN DER VLEUTEN

Much has been written about the way in which the EU 'exports' its norms, including gender equality norms. However, in the domain of trade the EU has not acted as an exporter of gender equality. This is striking as the EU has formally committed itself to gender-mainstreaming and the integration of gender in all its policies. Also, trade agreements have gendered consequences. In order to explain the weakness of gender equality norms in EU trade policies, this chapter uncovers the underlying logics of norms and regional governance. It shows how the dominance of a non-interventionist market logic in economic integration and the conflicting logics of trade liberalisation and gender mainstreaming create actor constellations in which actors promoting gender-mainstreaming are disempowered. This hinders the promotion of gender equality in EU trade policies such as the European Partnership Agreements (EPAs) which were concluded between the EU and Southern Africa.

1. Introduction[1]

The EU has a strong though also contested reputation as promoter of gender equality. Especially since the adoption of a gender mainstreaming obliga-

---

[1] The arguments put forward in this chapter took shape in discussions with Conny Roggeband and Anouka van Eerdewijk (see Roggeband, Van Eerdewijk and Van der Vleuten, 2014). I would like to thank Gill Allwood, Thomas Kruessmann, Rachel Minto and Conny Roggeband for comments on earlier versions of this chapter.

tion in the Treaty of Amsterdam (1997), the EU is supposed to promote gender equality in all its policies. However, trade agreements with third countries are not gender-mainstreamed. This is all the more striking for several reasons. First, the EU cherishes its reputation as norm promoter. Its power position in the global arena is not based on hard military capabilities, but on its economic power as the biggest trade bloc in the world, as well as its 'soft power' and its role as exporter of democracy and good governance (Orbie, 2008). Second, in several other policy domains the EU has incorporated gender concerns, even if feminist scholars and activists challenge the quality of gender mainstreaming policies which the EU has implemented (Lombardo and Meier, 2006). Third, trade agreements have a clear gender dimension as they are likely to affect gender relations in the target countries as well as in the EU (Thomson, 2007).

The next section will substantiate the claim that trade agreements between the EU and third parties are not gender-mainstreamed, using the case of the three European Partnership Agreements (EPAs) which have been concluded over the past few years between the EU and Southern Africa. Subsequently, a model is presented which may help understand why the EU fails to gender-mainstream its trade policies. It is based on the ideas of (mis-)matching logics, and the extent to which the dominant logic enables or constrains access for actors promoting gender mainstreaming (Roggeband, Van Eerdewijk and Van der Vleuten, 2014). As such it resonates with feminist institutionalist approaches, their focus on the ways in which formal and informal institutions shape and are shaped by gendered power relations (Curtin, 2014) as well as the idea of bounded agency (Mackay et al. 2010). Furthermore, not only organisations but also policy domains display a certain logic which favours or hinders the application of gender mainstreaming. I will argue that gender mainstreaming is a transformative policy strategy which is incompatible with a non-interventionist logic. The last section will show how the integration of gender concerns in the EPAs between the EU and Southern Africa was hindered by the dominance of the hegemonic logic of market integration in regionalism and the conflicting logics of trade liberalisation and gender mainstreaming, which disempower actors promoting gender mainstreaming.

2. GENDER MAINSTREAMING AND THE EPAS BETWEEN THE EU AND SOUTHERN AFRICA

2.1. GENDER MAINSTREAMING

Gender mainstreaming as a strategy for the achievement of gender equality was launched worldwide in Beijing at the Fourth UN World Conference on Women in 1995. It started its way through the institutions during the decade preceding 'Beijing', when Scandinavian gender experts and policy makers from the domain of development policies at the UN Headquarters started developing the strategy as a better alternative to the previous Women-in-Development approach. They argued that women should be brought 'into the mainstream of the development process on the same basis as men' (UN, 1986). The key differences between previous policies and gender mainstreaming were the shift from an exclusive focus on women towards a focus on gender and on women in relation to men; and the shift from designing specific policies for women as a complement to regular policies towards the incorporation of 'a gender equality perspective [...] in all policies at all levels and at all stages, by the actors normally involved in policy-making' (Verloo, 2005: 350). After 'Beijing', gender mainstreaming became a formal EU strategy. It was included in the Treaty of Amsterdam (1997) as a horizontal principle for the EU in all its activities, including its dealings with external partners (Woodward and Van der Vleuten, 2014). According to the definition of the EU, gender mainstreaming is 'the integration of the gender perspective into all policies with a view to promoting equality between women and men' (European Commission, 2013). In addition, the Commission has proclaimed that 'Gender equality must be fully incorporated into our external policies too ... Reducing gender inequalities ... , and promoting women's rights are essential for developing sustainable democratic societies ... We will promote and strengthen co-operation with international and regional organisations on advancing gender equality' (European Commission, 2010).

What would a gender-mainstreamed trade policy look like? In their assessment of gender mainstreaming in the EU, Hafner-Burton and Pollack argue that 'a gender-mainstreaming mandate in the EU or in any other political system should, in principle, result in developments at three different levels: process, outputs and outcomes' (Hafner-Burton and Pollack, 2009:

117). They limit their assessment to the policy outputs from the Commission's relevant DGs, and I will follow their approach for two reasons: first, the trade agreements have been concluded only very recently, and therefore there is no observable impact of the agreements yet; and secondly, in the domain of EU trade agreements, the Commission is the key actor who writes the drafts and is the chief negotiator. What I would expect to observe is that 'policies are explicitly gendered to anticipate their respective impacts on men and women and to reduce gender inequality' (Hafner-Burton and Pollack, 2009: 117). And more specifically, gender mainstreaming of trade agreements would require 'explicit[ly] links between trade policy and women's empowerment and gender equality and [...] provisions in trade agreements and trade negotiations that work towards these objectives and, thus, are supportive to women in their multiple roles in trade' (Williams, 2013: 99).

2.2. GENDER MAINSTREAMING AND TRADE AGREEMENTS: THE EPAS WITH SOUTHERN AFRICA[2]

The EU and Southern Africa have a long history of trade agreements, offering non-reciprocal duty-free access for Southern African exports to the European market. In the wake of the neoliberal wave of the 1990s, the World Trade Organisation (WTO) decided that this type of agreements was no longer permissible. Instead of preferential treatment, developing countries should receive financial and technical assistance to help them improve their capacity to trade and foster their integration into the world economy. 'Trade-driven development' became the new buzz-word. These ideas were laid down in the Cotonou Agreement which was signed in 2000 between the EU and 79 countries from Africa, the Caribbean and the Pacific (ACP). The Cotonou Agreement formed the basis for new-style trade agreements, called Economic Partnership Agreements (EPAs), that were negotiated between the EU and regional groupings of the ACP countries.[3] The EPAs were

---

[2]   'Southern Africa' here refers to the 15 Member States of the Southern African Development Community (SADC), a regional organisation which was established in 1992: Angola, Botswana, Democratic Republic of Congo, Lesotho, Madagascar, Malawi, Mauritius, Mozambique, Namibia, Seychelles, South Africa, Swaziland, Tanzania, Zambia, and Zimbabwe (Van der Vleuten and Hulse, 2013).

[3]   SADC Member States have been negotiating as part of different regional groupings, and therefore have signed different regional EPAs.

celebrated as a new type of trade agreement, in the sense that they linked trade with development and represented a partnership between equals, a 'joint [EU-ACP] answer' to the challenges of globalisation and development; a trade agreement that would allow the people of Southern Africa to 'take their rightful place in the world' (European Commission, 2005:3). In that respect, the EPAs are a most-likely case for gender mainstreaming as they are not limited to the elimination of tariff and non-tariff barriers. After years of protracted negotiations, eventually, in 2014, the EU concluded agreements with the East African Community (EAC) and SADC, while the Eastern and Southern African (ESA) region is covered by an interim-EPA. The Cotonou Agreement does not refer explicitly to the EU treaty obligation to gender mainstream all policies, but Article 1 includes a general commitment to gender equality which basically reflects the same idea. It states that 'Systematic account shall be taken of the situation of women and gender issues in all areas – political, economic and social' (Cotonou Agreement 2000: 6). Taking Article 1 as the yard stick to assess whether the Southern African EPAs have been gender-mainstreamed, however, the results are deceiving. They are summarised in Table 1.

The interim-EPA between the EU and the Eastern African states (ESA) does not mention gender in the trade chapter. There is a reference in the chapter on fisheries, where it aims to encourage 'participation of marginal groups in the fishing industry, for example, through the promotion of gender equality in fisheries by developing the capacity of women engaged in fisheries' (EU-ESA EPA 2012, Art. 35). In the section on development, 'gender mainstreaming' (just the two words) is mentioned as one of ten areas for co-operation, but without further details, deadlines or targets (EU-ESA EPA 2012, Art.38).

The EU-EAC EPA, which was concluded in 2014, does not mention gender mainstreaming, gender equity or gender equality as a general objective or principle of the agreement, and the trade chapter does not contain a single reference to gender (EU-EAC EPA, 2015). In the chapter on development co-operation, gender concerns pop up twice. First, the EU and the EAC will co-operate in order to promote rural development by, among many other things, 'addressing socio-cultural barriers such as language differences, literacy levels, gender biases, community health that influence the nature of farming systems' (EU-EAC EPA, 2015: 41). A second reference is found in the article on Inland Fisheries as part of the measures to alleviate poverty through '(. . .) (ii) participation of marginal groups in the fishing industry for example, the promotion of gender equity in fisheries, and particularly developing capacity of women traders involved and intending to engage in fisheries' (EU-EAC EPA, 2015: 46).

Table 1: Gender in the EPAs between the EU and Southern Africa

European Partnership Agreement (EPA) concluded	SADC member states involved	Gender in the EPA?
EU-ESA *interim*-EPA (2012) Common Market for Eastern and Southern Africa (COMESA)	Madagascar, Malawi, Mauritius, Seychelles, Zimbabwe (and other states)	– Promotion of gender equality in fisheries (Art. 35); – Gender mainstreaming as area for co-operation (Art. 38)
EU-EAC EPA (2014) East African Community (EAC)	Tanzania (and other states)	– Address sociocultural barriers in agriculture, 'such as […] gender biases'; – Promotion of gender equity in fisheries
EU-SADC EPA (2014) Southern African Development Community (SADC)	Angola, Botswana, Lesotho, Mozambique, Namibia, South Africa, Swaziland	– Reference to Articles 1 and 9 of the Cotonou Agreement

Source: compiled by Author

Finally, the EU-SADC EPA mentions 'gender' only once, in the section which defines key concepts. It stipulates that 'any reference to the male gender simultaneously means a reference to the female gender and vice versa' (EU-SADC EPA, 2015: 96). Actually, checking the full text of the agreement, this stipulation is relevant only twice, in one case where 'the exporter' is referred to as 'he' and a case where 'the consumer' is referred to as 'he'. Very indirectly, however, the EPA addresses gender concerns twice. The parties acknowledge that the agreement is based on the general principles in Article 9 of the Cotonou Agreement, and one of these principles is 'the equality of men and women' (Cotonou Agreement, 2000: 8). Furthermore, the EPA indirectly reiterates the general commitment to take gender into account where it states that the economic partnership should contribute to the 'fulfilment of the overriding commitments set out in Articles 1, 2 and 9 of the Cotonou Agreement'(EU-SADC EPA, 2015: 9).

Based on the parsimony and vagueness of the references to gender concerns in the three EPAs between the EU and Southern Africa, we may conclude that the EPAs are not gender-mainstreamed: they do not contain definite commitments to assess the consequences of the trade agreement for gender equality and they do not propose measures to ensure that trade liberalisation would contribute to gender equality. The parsimony and vagueness are worrisome, as it is widely feared that EPA-style trade liberalisation will threaten women's employment in fisheries and agriculture (small-scale farming) in Southern Africa (Kiraty and Roy, 2010; Ulmer, 2004). As Southern African governments will suffer tariff revenue losses, they might have to cut the provision and subsidies of social services which negatively impacts on women's employment, and if women themselves have to provide – free of charge – these services, they will be less able to engage in paid work (Pheko, 2006). Finally, women in Southern Africa are not well equipped to enjoy potential benefits (Nyakujarah and Morna, 2012). As Karin Ulmer aptly summarises,

"women are disproportionately faced with limited access to capital; lack of collateral for guarantees; greater exclusion from productive resources; fewer employment opportunities; weak property rights and tenures; and a lack of influence in decision making at high levels of government and industry" (Ulmer, 2007: 8).

In spite of demands from civil society representatives (Ulmer, 2007), the European Commission has decided that no further impact assessment is required (let alone a gender impact assessment), because a sustainability impact assessment (SIA) was conducted in 2007 (Commission 2014, Annex, p. 4; DG Trade, 2015). This impact assessment has not addressed gender concerns (PriceWaterhouseCoopers, 2007). Elina Viilup found that the SIA of the ACP EPA broadly predicted positive effects for food processing, fish processing in the pacific region, and tourism, and the only recommendation was to extend the civil society dialogue and increase women participation in it (Viilup, 2015). For lack of better and more comprehensive assessments, as there is good reason to suppose that trade agreements have gendered consequences, and as the EU has committed itself to gender mainstreaming of its external actions, why have the EPAs not been gender-mainstreamed?

3. LOGICS AND ACTOR CONSTELLATIONS

Obviously, the promotion of policies and norms is not a linear process but seems to be influenced by the compatibility of the underlying logic of such norms with regional governance and the policy fields in which these norms travel (Roggeband, Van Eerdewijk and Van der Vleuten, 2014). First the logics of regional governance by the EU are explored, and next the logics of gender mainstreaming, trade and development.

3.1. LOGICS OF REGIONAL GOVERNANCE

The regional level is situated between the global and the national level. Regional governance refers to a 'system of rule at the regional level where authority is exercised by state and non-state actors in formal and informal ways, and where global, regional, national and subnational levels are linked' (Van der Vleuten and Van Eerdewijk, 2014: 18). Key actors in regional governance are regional organisations such as the EU, EAC and SADC. They have developed regional governance as a political reaction to globalisation in order to manage cross-border problems and strengthen their position in the world economy and in international politics. In this respect regional organisations are similar. However, they differ as to their identity which constructs the region, and the mission which was formulated when the organisation was established. The specific identity of a regional organisation enables and constrains its activities and opens up or restrains the access for specific actors.

The identity of the EU and its predecessors was based on the reconciliation of France and Germany, and on market integration as a means of locking-in this reconciliation (Van der Vleuten, 2007). From the start, integration in Western Europe through market integration was based heavily on deregulation and the removal of barriers to free movement of goods, services, capital and people. This market-oriented logic requires the state to gear its role towards improving the functioning of the market. Regulation is meant to create a level playing field and avoid unfair competition, but should remain limited to what is necessary to achieve this. Interventionist policies such as social policy are merely add-ons that are pursued as far as they are necessary to legitimise market integration policies and better prepare workers for economic integration.

After the fall of the Berlin Wall in 1989 and the prospect of former communist countries applying for membership, the EU developed an additional identity based on its opposition to totalitarian regimes and the promotion of human rights and democracy, summarised by the label of Normative Power Europe (Manners, 2002). Its new mission was codified in the Treaty of Amsterdam in 1997, which enabled the inclusion of democratic conditionality, good governance clauses and anti-discrimination requirements in accession treaties, development policies and trade agreements. However, the new mission does not replace the older one. Economic power remains the main asset of the EU and neoliberal-style market integration remains the predominant logic. Human rights instruments are mainly non-binding, except for candidate countries, and they are mainly addressed at third countries rather than applied to the EU internally (Börzel and Van Hüllen, 2015; Van der Vleuten and Ribeiro Hoffmann, 2010).

Given the predominant logic of market integration, it is expected that the EU will accommodate 'non-interventionist policies' such as non-binding recommendations, positive incentives, and removal of obstacles more successfully than 'interventionist policies' which have a binding character or impose certain norms, unless they are required for the sake of 'fair' competition. Also, gender concerns will be framed as eliminating discrimination in the labour market and enable women and men to be better (educated, available, healthy) workers. Table 2 summarises the key elements of the logics.

Table 2: The identity, mission and logics of the EU

	EC/EU until 1997	EU since 1997
Identity: what the organisation opposes	Second World War	Communism, fascism, totalitarianism
Mission	Transcend Franco-German enmity	Consolidate democracy and human rights
Means	Market integration	Conditionality, market integration
Logic market/state	Non-interventionist	Interventionist
Gender equality framed as	Non-discrimination in the labour market to prevent unfair competition	Human right

3.2. LOGICS OF NORMS

The perspective of enabling and constraining logics may help us understand the difficult trajectory of gender mainstreaming in the policy field of trade. Gender mainstreaming is usually defined as a strategy with a transformative logic which challenges the existing gender order and aims to redress structural power asymmetries between women and men (Beveridge and Nott, 2002). For that reason, gender mainstreaming is arguably based upon an interventionist logic, as the state is supposed to promulgate an obligation to include gender concerns in all policy-making processes and outcomes, including market-making policies.

This contrasts sharply with the logic of trade liberalisation. Whereas gender mainstreaming requires heavy policy intervention by the state, the aim of trade liberalisation is actually to reduce the level of state intervention in the market. With their emphasis on eliminating barriers, trade liberalisation policies are, unsurprisingly, based on a non-interventionist logic which seeks to improve the functioning of markets by freeing them of distorting obstacles such as tariff and non-tariff trade barriers. As a result, trade policies tend to confirm power asymmetries between the parties involved as they offer opportunities 'equal to all' which however are easier accessed, seized and exploited by states, business and individuals with more capital, knowledge and other assets than those with less. Given the gendered character of opportunities in business and in the labour market, women are expected to benefit less than men from the opportunities created by the elimination of trade barriers (Ulmer, 2007).

For that reason, feminist economists argue that the ideology underlying trade liberalisation and neoliberal economic policies is detrimental to equitable growth, gender equality and the empowerment of women (Hoskyns, 2008). A transformative approach to trade policies, meanwhile, would focus on the interrelationship between the formal and informal, productive and reproductive sectors of the economy, and the distributional consequences of liberalisation across these sectors. It would prioritise the elimination of poverty instead of shifting the burden of adjusting to global economic processes to unpaid labour (Williams, 2013). The mismatch of underlying logics helps understand the weak presence of gender equality concerns in the trade policies of a regional organisation, as well as the de-gendered frames that are used in the rare instances where gender is referred to. As Table 3 summarises, the ostensibly gender-neutral, neoliberal, rational economic framework does not sit easily with the logic of gender mainstreaming.

Table 3: Logics of norms

	Aim	**Logic**	**Power asymmetry**
Gender mainstreaming	Transform gender relations	Interventionist: state intervention in the market	Redress
Trade liberalisation	Eliminate trade barriers	Non-interventionist: reduction of state intervention in the market	Confirm

A next step is to investigate the compatibility between the logic of regional governance and the logic of the norms. The non-interventionist logic of the EU and its focus on market integration clearly constitute an obstacle to gender mainstreaming, even more so because gender mainstreaming does not aim at opening up a new policy domain, but operates in existing terrain. When there is incompatibility with the logics of governance operating in that terrain, the transformative promise of gender mainstreaming will be undermined and gender mainstreaming may either not be articulated at all, or only on the sidelines, in a mainly symbolic 'checklist' way (Roggeband, Van Eerdewijk and Van der Vleuten, 2014).

Yet, the development of a secondary identity of the EU and the increased emphasis by the EU on human rights issues have created an opening which might enable actors to put gender mainstreaming on the regional agenda, especially in the dealings of the EU with third parties. However, in spite of a general commitment to combating poverty and promoting social sustainability, no explicit reference to human rights was found in the EPAs.

3.3. ACTOR CONSTELLATIONS

A final step as regards the way in which logics influence the dynamics of gender mainstreaming relates to their effect on access for and inclusion of different actors in the policy-making arena. In the EU, the non-interventionist logic of market integration, with social policies as an add-on, has generated an informal hierarchy within the supranational bureaucracy which favours the directorates with expertise in market-oriented domains. As regards non-state actors, it depends on their resources in terms of regional mobilisation capacity, access and specific expertise to what extent they are able to exert influence on supranational and state actors. They may create regional advocacy networks (RANs) that link regional and national non-governmental organisations, social movements, regional institutions and politicians in domestic or regional parliaments (Adams and Kang, 2007). Such actor networks are not fixed but fluid and often highly informal; actors may simultaneously occupy different positions and use both insiders' and outsiders' tactics (Van Eerdewijk and Roggeband, 2014). Personal ties may develop among committed individuals and create velvet triangles (Woodward, 2003) and pentangles (Roggeband, 2010), enabling them to share knowledge and establish shared 'world views'. However, when the ideas they promote do not fit the dominant logic, such dynamics will not result in an entrance into the central policy arena, but to marginalisation and the development of a 'counter-perspective' which can be easily sidelined by the dominant forces as irrelevant. The dominant logic of market integration in the process of regionalisation has, therefore, implications for the opportunities for gender mainstreaming, because it sidelines feminist actors that seek to transform the processes of market integration. The next section maps the actor constellations in trade negotiations.

4. Logics at play and actor constellations at work in EU trade negotiations

Who's who in trade negotiations on the EU side and where do activists for gender equality have access? This section discusses the role of the European Commission and the specific Directorate-General involved in trade negotiations, DG Trade; the European Parliament and its trade committee INTA; and several civil society actors at the European level.

4.1. The Commission

The Commission plays a crucial role in trade negotiations, as trade agreements are within the exclusive competence of the EU. The Commissioner for Trade, Cecilia Malmström (since October 2014), chairs DG Trade which is in charge of the negotiations on EPAs (more specifically, Directorate D, Unit D2). Decision-making concerning international trade negotiations broadly follows the so-called community method. This means that the Commission has the right of initiative. It tables a proposal; it discusses it with Member States' representatives (top trade officials) in the Trade Policy Committee (formerly known as the Article 133 Committee), and subsequently the Council composed of the Ministers of Trade authorises DG Trade to negotiate. During the negotiations, DG Trade provides output to and receives input from interest groups, from the Trade Policy Committee and from the International Trade Committee of the European Parliament (INTA). When the negotiations are successful, the Commission initials an agreement, which has to be endorsed by the Trade ministers. The Foreign Affairs Council (by qualified majority) and then the European Parliament (by simple majority) adopt the results. Because of exclusive EU competence in the matter, national parliaments of EU member states are not involved in the ratification process; the EPAs have to be ratified, however, by the national parliaments of the ACP counterparts.

This description shows how DG Trade plays a key role in the negotiations. Added to its formal prerogatives are its institutional memory, its technical capacity and its access to specific information (Woolcock, 2012). Traditionally, DG Trade has a liberal leaning (Woolcock, 2012). David Martin, Member of European Parliament (MEP) and several times rapporteur on EPAs, stated it elegantly:

"Trade experts by their nature aim to get the best possible deal for the European Union. They did not necessarily aim to get the best development outcome. I repeat: that is not a criticism; that is what they are trained to do. But that is the reality of the negotiations." (European Parliament, 2009a)

DG Trade has no strong record in gender mainstreaming (True, 2009). It holds the opinion that gender concerns are to be addressed within the framework of development co-operation, and that an EPA is not an appropriate instrument for doing this (APRODEV, 2007). Its mission statement says that 'DG Trade is committed to liberalising world trade and fostering sustainable economic, social and environmental development, thereby boosting competitiveness, jobs and growth' (DG Trade, 2013a: 5), which depicts a broader perspective than a strictly neoliberal one. However, its key policy performance indicators speak a standard neoliberal language, as the five targets refer to the value or percentage of EU trade covered by zero or preferential duties, the level of EU investment in third countries and the level of investment of third countries in the EU, the value or diversificati-on of preferential imports from developing countries into the EU, and the extent to which operators use the EU preferential agreements (DG Trade, 2013a: 7). Social development or gender concerns do not figure among its targets. Hafner-Burton and Pollack (2009) in their quantitative assessment of gender mainstreaming found a single reference to gender in the reports of DG Trade for 2006-2008. The most recent DG Trade Activity Reports available do not contain any reference to gender, gender mainstreaming or women (DG Trade, 2013b; DG Trade, 2014). Interestingly, in its manage-ment plan, DG Trade does mention the requirement to improve the gender balance in staff. It aims to further increase the percentage of women in ma-nagement positions in order to reach the Commission target of 43 percent women (DG Trade, 2013a: 39). However, 'more women in management' of course is not the same as gender mainstreaming and does not mean that more attention is paid to gender in trade agreements, especially as long as policy performance indicators and targets do not offer any incentive to do so.

4.2. THE EUROPEAN PARLIAMENT

A second key actor at EU level is the European Parliament, and most no-tably its trade committee INTA. INTA is responsible for reporting on trade issues, and DEVE (development) is the committee entitled to give an opini-on in this domain. DG Trade maintains close relations with INTA, as well as with the parliamentary committees IMCO (internal market and consumer protection), ITRE (industry research and energy) and LIBE (civil liberties, justice and home affairs) (DG Trade, 2013a). With FEMM, the parliamenta-ry committee on Women's Rights and Gender Equality, there are no regular contacts.

In his discussion of EU trade policies, Stephen Woolcock observes that "The EP has in the past interested itself in more general issues such as hu-man rights, labour standards, environmental sustainability and development issues rather than the detail of tariff schedules or other parts of an agreement that can impact on specific sectors. In general, then, the EP can be expected to push for the inclusion of such provisions in trade agreements" (Wool-cock, 2012: 61), or, in Martin's words "We have, as a Parliament, since the conclusion of the negotiations been trying to square the circle between tra-de and development" (European Parliament, 2009a). This attitude is further exemplified by the resolution which the EP adopted in 2013 on 'trade and investment-driven growth for developing countries', where it tries to bridge the different aims of development and trade policies. The resolution was prepared by INTA, but it literally copied some articles from the opinion from DEVE into the text, including the only mention of 'women':

"32. Urges the EU to design its trade agreements so as to foster responsible investor behaviour and compliance with best international practises of corporate social responsibility and good corporate governance; stresses, in particular, that in order for growth to be inclusive and efficient in terms of poverty reduction, it should be pursued in sectors in which poor people are active, should benefit and empower women, and should be associated with the creation of jobs as well as with the development of finance for micro-enterprises and small businesses (European Parliament, 2009a)."

FEMM is not a rapporteur or 'rapporteur for opinion' for trade agreements. In the actual parliamentary term, only one of the 35 members of the FEMM committee is also member of the INTA trade committee which suggests that there are few opportunities for sharing of information and that presumably there is limited knowledge about or commitment to gender mainstreaming in the trade committee, and limited knowledge about or commitment to trade issues in the FEMM committee. Invited by the network of MEPs for gender mainstreaming, INTA commissioned a study on gender and trade aptly labelled 'The EU's Trade Policy: from gender-blind to gender-sensitive' (Viilup, 2015). INTA discussed the study in September 2015, but did not take any decision concerning the follow-up of this exchange of views.

As regards the EPAs more specifically, the EP endorsed the ESA-EU interim-EPA in 2013 by a large majority, but it accompanied the consent vote with a resolution expressing its concerns about the human rights situation in Zimbabwe and deploring the absence of a human rights clause (European Parliament 2013b). The EP brought up the position of women only in its discussions of the SADC interim-EPA, when it stressed that:

'any full EPA must also include provisions regarding a commonly accepted definition of good governance, transparency in political offices, and human rights, in accordance with Articles 11b, 96 and 97 of the Cotonou Agreement, as well as specific provisions for the most vulnerable groups such as local farmers and women' (European Parliament, 2009b).

The EP did not refer to the gender mainstreaming obligation in Article 1 of the Cotonou Agreement.[4]

4.3.EXPERTS AND CIVIL SOCIETY

The European Institute for Gender Equality (EIGE) was established by the EU in 2007 to generate knowledge and provide expertise on gender equality issues. Trade and international trade agreements are not mentioned among the central themes of EIGE, and it does not have specific expertise in this domain. State representatives constituting the management board of EIGE do not come from Economic Affairs or Trade Ministries; the staff of EIGE and the experts forum have a wealth of expertise and connections, but not on trade and trade agreements. Here we see that even if there is access, no one is pushing the issue of gender mainstreaming in trade agreements.

Another set of actors are civil society groups. Since the mid-1990s, the European Women's Lobby (EWL) is the institutional platform for over 2000 women's organisations in Europe. It has strong links with the Commission (primarily DG JUST and DG EMPL) and the FEMM committee in the European Parliament. In the past years, international trade agreements have not been among the topics it has published reports or statements on, and in the context of Beijing +20, no attention is paid to EU trade policies.

EU trade policy has been criticised by the European Parliament and NGOs for a lack of transparency. Often it was characterised as 'technocratic in that national and Commission officials do much of the work' (Woolcock, 2012: 51). In order to address these criticisms, in 2000, DG Trade has created a Civil Society Dialogue to reach out to the NGO community, with meetings discussing major policy proposals.

The 359 organisations which have registered for this dialogue are mainly European producer associations (such as producers of renewable ethanol, tropical tuna fish), trade unions, chambers of commerce and business associations, as well as social, environmental and development NGOs (Coffey International Development, 2014: 20). Among them, ACT Alliance Advo-

---

[4]   At the moment of writing (April 2016), the final EPAs still have to come up for discussion.

cacy to the European Union[5] and WIDE+[6] are the main representatives of women's interests at the table, and they are considered to be very active within the Dialogue (Thomson, 2007). However, Dürr and De Bièvre (2007) and Hoskyns (2008) claim that the consultation process does not result in any influence by NGOs on trade policy outcomes but only provides NGOs with information on the position of DG Trade and each other's positions and provides DG Trade with some legitimacy. This assessment is confirmed by a critical evaluation of the Civil Society Dialogue. It states that 'Managers [officials from DG Trade] believe in the political and operational importance of listening and being seen to listen to civil society', but the objectives of the dialogue are not clear and therefore participants feel frustrated with being informed without having influence: 'DG Trade regards this as a briefing exercise, not a consultation' (Coffey International Development, 2014: 36 n15). Participation in the Civil Society Dialogue is limited to EU-based organisations.

In sum, the arena of trade negotiations is dominated by trade experts and there is no serious institutionalised access for representatives of women's interests or persons with gender expertise. Moreover, those who defend gender equality issues as MEPs, experts in EIGE or civil society organisations (EWL as flagship platform) tend to focus on other issues than international trade agreements. Therefore the actor constellation is not a well-established alliance of committed individuals at different nodes of the arena, but consists of unconnected spots of commitment and expertise.

Depicted in this way, it might seem that the dominant logic constrains agency in such a way that change is excluded. However, there are some openings. First, the legitimacy of EU trade policies is contested by external partners and as EU public opinion as has become visible in protests against the trade agreement under negotiation with the US (the Transatlantic Trade and Investment Partnership, referred to as TTIP). Trade agreements are perceived as detrimental to citizens' interests. Commissioner for Trade Malm-

---

[5]   ACT Alliance is a coalition of 146 churches and affiliated organisations working together in the areas of humanitarian aid, development and advocacy, with the purpose of influencing EU decision-making processes as they affect developing countries in order to promote justice and peace and the eradication of poverty.

[6]   WIDE+ (previously WIDE) is the European network around women's rights and development which works on economic and development issues, including trade negotiations.

ström seems to take the legitimacy issue very seriously, which fits her record in fundamental rights issues. She argues for more transparency in trade
affairs and stepping up the contacts with INTA, which might open up the
rather closed arena. During her first month in office she addressed the Civil
Society Dialogue meeting directly to stress its fundamental importance for
European democracy (Malmström, 2014a; Malmström, 2014b). Secondly,
against the background of a rise of eurosceptic attitudes among the European population and an increase of members of the European Parliament
representing such views, the Commission under the presidency of Jean-
Claude Juncker has decided to align EU actions in different domains and
improve their effectiveness. Smart regulation guidelines have resulted in
strengthening the attention to the impact of trade-related policies on gender
equality (Viilup, 2015). These openings, however, will only result in the recognition of gender equality and gender mainstreaming as part and parcel
of EU trade policies if actors promoting these issues are able and willing to
constitute alliances with actors at the tables.

5. CONCLUSION

In spite of its commitment to gender mainstreaming and its ambition to fully incorporate gender equality into its external policies, the EU has not lived
up to its promises with regard to gender mainstreaming as regards the trade
agreements which it has concluded with Southern Africa. The three European Partnership Agreements contain hardly any reference to gender. This
chapter argues that this paucity can be understood against the background
of the predominant logic of the EU. Underlying its activities is a non-
interventionist logic, aimed at liberalisation, deregulation and the removal
of obstacles. It empowers actors which promote such policies, and it dis-
empowers others. International trade agreements aim to remove obstacles
to free trade, based on a non-interventionist logic (strengthening the market
vis-à-vis the state) which sits uneasily with the need for intervention aimed at a transformation of political and economic structures and practices
which is the core of the gender mainstreaming strategy. The implication is
that the conflicting logics of trade liberalisation and gender mainstreaming
disempower actors promoting gender mainstreaming because the measures
linked to trade negotiations do not accommodate interventionist aims and
empower actors promoting trade liberalisation and other objectives which

fit the neoliberal discourse. As a result, EU-style trade policies are very difficult 'territory' for gender mainstreaming. Policy domains with an interventionist logic will offer more possibilities, such as development aid (but see Debusscher, 2014). Mapping the actors involved in promoting gender concerns at the European level and the parties represented at the EPA negotiating tables shows that they are part of different, mainly separate networks. Feminist actors active in the EU do not focus on international trade, whereas actors involved in trade policymaking do not consider gender mainstreaming to be part of their agenda.

REFERENCES

Adams, Melinda and Alice Kang (2007). 'Regional Advocacy Networks and the Protocol on the Rights of Women in Africa', *Politics & Gender*, 3: 4, 451-474.

Aprodev (2007). 'Continental Review of the EPA Negotiations: A Survey of African Countries' Perspectives', *Trade Negotiations Insights*, 6: 2, 5-7, available at http://aprodev.eu/files/Trade/TNI_EN_6.2.pdf.

Beveridge, Fiona and Sue Nott (2002). "Mainstreaming: A Case for Optimism and Cynicism", *Feminist Legal Studies*, 10:3, 299–311.

Börzel, Tanja and Vera van Hüllen (Eds) (2015). *Governance Transfer by Regional Organizations. Patching Together a Global Script*, Houndmills, Basingstoke, Palgrave.

Coffey International Development (2014). Evaluation of DG TRADE's Civil Society Dialogue: Final Report, available at http://trade.ec.europa.eu/doclib/docs/2014/december/tradoc_152927.pdf.

Commission (2014). Commission Decision amending Commission Decision C(2014)1269 adopting the 2014 work programme serving as a financing decision for the financing of projects in the area of external trade relations, including access to the markets of non-European Union countries and initiatives in the field of trade related assistance, Brussels, 19,8,2014 C(2014) 5817 final, available at http://trade.ec.europa.eu/doclib/docs/2014/august/tradoc_152729.pdf.

Cotonou Agreement (2000). Partnership Agreement between the Members of the African, Caribbean and Pacific Group of States of the one Part, and the European Community and its Member States, of the other Part, signed in Cotonou on 23 June 2000, *Official Journal of the European Communities*, 15.12.2000, L317, available also at https://ec.europa.eu/europeaid/sites/devco/files/cotonou-agreement-2000_en.pdf.

Curtin, J. (2014). 'Thematic Review: Contemporary and Future Directions in Feminist Institutionalism', *Politics & Gender* 10:4, 698-714

Debusscher, Petra (2014). Gender Mainstreaming in EU Development Policy towards Southern Africa and South America, in: Anna van der Vleuten, Anouka van Eerdewijk and Conny Roggeband (Eds), pp. 93-116.

DG Trade (2013a). Management Plan 2014, available at http://trade.ec.europa.eu/doclib/docs/2013/january/tradoc_150230.pdf.

DG Trade (2013b). Annual Activity Report 2012, available at http://trade.ec.europa.eu/doclib/docs/2013/july/tradoc_151629.pdf

DG Trade (2014). Annual Activity Report 2013, available at http://trade.ec.europa.eu/doclib/docs/2014/july/tradoc_152711.pdf

DG Trade (2015). Roadmap, available at http://ec.europa.eu/smart-regulation/impact/planned_ia/docs/2015_trade_014_015_epa_sadc_fta_en.pdf.

Dürr, Andreas and Dirk de Bièvre (2007). 'Inclusion without Influence? NGOs in European Trade Policy', *Journal of Public Policy*, 27: 1, 79-101.

European Commission (2005). 'Trade for Development: EU-SADC Economic Partnership Agreement', available at http://trade.ec.europa.eu/doclib/docs/2006/february/tradoc_127350.pdf

European Commission (2010). Communication from the Commission of 5 March 2010 – A Strengthened Commitment to Equality between Women and Men – A Women's Charter: Declaration by the European Commission on the occasion of the 2010 International Women's Day in commemoration of the 15th anniversary of the adoption of a Declaration and Platform for Action at the Beijing UN World Conference on Women and of the 30th anniversary of the UN Convention on the Elimination of All Forms of Discrimination against Women (COM(2010) 78 final).

European Commission (2013). Gender Equality, available at http://ec.europa.eu/justice/gender-equality/glossary/index_en.htm.

European Parliament (2009a). Joint Debate on Partnership Agreements, available at http://www.europarl.europa.eu/sides/getDoc.do?type=CRE\&reference=20090323\&secondRef=ITEM-014\&language=EN\&ring=B6-2009-0144.

European Parliament (2009b). Resolution of 25 March 2009 on an Interim Economic Partnership Agreement between the European Community and its Member States, on the one Part, and the SADC EPA States, on the other Part, available at http://www.europarl.europa.eu/sides/getDoc.do?pubRef=-//EP//TEXT+TA+P6-TA-2009-0179+0+DOC+XML+V0//EN.

European Parliament (2013a). Resolution of 16 April 2013 on Trade and Investment-driven Growth for Developing Countries (2012/2225(INI)), available at http://www.europarl.europa.eu/sides/getDoc.do?pubRef=-//EP//NONSGML+TA+P7-TA-2013-0120+0+DOC+PDF+V0//EN.

European Parliament (2013b). Stepping-stone Economic Partnership Agreement between the EC and Central Africa, Debate, available at

http://www.europarl.europa.eu/sides/getDoc.do?pubRef=-//EP//TEXT+CRE+
20130613+ITEM-002+DOC+XML+V0//EN.

EU-EAC EPA (2015). Economic Partnership Agreement between the East African
Community partner states, of the one part, and the European Union and its
member states of the other part, Consolidated text, available at http://trade.ec.
europa.eu/doclib/docs/2015/october/tradoc_153845.compressed.pdf.

EU-ESA EPA (2012). Interim Agreement establishing a framework for an Economic Partnership Agreement between the Eastern and Southern Africa States,
on the one part, and the European Community and its Member States, on the
other part, available at http://eur-lex.europa.eu/legal-content/EN/ALL/?uri=
OJ:L:2012:111:TOC

EU-SADC EPA (2015). Economic Partnership Agreement between the European
Union and its Member States, of the one Part, and the SADC EPA states, of
the other Part, Consolidated text, available at http://trade.ec.europa.eu/doclib/
docs/2015/october/tradoc_153915.pdf.

Hafner-Burton, Emily M. and Mark A. Pollack (2009). 'Mainstreaming Gender
in the European Union: Getting the Incentives Right', *Comparative European
Politics* 7: 1, 114-138.

Hoskyns, Catherine (2008). 'Governing the EU: Gender and Macroeconomics',
in Shireen M. Rai and Georgina Waylen (eds.), *Global Governance: Feminist
Perspectives*, Basingstoke: Palgrave Macmillan, pp. 107-128.

Kiratu, Sheila and Suryapratim Roy (2010). 'Beyond Barriers: The Gender Implications of Trade Liberalisation in Southern Africa', Winnipeg: International Institute for Sustainable Development, available at http://www.iisd.org/tkn/pdf/
beyond_barriers_gender_south_africa.pdf.

Lombardo, Emanuela and Petra Meier (2006). Gender Mainstreaming in the
EU: Incorporating a Feminist Reading, *European Journal of Women's Studies*
13(2), 151-166.

Mackay, Fiona, Meryl Kenny and Louise Chappell (2010). New Institutionalism
Through a Gender Lens: Towards a Feminist Institutionalism? *International
Political Science Review* 31:5, 573-88.

Malmström, Celia (2014a). Answers to the European Parliament Questionnaire
to the Commissioner Designate, available at http://ec.europa.eu/commission/
sites/cwt/files/commissioner_ep_hearings/malmstrom-reply_en.pdf.

Malmström, Celia (2014b). Trade and European Tradition of Civil Society, Speech
by EU Trade Cecilia Malmström, Civil Society Dialogue Meeting Brussels, 4 December 2014, available at http://trade.ec.europa.eu/doclib/docs/2014/
december/tradoc_152938.pdf.

Manners, Ian (2002). 'Normative Power Europe: A Contradiction in Terms?' *Journal of Common Market Studies,* 40: 2, 235-258.

Nyakujarah, Loveness J. and Morna, Colleen L. (2012). SADC Gender Pro-

tocol 2012 Barometer, available at http://www.genderlinks.org.za/article/
sadc-gender-protocol-2012-barometer-2012-09-18.

Orbie, Jan (ed.) (2008). *Europe's Global Role: External Policies of the European Union*, Aldershot: Ashgate.

Pheko, Lebohang (2006). 'Gender Review of the European Partnership Agreements', Paper to the European Commission, 6.12.2006.

PriceWaterhouseCoopers (2007). EU-ACP Sustainability Impact Assessment. Key findings, policy recommendations and lessons learned, available at http://trade.ec.europa.eu/doclib/docs/2007/march/tradoc_133852.pdf.

Roggeband, Conny (2010). 'Double Triangles: How the Transnationalization of Gender Politics Affects Feminist Cooperative Constellations', Paper presented at the 51st Annual Convention of the International Studies Association (ISA) in New Orleans, 17-20 February 2010.

Roggeband, Conny, Anouka van Eerdewijk and Anna van der Vleuten (2014). Reconceptualizing Gender Equality Norm Diffusion and Regional Governance: Logics and Geometries, in: Anna van der Vleuten, Anouka van Eerdewijk and Conny Roggeband (Eds), pp. 221-246.

Thomson, Marilyn (ed.) (2007). *EU Bilateral and Regional Trade Agreements: Bringing Women to the Centre of the Debate*, Brussels: WIDE, available at http://biblioteca.hegoa.ehu.es/system/ebooks/16816/original/WIDE_EU_BILATERAL.pdf.

Traidcraft Exchange (2012). 'Economic Partnership Agreements – still pushing the wrong deal for Africa?', available at http://www.bothends.org/nl/Publicaties/document/76/Economic-Partnership-Agreements.

True, Jacqui (2009). Trading-in Gender Equality: Gendered Meanings in EU Trade Policies. In Emanuela Lombardo, Petra Meier and Mieke Verloo (Eds) *The Discursive Politics of Gender Equality: Stretching, Bending and Policy-Making*. New York: Routledge.

Ulmer, Karin (2004). 'EU-ACP Trade Negotiations on Economic Partnership Agreements: A Gender Approach', Global Center for Women's Politics, available at http://www.glowboell.de/media/de/txt_rubrik_5/SuS_Ulmer_Gender_EUPartnership.pdf.

Ulmer, Karin (2007). 'Equity in Trade Negotiations: a Gender Review of the EPAs', *Trade Negotiations Insights* March-April, pp. 8-9 available at http://aprodev.eu/files/Trade/TNI_EN_6.2.pdf.

UN (1986). Report of the World Conference to Review and Appraise the Achievements of the UN Decade for Women: Equality, Development and Peace: Nairobi 15-26 July 1985, New York: United Nations, available at http://www.un.org/womenwatch/daw/beijing/otherconferences/Nairobi/Nairobi\%20Full\%20Optimized.pdf.

Van der Vleuten, Anna (2007). *The Price of Gender Equality: Member States and Governance in the European Union*, Aldershot: Ashgate.

Van der Vleuten, Anna and Merran Hulse (2013). Governance Transfer by the Southern African Development Community (SADC). A B2 Case Study Report, *SFB Working Paper* 48, available at http://www.sfb-governance.de/en/publikationen/working_papers/wp48/index.html.

Van der Vleuten, Anna and Anouka van Eerdewijk (2014). Regional Governance, Gender and Transnationalism: A First Exploration, in: Anna van der Vleuten, Anouka van Eerdewijk and Conny Roggeband (Eds), pp. 17–41.

Van der Vleuten, Anna, Anouka van Eerdewijk and Conny Roggeband (Eds) (2014). *Gender Equality Norms in Regional Governance. Transnational Dynamics in Europe, South America and Southern Africa*, Houndmills, Basingstoke: Palgrave.

Van der Vleuten, Anna and Andrea Ribeiro Hoffmann (2010). 'Explaining the Enforcement of Democracy by Regional Organisations: Comparing EU, Mercosur and SADC', *Journal of Common Market Studies* 48:3, 737-58

Van Eerdewijk, Anouka and Conny Roggeband (2014). Gender Equality Norm Diffusion and Actor Constellations: A First Exploration, in: Anna van der Vleuten, Anouka van Eerdewijk and Conny Roggeband (Eds), pp. 42-66.

Verloo, Mieke (2005). 'Displacement and Empowerment: Reflections on the Council of Europe Approach to Gender Mainstreaming and Gender Equality', *Social Politics*, 12: 3, 344-366.

Viilup, Elina (2015). The EU's Trade Policy: from gender-blind to gender-sensitive?, PE 549.058, http://www.europarl.europa.eu/RegData/etudes/IDAN/2015/549058/EXPO_IDA(2015)549058_EN.pdf

Williams, Mariama (2013). 'A Perspective on Feminist International Organizing from the Bottom Up: The Case of IGTN and the WTO', in G. Caglar, E. Prügl and S. Zwingel (eds.), *Feminist Strategies in International Governance*, London and New York: Routledge, pp. 92-108.

Woodward, Alison E. (2003). 'Building Velvet Triangles: Gender and Informal Governance', in Thomas Christiansen and Simone Piattoni (eds.), Informal Governance in the European Union, Cheltenham: Edward Elgar, pp. 76-93.

Woodward, Alison E. and Anna van der Vleuten (2014). EU and the Export of Gender Equality Norms: Myth and Facts, in: A. van der Vleuten, A. van Eerdewijk and C. Roggeband (Eds), pp. 67-92.

Woolcock, Stephen (2012). *European Union Economic Diplomacy. The Role of the EU in External Economic Relations*, Farnham: Ashgate.

CHAPTER 6:

GENDERING GREEN CLIMATE FINANCE: POTENTIAL AND LIMITATIONS

Sam WONG

Using a 'gender-sensitive approach' and 'country ownership' as the two guiding principles, so-called green climate finance has generated great expectation about how it manages climate finance differently. This paper, however, argues that the Green Climate Fund (GCF) is not effective in achieving gender equity for four reasons: (1) the low representation of women on the GCF Board reinforces women's subordination in climate finance; (2) the idea of 'country-ownership' and enhanced direct access, without adequate governance mechanisms, is vulnerable to elite capture and corruption; (3) increasing participation of the private sector worsens, not improves, the imbalance of mitigation and adaptation; (4) the 'women-focused' approach fails to understand that poor men in developing countries are equally vulnerable to climate change.

1.INTRODUCTION

Climate finance has become a key element in climate change debate and policies since substantial financial resources are required in order to achieve the goal of limiting the rise of global temperature to less than 2°C. It is contentious and confusing because climate finance is a collective term which includes many players (World Bank, United Nations and many individual countries), has different emphasis in strategies (mitigation and adaptation), involves different funding sources (bilateral, multilateral, private and public), and works with a wide range of sectors (forest, water and agriculture). Climate finance discussion has been criticised for focusing too much on the amounts and the types of finance, and too little on the politics, effectiveness and equity (Curtin, 2013; Buchner *et al.*, 2012).

Amongst all climate funds, the Green Climate Fund (GCF) has caught most attention, although it has become operational only 2014. It is expected to replace the World Bank's Climate Investment Funds (CIFs) to become the globe's biggest climate fund and to provide long-term finance to assist developing countries. Apart from the sheer size, there are two particular guiding principles underlying GCF that have generated much anticipation: country ownership and a gender-sensitive approach (GCF, 2011). The former advocates fiscal de-centralisation in which developing countries get direct access to climate funds, whereas the latter promotes gender equality by responding to the criticism of 'gender-blindness' of many climate funds (UNDP, 2011).

This paper focuses on these two principles and examines if, and how, GCF is able to achieve gender equality through climate financing. Conceptually, it draws on the concept of political economy to analyse 'who gets what, when and how' in climate finance, as suggested by Calland and Dubosse (2011: 4). Methodologically, it reviews GCF-related documents, such as the governing instrument and Minutes of the Board meetings as well as academic literature and NGO reports, to provide evidence.

This paper makes four key arguments: firstly, women representation in the GCF Board is between 15% and 25%, much lower than the World Bank's administrated Pilot Program on Climate Resilience (PPCR) and the Global Environment Facility's Least Developed Country Fund. Secondly, the country ownership approach is prone to elite capture and the risk of corruption. Neither poor women nor men in developing countries will benefit from the increased funding. Thirdly, adaptation strategies matter to gender equality because they are related to poor people's daily livelihoods, but GCF's advocacy for the involvement of the private sector may make adaptation under-funded. Lastly, the gender policies, promoted by existing advocacy groups, are too women-focused. This pays inadequate attention to the needs of vulnerable men in climate finance in developing countries.

The structure of the paper is as follows: it will first discuss the nature and meaning of global climate finance, with a special focus on GCF. It will then examine the concept of gender and analyse the guiding principles of GCF. After looking into the women representation on the GCF board, the nature of country ownership, the politics of adaptation and mitigation, and the inclusion and exclusion of men in climate finance, it will conclude by offering suggestions for making GCF more gender-sensitive.

2. NATURE OF CLIMATE FINANCE

Climate finance can be generally defined as 'the transfer of funds from the North to the South to help developing countries adapt to the unavoidable impacts of climate change, reduce greenhouse gas emissions and embark on clean energy development paths' (Friends of the Earth, 2010: 1).[1] Climate Policy Initiative estimates that the annual global climate flows reached USD 331 billion in 2013, rising from USD 97 billion in 2011 (Buchner *et al.*, 2014). This marks a 241% increase between 2011 and 2013.

According to the Climate Policy Initiative, the private sector plays a significant role in climate finance, its shares in 2012 was 63%. Two-thirds of the investment came from developed countries. In contrast, the contribution of the public sector has decreased, from USD 21 billion in 2011 to USD 19.5 billion in 2012. The financial sources of the public sector include domestic government support to renewable energy projects and related infrastructure. Compared to the private sector, the public sector seems small. However, Whitley (2013) stresses that the public sector plays a crucial role in catalysing investments from the private sector. The intermediaries include multilateral, bilateral and national agencies. Their share has also increased from USD 21 billion in 2011 to USD 115 billion in 2012, which marks a 21.6% rise.

The international climate finance landscape is highly complex and confusing. It is sometimes synonymous with carbon finance, used by Groupe Energies Renouvelables, Environnement et Solidarites (GERES). It is sometimes used in a sector-specific way, such as forest financing, or function-specific, such as mitigation financing. Climate finance is actually a collective term which includes a bundle of climate funds in different scale and location, such as the African Green Fund by African Development Bank and People's Survival Fund in the Philippines. So far, there is no single climate fund to collect and disperse all climate-related finance. Stewart *et al.* (2009: 7) predict that such a proposal for a single global fund is 'political-

---

[1]   Fossil fuel subsidies and reforms are highly related to climate finance because they affect whether low-CO_2 policies are financially attractive. Whitley (2013) estimates that global fossil fuel subsidies alone are between USD 775 billion to as much as USD 1 trillion in 2012. However, phasing out fossil fuel subsides is often considered not simply an economic issue, but also a political agenda (Craeynest, 2010).

ly infeasible and unsuited to advance the policy needs of decentralisation, innovation and experimentation'.

Climate finance comes from four different sources: bilateral, multilateral, public and private. Bilateral fund means that donors provide finance directly to recipient countries. This approach gives donor countries more control. Multilateral, in contrast, indicates that funds are disbursed through intermediary agencies, such as the World Bank and the United Nations. The public sources of financing take a number of forms, such as concessional debt, loan guarantees and technology transfer arrangements. The private source includes investments from private companies and the carbon market (Clapp *et al.*, 2012). Climate finance is often a finance mix and combines different sources.

Another reason for causing confusion is what is considered as 'climate-specific' and 'climate-relevant'. The former denotes capital flows which target low-carbon and climate-resilient development, whereas the latter includes any funding that influences, directly or indirectly, carbon emissions and vulnerability to climate change in developing countries. Although only the former is counted as climate finance, Buchner *et al.* (2012) warn that their differences are not so clear-cut that it is sometimes not easy to make judgement. The lack of an internationally acknowledged definition and the absence of a common measurement and reporting system also make accurate data collection and comparison difficult (Curtin, 2013). It is also difficult to track private finance because of confidentiality and multiple ownership issues (Caruso and Ellis, 2013). In the light of these difficulties, there are high risks of double counting (Forstater and Rank, 2012). For example, stakeholders at various stages of the same project report their own financial mobilisation.

2.1. FOUR MAJOR INTERNATIONAL CLIMATE FUNDS

Here, we will only introduce four major global climate funds, based on the sizes of the funds and the impact (see Table 1).

Table 1: Comparing the changes in financial flows of Climate Investment Funds (CIFs) to the Adaptation Fund (AF) and the Global Environment Facility (GEF) between 2011 and 2012

Climate funds	2012 (USD million)	2011(USD million)	Change in %
CIFs (including CTF & SCF)	929.5	1,015.0	-8.4
AF	85.6	34.5	+148.1
GEF (including LDCF & SCCF)	220.5	301.6	-25.9

(sources: Buchner et al., 2011; Buchner et al., 2012)

2.1.1. CLIMATE INVESTMENT FUNDS (CIFs)

CIFs were jointly established by the World Bank and regional multilateral development banks in 2009. They aim to leverage private and public resources to assist developing countries to transit to a low-carbon and climate-resilient future. They are composed of two funds: the Clean Technology Fund (CTF) and the Strategic Climate Fund (SCF). CTF supports 15 to 20 countries or regional investment plans that meet the criteria of significant greenhouse gas emission savings. The arrangements of the SCF are different. Under the SCF, there are three programmes: the Pilot Programme on Climate Resilience (PPCR), the Forest Investment Programme (FIP), and the Scaling Up Renewable Energy in Low-Income Countries (SREP). PPCR assists countries to integrate climate resilience into national development planning. FIP focuses on reducing CO_2 emissions from deforestation and forest degradation. SREP helps poor countries adopt renewable energy solutions (Oxfam, 2011). According to Table 1, CIFs received USD 929.5 million funding in 2012, which is lower than 2011 by 8.4%.

2.1.2. ADAPTATION FUND (AF)

The AF was established under the Kyoto Protocol in order to provide funds for adaptation programmes in developing countries. It became operational in 2009. Similar to the GCF, it is independent of development finance institutions. It is managed by a Board that equally represents developing and developed countries. It is financed with 2% of revenues generated from the trade of certified emission reductions allocated to the Clean Development Mechanism. According to Fankhauser (2013), there are some concerns about the financial sustainability of the AF owing to the collapse of the international carbon pricing. In contrast to CIFs, the AF received a nearly 150% rise in funding, up to USD 85.6 million in 2012, although it is only one-tenth of CIFs, in term of the size of funding.

2.1.3. GLOBAL ENVIRONMENT FACILITY (GEF)

Founded in 1991, the GEF was a USD 1 billion pilot programme of the World Bank. It is now an independent financial organisation representing 182 member governments in partnership with international institutions, NGOs and the private sector. It assists developing countries by providing grants in support of the UN environmental agreements. There are two components under the GEF: the Least Developed Countries Fund (LDCF) and the Special Climate Change Fund (SCCF). The LDCF assists the least developed countries to implement National Adaptation Programmes of Action (NAPAs). The nature of the SCCF is slightly different. It provides not only adaptation, but also technology transfer to all developing country parties to the UNFCCC (Oxfam, 2011). The size of the climate finance of the GEF is bigger than the AP, but smaller than CIFs.

2.1.4. GREEN CLIMATE FUND (GCF)

The existing architecture of climate change finance, shown above, is composed of several bilateral and multilateral agencies which may not be able to offer long-term, predictable and stable sources of finance. In the light of this, developed countries signed the Copenhagen Accord in 2009 and agreed a ten-year financing plan to assist developing countries to combat climate change. This financial agreement was divided into two parts: firstly, the developed countries would offer fast-track finance of USD 10 billion per year for the first three years from 2010. Secondly, they will increase the funds to USD 100 billion per year by 2020.

The funding was initially channeled by the GEF and administered by the World Bank. However, this arrangement was not popular amongst developing countries because they did not like the fact that access to funding was subject to the rules and conditions of the World Bank (Fankhauser, 2013). After a few rounds of negotiation, the Conference of Parties in Cancun agreed to establish a new fund, called the Green Climate Fund, under the UNFCCC in 2012 as a mechanism to deliver adaptation and mitigation finance in developing countries. Headquartered in South Korea, the new fund is overseen by a Board of 24 members, equally representing both developing and developed countries.

According to the Governing Instrument, the GCF will "play a key role in channelling new, additional, adequate and predictable financial resources to developing countries" (GCF, 2011, para 1). The funding is expected to come from public, private, bilateral and multilateral sources. The GCF is based on three principles: (i) enhanced direct access to create country ownership; (ii) multi-stakeholder engagement with local government and communities; (iii) a gender-sensitive approach.

Dasgupta *et al.* (2013) suggest that the design of the GCF is a combination of a top-down and bottom-up approach to bridge the gap between international funding and bottom-up climate solutions. Having learned from the AF, recipient countries are now required to nominate competent subnational, national and regional implementing entities for accreditation in order to receive funding (GCF, 2011, para 47). This decentralised approach to provide direct access funding is a response to the dissatisfaction of developing countries in accessing funds to CIFs and the GEF. This system intended to reduce the costs of disbursement using traditional centralised funding modalities and to increase flexibility over how climate finance is disbursed. This approach also creates stronger incentives for governments to integrate funding into existing development strategies and to provide cross-sectoral climate change policies that are locally appropriate (Muller et al., 2013: 4). GCF is also keen to give local people a greater say in how funds are used. Local communities and NGOs are encouraged to get involved in the consultation and decision-making process (Marston, 2013). The private sector is also welcome to seize any business opportunities it may identify.

The Board has already met ten times between 2012 and 2015 to discuss the details of the funding mechanisms. Four observers and eight non-business UNFCCC civil society constituencies, including women and indigenous representatives, are allowed to sit in the meetings. The idea of a 'gender-sensitive approach' will be discussed later.

3. THE POLITICAL ECONOMY OF CLIMATE FINANCE

Climate finance, according to Calland and Dubosse (2011: 4), is "fundamentally a matter of political economy". On the surface, it underlines the philosophy of 'climate-smart development' which means that countries can enjoy economic growth and simultaneously become climate-resilient (Forstater and Rank, 2012). However, political economists would argue that achieving 'climate-smart development' is not cost-free. There are winners and losers in the process, and the uneven distribution of costs and benefits reflects unequal power relationships. For example, Schroeder (2010: 2) suggests that climate finance is intertwined with the present, and past, global (climate) politics. The mistrust of developing countries over the commitment of developed countries in the GCF is related to the "failure to deliver on past promises" and "concerns about the inequity of the current situation".

Global climate finance, as discussed in the previous section, has increased between 2011 and 2013. Yet, the benefits are not equally distributed. While 53% of climate finance goes to developed countries, developing countries only receive 47% (Buchner *et al.*, 2012). The politics of mitigation and adaptation is also embedded in climate finance. While adaptation activities receive only 4% of total climate finance, approximately USD 14 billion, mitigation strategies get the rest. The Fast Start Finance may perform better; 21% of the funding has been used for adaptation purposes.

Geographically, 92% of approved climate finance has been directed to the developing countries and middle income countries to support primarily mitigation action to reduce greenhouse gas emissions (ODI, 2013). In Asia, 113 mitigation projects were launched compared to 40 for adaptation. As a consequence, Africa is left out and receives the lowest level of climate funding (Whande and Reddy, 2011). The big financial gap between mitigation and adaptation and the uneven geographical distribution of climate funding have significant impact on gender equality, which will be discussed in Section 5.3.

In the 2009 Copenhagen Accord, developed countries agreed to mobilise 'new and additional' funds to assist developing countries. According to Official Development Assistance, 'new' means that finance should not include any commitments announced before the Accord. However, Oxfam found out that only 17% (around USD 5.2 billion) of the Fast Start Fund is considered new. Report by the African Climate Policy Centre of the Economic Commission for Africa shows that only 45% has been committed, 33% allocated and about 7% actually disbursed (Ciplet *et al.*, 2013).

Another debate is about whether climate finance should be considered as aid, loan or debt. Michael Tierney in the 'Aid and Our Changing Environment Conference' (2013) suggested that climate finance can be considered as 'the greening of aid' which means that climate change has become a key priority in foreign aid. However, Peralta (2008) argues that it should be conceptualised as 'climate debt' or 'ecological debt', but the debt is not paid by developing countries to developed countries, but the other way round. The developed countries need to fulfill their historical responsibilities of helping developing countries which are least responsible for causing climate change but are worst hit by the impact. Despite the debate, a study by the European Network on Debt and Development shows that only one-sixth of the CIFs have been disbursed in the form of grants (quoted in Calland and Dubosse, 2011: 6). This leaves developing countries in heavy debt.

Furthermore, the aim of climate mitigation is to 'reduce the sources or enhance the sinks of greenhouse gases', whereas climate adaptation refers to the adjustment capability of the natural and/or human systems in response to the changing climate (IPCC, 2001). Helgeson and Ellis (2015) criticise that most of the climate funds have been allocated to tackling mitigation, rather than adaptation. Yet, this imbalanced resource allocation risks putting women at a disadvantage, which will be further explained in the later section.

4. GENDERING CLIMATE FINANCE

Climate finance is not gender-neutral. Access to climate finance shapes, and is shaped by, gender relationships (UNDP, 2012). Gender is defined as the "socially constructed roles and socially learned behaviours and expectations of women and men in a particular society" (World Bank, 2001: 34). Gendered relations involve 'difference, inequality and power', and that shapes "access to, and control over, material and symbolic resources" (Wilson, 2004: 8). Gendered relations are 'contextually specific and often changing in response to altering circumstances' (Moser, 1993: 230). Here, it is crucial to point out that gender is about power relationships between women and men. Both poor women and men encounter differing vulnerabilities to climate change, owing to their gender roles and social norms. This paper is, therefore, 'gender-focused', not 'women-specific'. Cleaver (2003) argues that, while not all men are powerful, not all women are powerless. Focusing solely on women in climate finance fails to understand how men are also affected due to masculinity. It also restricts diverse experiences and capabilities of different women in response to climate finance.

Changing farming and water management practices, induced by climate change, has significant gender impact. Research by the Institute of Development Studies (IDS, 2008) shows that 80% of women in Sub-Saharan Africa are involved in food production. Women and girls are also expected to secure water, energy and food resources for their families. Water stress, caused by prolonged droughts, means that they have to walk a longer distance to find water in rural areas or spend more time queuing for intermittent water supplies in urban areas. These changes have long-term implications for their health in light of the rising workload and physical exhaustion (Bathge, 2010). Rural women and girls often take up the role as domestic carer. This gender norm constrains them from migrating to cities and towns (Oxfam, 2011).

Women feel more constrained from building adaptive capacities because they are deprived of 'land rights, ownership rights for the means of production, technology, finances, information and training in climate adaptation' (Bathge, 2010: 5). Being weak in decision-making power and without control over productive resources and access to loans, credits and agricultural extension services, Olson *et al.* (2010) argue that women do not have the power to decide what changes are needed in their farms. All these constraints, IDS (2008: 4) suggests, reduce their incentives 'to engage in environmentally sustainable farming practices and make long-term investments in land rehabilitation and soil quality'.

However, Cleaver (2003) warns that the focus should not simply be placed on women's vulnerabilities. Instead, examining the intricate relationships between masculinity and climate change help understand how men perceive climate change differently from women. For instance, Lipset (2011) conducts an anthropological research with the Murik tribe who have long lived on the coast of Papua New Guinea. After the impact of the Asian Tsunami in 2007, Lipset talked to the Murik men in order to understand how they constructed the causes of the tsunami. Some men, in interviews, suggested that the 'high tide' was a sign of anger of the sea-spirits. The spirits sought retribution on them because they abandoned their traditional lifestyle in which they manoeuvred outrigger canoes to a modern one in which they steer dinghies powered by outboard motors (p 39-40).

Knowing men's perspectives in climate change has significant implications for disaster management and planning. Using the Asian tsunami as an example once again, the UN (2011) shows that men and boys considered saving their families as heroic and placed themselves at risk. That masculine notion could undermine the effectiveness of information and communication technologies (ICTs) in saving lives during disasters.

4.1. GENDER INSENSITIVITY IN EXISTING CLIMATE FINANCE

The above section provides just a few examples to demonstrate that women and men experience climate change differently and that gender relationships shape the effectiveness of climate change policies, it is surprising to find out that gender is not adequately considered in the climate finance design. Although both the World Bank and the Global Environment Facility have been advocating gender-mainstreaming strategies in their climate change policies, Schalatek (2011) criticises that gender is simply an 'add-on' in their climate funds' strategy. By not taking gender seriously, Oxfam (2011) has expressed its misgiving that it would limit the impact of climate financing in achieving gender empowerment.

4.1.1. WORLD BANK'S CIFs

UNDP (2009: 2) criticises that CIFs have not considered the gender-differentiated impact of climate change in programme design and financing criteria. They also have not paid sufficient attention to the existing gender bias in the distribution of risks and benefits. Additionally, 80% of its pledged funding is allocated to large-scale energy and transportation programmes and projects. According to UNDP, these sectors are 'traditionally male-dominated working sectors of the formal economy'. In contrast, smaller scale mitigation and adaptation programmes, such as organic farming and natural resource management, have the potential to improve local livelihoods of women because the women depend on food, fuel, medicine and income, but they are not actively promoted. As a result, just focusing on mitigation financing risks reproducing the existing gender imbalance in climate change financing.

The verdict by Oxfam (2011) over FIP is mixed. While Oxfam appreciates that gender-sensitive consultation and consulting women's groups in the operational guidelines and inclusive processes and participation of all important stakeholders are highlighted in the project review criteria, there is no explicit call for collecting sex- disaggregated data in terms of gender-sensitive monitoring and evaluation.

As far as PPCR is concerned, gender is not included in the operational principles. Oxfam (2011) suggests that consultation with 'key stakeholders' is mentioned in the evaluation, but it does not make it specific to women. Despite the criticisms, Schalatek and Burns (2013) believe that PPCR has great potential in helping those with the least adaptive capacity since it promotes adaptation projects, such as promoting drought-resistant cultivation.

4.1.2. AF

Arend and Lowman (2011: 16) are highly critical of the gender performance of the AF. They suggest that the Fund considers gender merely an additional component which means 'adding bureaucratic layers to the direct finance design'. They also accuse the Fund of making a big mistake in depicting women mostly as victims of climate change, rather than agents of change who have valuable resources in adaptation strategies (ibid.). In term of gender capacity, although 60% of the staff members of the secretariat are female, they suggest that these staff members have no formal gender expertise (at p 15). They recommend that the Fund considers gender integration through all project cycles, including mandatory gender project review criteria, and also provides smaller funding channels for poor women to apply for climate funds directly.

Marston (2013) suggests that the Fund lacks clear mechanisms for including local strategies and vulnerability and impact assessments. Similarly, Oxfam (2011) suggests that the Fund can make improvements by making consultation more specific. For instance, the Fund only mentions 'necessary' stakeholders in gender-sensitive monitoring framework and 'vulnerable' groups in evaluation. That said, the Fund has produced new guidelines to include gender in programme planning.

4.1.3. GEF

GEF has achieved a good gender balance in staff recruitment. 49% of staff members are female and three gender experts, including one external, work closely with GEF. However, Schalatek and Nakhooda (2011) criticise its administrated LDCF for not making gender one of the obligatory decision criteria for project review and approval. Only one third of the NAPAs include gender analysis or indicators (p 3). Arend and Lowman (2011: 12) are equally critical of the GEF. They suggest that the GEF inserts an 'added layer of complexity' which is 'often subordinated to other concerns'. They complain about the GEF's weak gender budgeting because it assumes that projects benefit women and men equally, so they do not feel the need to collect sex-disaggregated data. They also criticise the GEF for focusing on mitigation policies, assuming that 'mitigation interventions addressing global environmental issues should theoretically benefit everyone on the planet, regardless of their sex'.

In response to these challenges, the GEF approved a gender mainstreaming policy in both LDCF and SCCF in 2011. It also introduced a new monitoring and evaluation tool for adaptation projects that evaluates gender-differentiated impact. For instance, eight out of its 47 outcome indicators monitor gender-sensitive effectiveness (GEF, 2011).

4.2. THE GCF'S GENDER-SENSITIVE APPROACH

What makes the GCF different from other climate funds is that it makes gender an explicit guiding principle. Its 'gender-sensitive approach' is announced in the Governing Instrument (para 3). Although no proper definition is given, gender is mentioned in other three areas within the Governing Instrument which gives some hints of how the 'gender-sensitive approach' is operationalised. In the selection of board members, it states that: due consideration should be 'given to gender balance' (para 11). In the establishment of the secretariat, gender balance should be taken into in the processes of staff selection (para 21). In the operational modalities, the GCF should simplify funding processes and 'encourage the involvement of relevant stakeholders, including vulnerable groups and (also) addressing gender aspects' (para 31).

Schalatek and Burns (2013: 1) call it an 'unprecedented step' in integrating gender into climate finance. It acknowledges gender-differentiated vulnerabilities and capacities in the context of climate change and in accessing climate finance. It also indicates that achieving funding efficiency and policy effectiveness can be compatible. This makes the Friends of the Earth (2010) to conclude that there is high expectation on the GCF to achieve gender empowerment. It will also give some pressure on other finance funds to examine their own gender policies and practices.

5. DISCUSSION

5.1. LOW REPRESENTATION OF WOMEN ON THE GCF BOARD

The GCF makes a special reference to pursuing a 'gender-sensitive approach' in the Governing Instrument. To show its seriousness about gender, it states explicitly that it will pay 'due consideration given to gender balance' in the composition of the Board members (GCF, para 11). Oxfam (2011) welcomes this high-profile intervention, suggesting that gender balance matters in decision-making forums, so that women's voices are equally represented.

The high expectation has, however, led to disappointment. The Board of the GCF is composed of 24 principal members. The GCF has held ten meetings over the past three year, but there were no more than six women at each Board meeting (see Table 2). This is far below the World Bank's administrated PPCR and the GEF's LDCF and SCCF. Petherick (2013: 86) argues that the numbers of women in committees matter since creating a critical mass of qualified women is necessary for women to 'influence key outcomes and be taken seriously in political circle(s)'.

Table 2: Women representation at Board meetings of various climate funds

Climate Fund	Women	Men	Women representation at Board Meeting (%)
GCF (1st meeting in Geneva, 23-25 Aug 2012)	5	19	20.5
GCF (2nd meeting in Songdo, 18-20 Oct 2012)	6	18	25.0
GCF (3rd meeting in Berlin, 12-15 Mar 2013)	5	19	20.5
GCF (4th meeting in Songdo, 26-28 June 2013)	5	19	20.5
GCF (5th meeting in Paris, 8-10 Oct 2013)	3	21	14.3
GCF (6th meeting in Bali, 19-21 Feb 2014)	3	21	14.3
GCF (7th meeting in Songdo, 18-21 May 2014)	3	21	14.3

(sources: Green Climate Fund website www.gcfund.org/; Heinrich-Böll-Stiftung website www.us.boell.org)

Table 2: Women representation at Board meetings of various climate funds

GCF (8th meeting in Bridge-town, 14-17 Oct 2014)	4	20	20.0
GCF (9th meeting in Songdo, 24-26 Mar 2015)	4	20	20.0
GCF (10th meeting in Songdo, 6-9 July 2015)	4	20	20.0

(sources: Green Climate Fund website www.gcfund.org/; Heinrich-Böll-Stiftung website www.us.boell.org)

One year before the GCF became fully operational in 2014, Schalatek (2013b), a key gender observer in the GCF, could not hide her frustration that the GCF has, so far, 'paid little to no attention to gender issues as an area to be addressed implementing a vision for the Fund' (p. iv). Oscar Reyes suggests that he is not too surprised by such a low representation of women in the GCF. Before the GCF was established, the UN Secretary General's High Level Advisory Group on Climate Change Finance (AGF) was charged with the preparation of the GCF. In the Board meeting of AGF, women's representation was only at 5%. That is why Reyes calls it a 'UN Boy's Club' (2010).

Although UNDP (2009) suggests that merely including women in boards or in meetings is not sufficient to ensure that climate funds would respond to the needs of both women and men, Petherick (2013: 86) argues that numbers still matter, since creating a critical mass of qualified women is necessary for women to 'influence key outcomes and be taken seriously in political circle(s)'. Bhowmik (2013) also stresses that the Board of GCF needs to set an example otherwise this will make the idea of achieving equal sex representation at the national level even harder.

5.2. COUNTRY OWNERSHIP, ELITE CAPTURE AND CORRUPTION

The underlying principles of the GCF in championing country ownership and multi-stakeholder governance are well-intended. They aim to enhance the efficiency of public climate finance delivery by devolving the decision-making power to national and local governments (Bird *et al.*, 2013). They also help improve effectiveness by promoting local voices and reflecting funding priorities at the community level. In decentralised forest financing,

Kanel (2012) argues that the production of forest products and services meets the needs of local people and enables them to use the incomes from community forestry for livelihood support and community development. In the light of these arguments, some gender experts consider the idea of fiscal decentralisation a good opportunity for gender empowerment. Schalatek (2011) believes that this approach would encourage more women's groups to apply for finance directly for adaptation and mitigation activities. Women entrepreneurs can also use grants for increasing their business opportunities. To maximise the impact, gender experts such as Arend and Lowman (2011) recommend better gender training for national implementing agencies and effective local capacity-building and monitoring.

While these gender-sensitive suggestions are valid, the success of anchoring climate finance locally, however, hinges on complex power dynamics between national and sub-national governments and local communities. Hoffmann (2013: 5) warns that decentralising the decision-making power of climate financing is a 'highly contentious and contested process'. Without effective monitoring and adequate local capacity building, the newly-created participatory space would easily be captured by national and local elites. The risks of corruption would simply increase vulnerability of poor women and men, and reinforce gender inequalities.

The principle of country ownership inevitably strengthens the role of central government in allocation and delivery of climate finance (Calland and Dubosse, 2011). There are concerns that some national institutions and ministries may not have adequate capacity in ensuring efficient financial allocation in climate funds. That said, the International Institute for Environment and Development (IIED, 2013) found out that having strong country leadership may not always bring positive outcomes. Using their experiences of the Pilot Programme for Climate Resilience projects in Bangladesh as an example, IIED indicates that the decisions to use loan finance for adaptation projects are often hijacked by one or two dominant ministers who often prefer large-scale engineering interventions. The country ownership may allow strong cross-sectoral coordination for climate change, but Otzelberger (2011) warns that competing priorities for scarce resources between ministries may undermine the integration.

Whether multi-level governance works also depends on whether or not the state is willing to share and transfer fiscal decision-making power and management responsibility to lower levels. Larson and Ribot (2009: 176) suggest that, in reality, central government 'either transfers too little power to be meaningful, or transfers these powers to local authorities that are not representative'. In the governing instruments, the GCF may set up some mechanism for ensuring inclusion of local level strategies, but national leaders can make use of the opportunity to work with sub-national elites to retain their authorities. Additionally, UNDP (2013) suggests that the participation of local authorities in climate finance varies widely. While it works quite well in Papua New Guinea and Nepal, little effective devolution of forest-related authority to local governments is recorded in Ghana and Kenya. Civil society and NGOs are also left off the boards and committees of national and local institutions.

Another concern is elite capture and the risk of corruption. Platteau *et al.* (2012: 3) suggest that a decentralised, participatory development is 'highly vulnerable to the risk of elite capture'. Elites are a small group of well-connected and resourceful individuals who exert disproportionate influence over collective action. The local elites, mostly men, are in better positions to capitalise on newly-created participatory space and to make decisions on behalf of their communities. US 600 million was reported to be stolen from Indonesia's reforestation fund during the mid-1990s (U4 Brief, 2012: 2). Bribery speeds up illegal logging because corrupt officials create fake land titles. According to the Asia Pacific Human Development Network (2007), 20 to 40% of water sector finances are lost to corruption. In addition, whilst climate finance and adaptation may bring investments to local communities, it also generates new forms of corruption, such as fraud in carbon accounting, cheating over carbon rights and excuses for land grabbing (UN, 2008: 4). Built on unequal patron-client structures, poor people rarely challenge their domination, and unwittingly, reinforce existing inequalities. Devolving climate finance to the local level may also risk legitimising customary authorities, and thus reproducing gender stereotypes. Ribot (2003) suggests that power over natural resources is often transferred to chieftains and religious leaders who are considered able to make indigenous claims.

5.3.IMBALANCE BETWEEN ADAPTATION AND MITIGATION

As discussed at the end of section 3, climate finance tilts towards mitigation, which receives 96% of total global funding, which leaves adaptation activities under-funded. Additionally, most of the climate finance goes to emerging developing countries, such as China, Brazil and India, which attract many big-scale mitigation projects. This leaves poor African women and men behind.

Gender scholars and practitioners are deeply concerned about these two uneven financial and geographical distributions of climate finance. Otzelberger (2011) suggests that focusing too much on mitigation puts women at a disadvantage because women have less access to property and information than men, so they are less likely to benefit from technology-based mitigation activities. Instead, making adaptation a priority matters to gender equity. Firstly, adaptation projects focus on water management, agriculture and rural development. They are most relevant to the livelihoods and food security of poor women and men who rely on natural resources for everyday survival. Secondly, IDS (2008) argues that the majority of small-scale farmers in developing countries are women. Their understanding of traditional land management techniques and knowledge of soil enrichment and drought-resistant measures are relevant to climate change adaptation. Therefore, adaptation policies, targeting rural women in capacity building and agricultural extension services, would make a difference to gender equality in food security and distribution, both within households and in retail markets.

The GCF has shown awareness of these concerns. It makes it explicit in the Governing Instrument that: 'the Board will balance the allocation of resources between adaptation and mitigation activities under the Fund' (para 50) and 'the Board will aim for appropriate geographical balance' in financial allocation (para 52). While these promises are encouraging, how much adaptation activities would receive remains a great concern. That is the reason why gender lobby groups have campaigned for splitting the GCF funding equally between adaptation and mitigation (Schaletek, 2013a).

A foreseeable challenge for the GCF to increase the budget for adaptation is about how to make adaptation strategies in not-so-fast-growing economies, such as African countries, attractive to private investment (UNDP, 2011). As discussed in Section 2, it is the market mechanisms that lead to the investment imbalance between mitigation and adaptation because the private sector makes more profits in mitigation projects. The GCF is keen to get the private sector involved in order to catalyse additional finance

(GCF guiding instrument, para 54). Yet, the private sector will not invest in adaptation policies if they do not offer sufficient financial incentives. The GCF can use more public funds to promote adaptation, but how it strikes a financial balance between mitigation and adaptation, as it has committed, remains unclear.

Finally, there is concern about how adaptation financing is delivered. At present, most adaptation funds are distributed in the form of concessional loans, rather than grants. The debt payment will add extra financial burden on poor countries and vulnerable communities. Calland and Dubosse (2011) are worried that, in order to pay up the debts, developing countries may have to reduce social expenditures which have greater negative impact on women and thus increase gender inequalities.

5.4.INCLUSION OF VULNERABLE MEN IN CLIMATE FINANCE

The GCF, championing gender sensitivity in climate finance, mentions 'women' only once in para 71 of the Governing Instrument. Instead, the Governing Instrument mentions 'vulnerable group' twice, in the operational modalities (para 31) and stakeholder input and participation (para 71). This reflects that the GCF does not consider men and women two separate groups in pursing gender equality.

However, in pursuing gender equality, the gender lobby groups and experts in the GCF, wittingly or unwittingly, promote 'women-specific' policies. It may be understandable why the discussion tends to focus on women. As discussed before, climate change disproportionately affects women. They suffer from multiple discriminations in accessing climate finance. Their voices are often silent in the decision-making process (Marston, 2013). Therefore, taking women seriously in climate finance would make a considerable impact. Criticising gender scholars for excluding men in the GCF is unfair. Bhowmik (2013), for example, advocates equal gender representation and recommends conducting gender-sensitive consultation with both women and men.

Having said that, the gender discussion remains too much about women, and does not adequately consider vulnerable men, who equally suffer from gender-insensitive policies. For instance, in explaining the meaning of the gender-sensitive approach, Schalatek (2011) suggests that: it 'requires that women, as essential stakeholders, are fully considered and represented and that gender roles and dynamics, including constraints and capacities, are taken into account and proactively addressed in program and project design, implementation and monitoring and evaluation' (p 1-2). Vulnerable men are completely invisible in the discussion. While women are praised for being transformative agents who have specific knowledge relevant to adaptation, Cornwall *et al.* (2007) stresses that vulnerable men have similar, but unrealised, potential. Additionally, women specificity is equally obvious in policy recommendations. Many women-only interventions are proposed, such as setting up special women's sub-funds and women enterprises (Schalatek and Burns, 2013) as well as special training workshops for women (Oxfam, 2011).

The problem with replacing the 'gender-sensitive' perspective by the 'women-only' approach are that men are also 'gendered beings' (MacGregor, 2010). Poor men and boys are equally vulnerable to climate change. Older men, for instance, are less tied into social networks than women which puts them at a disadvantage when seeking help from their communities (IDS, 2008). As mentioned before, men could also become the victims of climate change because of socialised masculine and gendered roles and expectations. For example, more men than women died when Hurricane Mitch hit Central America in 1998 because of societal expectations that they should carry out high-risk rescue activities. Men have specific vulnerabilities that affect their health and safety, and that are linked to traditional norms and values, and the way in which prevailing ideas of masculinity are constructed (Blomstrom *et al.*, 2009) Drawing on examples in Usangu, Tanzania, Cleaver (2001) suggested that community forest protection is gendered. Male youths are recruited as foot-soldiers and the elders act as advisors on tactics. While women and girls are excluded from the forest policing teams, because the tasks are seen as dangerous and physically demanding, the full responsibilities fall on the shoulders of men and boys.

Understanding masculinity also helps understand how men and boys facilitate, as well as hinder, women and girls in accessing climate finance and building resilience. As Letherby (2003: 137) puts it: 'in order to fully understand what is going on in women's lives, we need to know what is going on in men's lives also'. This is the interdependence that shapes gender dynamics.

Another concern of the women-only interventions also risks homogenising women's experiences. UN (2002) suggests that single mothers, widows, disabled women, aged women and women in urban and rural areas have different identities, and their strategies to adapt to climate change can be very different. The diverse experiences of women and men are also related to the previous discussion about elite capture. Cleaver (2003) argues that, while not all men are powerful, not all women are powerless. Although many national and local elites are men, their wives and female family members enjoy privileges that vulnerable men do not. The exclusivity of women also reflects the sisterhood identity. For instance, in the process of climate change negotiation, Phakathi (2013) suggests that 'African women are in solidarity with their sisters throughout the world to shape an agreement'. The sisterhood approach, however, risks considering the power relationships between men and women a zero-sum game.

Many gender experts recommend the GCF to collect sex-disaggregated data to monitor gender impact. The quantitative approach may, however, fail to unpack the complex gender dynamics. IDS (2008) argues that a gender-sensitive approach requires more than a set of disaggregated data since it risks reinforcing fixed binary roles assigned to women and men. Instead, good quality data should reflect the 'contested, changed and reinforced' processes of gender and social inequalities (Resureccion, 2011: 7). Qualitative information, such as local power structures, control over key economic assets and social norms, is crucial to 'evaluate women's situation as compared to that of men in relation to specific environmental concerns' (Lambrou and Piana, 2006: 12).

6. CONCLUSION

The GCF has taken an unprecedented step in taking gender seriously by pursuing a 'gender-sensitive approach'. This has raised optimism about how it may enhance project efficiency by tapping into local knowledge in adopting adaptive farming. It may achieve gender effectiveness by promoting women entrepreneurship and access to loans and agricultural extension services. It may also achieve gender equity by challenging traditional practices in restricting women's land rights.

This paper has argued that whether or not climate finance has the power to transform gender inequalities depends on four aspects: (1) increasing women's decision-making power; (2) avoiding national and local elites capturing the benefits of increasing climate funds; (3) promoting adaptation policies that matter to gender equity and livelihood improvement; (4) understanding the needs of both vulnerable women and men. This paper has argued that the GCF is not effective in achieving these four elements. The low level of representation of women on the GCF's Board meetings is disappointing. Championing the principles of country ownership and fiscal decentralisation in distributing climate funds, without adequate governance measures to tackle elite capture and corruption, would undermine the impact of the GCF. How to make adaptation measures financially appealing to the private sector in order to adjust the current imbalance between mitigation and adaptation spending needs more strategic thoughts. Furthermore, having a deeper understanding of the impact of climate change on vulnerable men in developing countries would help shift back the attention from 'women-specificity' to 'gender-sensitivity'.

REFERENCES

Asia Pacific Human Development Network (2007). *Social Services: Water, Sanitation and Electricity.*

Arend, Elizabeth and Lowman, Sonia (2011). *Governing Climate Funds. What Will Work For Women?* Gender Action. Research report.

Bathge, Sandra (2010). *Climate Change and Gender: Economic Empowerment of Women Through Climate Mitigation and Adaptation.* Working Paper. Governance and Democracy Division, GTZ Governance Cluster.

Bhowmik, Debesh (2013). *'Key Features and Dimensions of Climate Finance'*, International Journal of Scientific and Research Publications, 3(4): 1-11.

Bird, Neil, Helen Tilley, Nella Trujillo, Godber Tumushabe, Bryn Welham and Pius Yanda (2013). *Measuring the Effectiveness of Public Climate Finance Delivery at the National Level.* Overseas Development Institute, UK.

Blomstrom, Eleanor, Cunningham, Sarah, Johnson and Owen, Cate (2009). *Climate Change Connections.* United Nations Population Fund and Women's Environment and Development Organization.

Buchner, Barbara, Falconer, Angela, Herve-Mignucci, Morgan and Trabacchi, Chiara (2012). *The Landscape of Climate Finance 2012.* Climate Policy Initiative.

Calland, Richard and Dubosse, Nancy (2011).*The Politics of Climate Finance*, in: *Perspectives.* Special issue: Mobilising climate change for Africa, pp 4-6.

Caruso, Randy and Ellis, Jane (2013). *Comparing Definitions and Methods to Estimate Mobilised Climate Finance.* OECD/IEA Climate Change Expert Group Papers.

Ciplet, David, Roberts, Timmons, Khan, Mizan, Fields, Spencer and Madden, Keith (2013). *Least Developed, Most Vulnerable: Have Climate Finance Promises Been Fulfilled for the LDCs?* European Capacity Building Initiative.

Cleaver, Frances (ed.) (2003). *Masculinities Matter! Men, Gender and Development.* London: Zeds Book.

Cleaver, Frances (2001). *Institutional Bricolage, Conflict and Cooperation in Usangu, Tanzania*, IDS Bulletin, 32(4): 26-36.

Cornwall, Andrea, Harrison, Elizabeth and Whitehead, Ann (eds.) (2007). *Feminisms in Development: Contradictions, Contestations and Challenges.* London: Zeds Book.

Craeynest, Lies (2010). *The Political Economy of Climate Finance.* Christian Aid, available at https://www.christianaid.org.uk/images/climate-finance-report.pdf.

Curtin, Joseph (2013). *Nine Steps to Unlock Climate Finance Flows.* Responding to Climate Change News, available at http://www.climatechangenews.com/2013/03/25/nine-steps-to-unlock-climate-finance-flows/.

Dasgupta, Dipak, Ghosh, Prodipto, Ray, Rajasree, Acharya, Abhishek, Mehta, Jyotsna and Grover, Kanika (2013). *Delhi Vision Statement: the Green Climate Fund.*

Fankhauser, Samuel (2013). *What Is Climate Finance and Where Will It Come From?*, The Guardian, available at https://www.theguardian.com/environment/2013/apr/04/climate-change-renewableenergy.

Forstater, Maya and Rank, Rachel (2012). *Towards Climate Finance Transparency.* AidInfo, available at http://www.publishwhatyoufund.org/files/Towards-Climate-Finance-Transparency_Final.pdf.

Friends of the Earth (2010). *International Climate Finance: An Overview.* Briefing, available at http://www.foe.org/projects/economics-for-the-earth/climate-finance.

Green Climate Fund (2011). *Governing Instrument of Green Climate Fund*, available at https://www.greenclimate.fund/documents/20182/574763/Governing_Instrument.pdf/caa6ce45-cd54-4ab0-9e37-fb637a9c6235.

Helgeson, Jennifer and Ellis, Jane (2015). *The Role of the 2015 Agreement in Enhancing Adaptation to Climate Change.* OECD.

Hoffmann, Anja (2013). *Decentralisation and Re-Centralisation in Morocco: A View from the Middle Atlas.* CERAM Working paper 2013/01.

Institute of Development Studies (IDS) (2008). *Gender and Climate Change: Mapping the Linkages – A Scoping Study on Knowledge and Gaps.* BRIDGE, Institute of Development Studies, Brighton.

IIED (International Institute for Environment and Development) (2013). *Climate Investment Funds: Understanding the PPCR in Bangladesh and Nepal, Briefing.* April.

Intergovernmental Panel of Climate Change (IPCC) (2001). *Climate Change 2001: Synthesis Report.*

Lambrou, Yianna and Piana, Grazia (2006). *Gender: The Missing Component of the Response to Climate Change.* Food and Agriculture Organisation of the United Nations.

Larson, Anne and Ribot, Jesse (2009). *Lessons From Forestry Decentralization. Enabling REDD+ Through Broad Policy Reform*, in: Angelsen, Arild (ed.) *Realising REDD+: National Strategy and Policy Options.* Centre for International Forestry Research, 175-190.

Letherby, Gayle (2003). *Feminist Research in Theory and Practice.* Backingham: Open University Press.

Lipset, David (2011). *The Tides: Masculinity and Climate Change in Coastal Papua New Guinea*, Journal of the Royal Anthropological Institute, 17: 20-43.

MacGregor, Sherilyn (2010). *Gender and Climate Change: From Impacts to Discourses.* School of Politics, International Relations and Philosophy, Research Centre for the Study of Politics, International Relations and Environment, Keele University.

Marston, Ama (2013). *Reaching Local Actors in Climate Finance. Lessons on Direct Access for the Green Climate Fund*, available at http://www.bothends.org/uploaded_files/document/Reaching_local_actors_in_climate_finance_Both_ENDS_.pdf.

Moser, Caroline (1993). *Gender Planning and Development: Theory, Practice and Training.* London: Routledge.

Overseas Development Institute (ODI) (2013). *Measuring the Effectiveness of Public Climate Finance Delivery at the National Level.*

Olson, Jennifer, Rubin, Deborah and Wangui, Edna (2010). *Gender, Agriculture and Climate Change. A Regional Analysis for USAID/East Africa.* United States Agency for International Development.

Otzelberger, Agnes (2011). *Gender-responsive Strategies on Climate Change: Recent Progress and Ways Forward for Donors.* IDS and Bridge.

Oxfam (2011). *Gender and the Green Climate Fund.* Oxfam Issue Briefing July 2011.

Peralta, Athena (2008). *Gender and Climate Change Finance. A Case Study from the Philippines.* Heinrich Boll Stiftung.

Petherick, Anna (2013). *Oblivious Money-Men*, Nature Climate Change, Vol.3, 96-7.

Platteau, Jean-Phillippe, Somville, Vincent and Wahhaj, Zaki (2012). *Elite Capture Through Information Distortion: A Theoretical Essay.* Centre of Research in the Economics of Development.

Resurreccion, Bernadette (2011). *The Gender and Climate Debate: More of the*

Same or New Pathways of Thinking and Doing? Asia Security Initiative Policy Series Working Paper no. 10.

Reyes, Oscar (2010). *The UN Boys Club Tasked with Redefining Climate Finance.* Carbon Trade Watch.

Ribot, Jesse (2003). *Democratic Decentralisation of Natural Resources: Institutional Choice and Discretionary Power Transfers in Sub-Saharan Africa*, Public Administration and Development, 23(1): 53-65.

Schalatek, Liane and Burns, Katya (2013). *Operationalising a Gender-Sensitive Approach in the Green Climate Fund*, available at https://unfccc.int/files/cooperation_and_support/financial_mechanism/standing_committee/application/pdf/final_schalatek_burns_gcf_gender-sensitive-approach.doc.pdf.

Schalatek, Liane (2011). *Engendering Climate Finance. An Opportunity for Africa*. Perspectives. Special issue: Mobilising Climate Change for Africa. 9-13.

Schalatek, Liane (2012a). *Taking Charge. At its First Meeting, the GCF Board Lays the Groundwork for the Functioning of the New Fund*. Heinrich Boll Stiftung. The Green Political Foundation.

Schalatek, Liane (2012b). *Inching Forward. The Second Meeting of the Green Climate Fund Board and the Nitty-Gritty of GCF Operationalisation*. Heinrich Boll Stiftung. The Green Political Foundation.

Schalatek, Liane (2013a). *Setting the Course. The Third Meeting of the Green Climate Fund Board*. Heinrich Boll Stiftung. The Green Political Foundation.

Schalatek, Liane (2013b). *Decision Time? The 4th Meeting of the Green Climate Fund Board Focuses on the Fund's Business Model and its New Executive Director*. Heinrich Boll Stiftung. The Green Political Foundation.

Schalatek, Liane and Nakhooda, Smita (2011). *Gender and Climate Finance Brief 10*. Heinrich Boll Stiftung and ODI.

Schroeder, Frank (2010). *A Shot in the Arm for Climate Finance? New Directions for Delivering on International Pledges and Development*. Friedrich-Ebert-Stiftung.

Stewart, Richard, Kingsbury, Benedict and Rudyk, Bryce (2009). *Climate Finance: Key Concepts and Ways Forward*. Working paper no. 09-69. Public Law and Legal Theory Research Paper Series. School of Law, New York University.

U4 Brief (2012). *Corruption and REDD+. Identifying Risks amid Complexity*. U4 Brief, No2, May. Anti-corruption resource centre. The U4 Anti-Corruption Resource Centre.

United Nations (2011). *Fact Sheet: Women, Gender Equality and Climate Change*. The UN Internal Gateway on Gender Equality and Empowerment of Women.

United Nations (2002). *Gender Issues in ICT Policy in Developing Countries: An Overview*. Division for the Advancement of Women. EGM/ICT/2002/EP.1.

United Nations Development Programs (UNDP) (2008). *Gender Responsive E-*

Governance: Exploring the Transformative Potential. United Nations Development Programme.

UNDP (2009). *Briefs on Gender and Climate Funds: Climate Investment Funds.* Working draft.

UNDP (2011). *Catalyzing Climate Finance. A Guidebook on Policy and Financing Options to Support Green,* Low-Emission and Climate-Resilient Development.

UNDP (2012). *Gender and Climate Finance.* Capacity Development Series Training Module 5.

UNDP (2013). *Consolidated Summary: E-discussion on Addressing REDD+ Corruption at the Local Level.*

Whande, Webster and Reddy, Trusha (2011). *The Governance of Climate Finance in Africa, Asia and Latin America: Some Critical Reflections.* Policy Brief No. 24, Hanns-Seidel-Stiftung.

Whitley, Shelagh (2013). *At Cross-Purposes: Subsidies and Climate Compatible Investment.* ODI: London.

Wilson, Melanie (2004). *A Conceptual Framework for Studying Gender in Information Systems Research,* Journal of Information Technology, 19, 81-92.

World Bank (2001). *Engendering Development. Through Gender Equality in Rights, Resources and Voice.* Washington D.C.: World Bank.

Promoting Gender Equality in Various Regions of the World

CHAPTER 7:

THE QUALITY OF GENDER POLICIES IN EU DEVELOPMENT CO-OPERATION WITH SOUTH AFRICA

Petra DEBUSSCHER

This chapter examines the quality of gender equality policies in EU development co-operation with South Africa to gain a deeper understanding of the EU as a global gender actor. In this chapter the perspectives of South African gender advocates are used as a touchstone for the evaluation of both process and content dimensions of quality. The research shows that EU-South African co-operation conforms with dominant development paradigms which seem to neglect the specific South African contextual legacy. If the EU wants to stay relevant as a global promotor of gender equality, it would do good to include national gender advocates' voices in external policy processes in a more meaningful and systematic way, as to avoid Eurocentric ideas on the meaning of "quality" in gender policy abroad.

1. INTRODUCTION

What can a systematic study of the EU's gender and development policies teach us about the EU's role as a global gender actor? Is the EU a transformative actor as regards the content of its external gender policy? Are its decision-making processes empowering to women in partner countries? Or are gender inequalities being reproduced in the content and processes of its co-operation policies? In this chapter I engage with these research questions by zooming in on the case of EU development co-operation with South Africa from 2007 to 2013. Specifically, I analyse the quality of the gender policies resulting from this co-operation based on policy document analysis and 15 in-depth semi-structured expert interviews[1] conducted in Pretoria

---

[1]   A list of the interviews cited in this article is provided in the Appendix.

and Johannesburg, South Africa. In the following section I will first discuss the methodological model I will use for the gender analysis of quality in EU external policy. Next I apply this specific operationalisation to the case of EU-South African development co-operation. Finally, in the conclusion I discuss the EU as a global gender actor based on the presented data.

2. ANALYSING THE QUALITY OF EU EXTERNAL GENDER POLICIES

Methodologically, this research builds on Krizsan and Lombardo's two-dimensional model for understanding gender policies' quality. The first dimension of this model looks at the substantive content of policies and includes criteria on genderdness, intersectionality and the transformative focus of policies (Verloo *et al.*, 2011). The second dimension of this model connects quality to procedural aspects and involves assessment criteria on the empowerment of women's rights advocates in the policy process and transformation in relation to the contextual legacies.

The first substantive content criterion analyses the genderdness of policies. This implies the extent to which gender is approached as an aim in itself, and not used instrumentally to achieve other policy goals. It also implies looking into the underlying equality perspectives that underpin policies: which norms and ideologies lie behind policies? what is the ultimate aim of policies? what kind of society do we ideally want to live in? In this respect feminist literature typically distinguishes perspectives of equal treatment, difference/specific actions and transformation (Verloo, 2005).

Second, feminist research has shown how gender policy that fails to incorporate an intersectional dimension excludes people at intersections of inequalities, such as race, age, class, sexuality, or disability. The extent to which policies pay attention to intersecting inequalities and are therefore inclusive is thus a second important criterion with regards the policy content (Krizsan & Lombardo. 2013).

Third, the structurally transformative focus of policies refers to the extent to which policies aim to dismantle deeply rooted hierarchies, societal norms and practices within which inequalities are embedded and which systematically discriminate women. According to Krizsan and Lombardo, such policies reveal quality in terms of their in-depth understanding of the problem of inequality being rooted in interconnected structures, such as the organisation of labour, intimacy and citizenship,[2] and the long-term transformative potential this understanding has for changing the social structures that maintain and reproduce gender inequality (2013).

The second dimension of the model connects quality to policy processes and involves two procedural criteria. As regards the first criterion, empowerment of women's rights advocates, empirical research has indeed shown that policies developed with the participation of women's organisations or in accordance with their agenda's produce better quality, insofar they help frame policy in more transformative ways. This is because the participation of external gender advocates increases the possibility that policy-makers become aware of their preconceptions induced by their institutional culture and its predetermined logics and norms.

The second procedural criterion, transformation with reference to the prevailing contextual legacies, is a clear attempt to contextualise quality criteria, as quality does not exist in a vacuum. Indeed, rather than attempting to pin quality down as a one-size-fits-all, quality needs to be understood in relation to the specific context, as what constitutes as "transformation of gender relations" often varies across countries, depending on the state of equality politics, the institutional setting, and the specific process of gender policy development (Krizsan and Lombardo, 2013).

Indeed, while transformative policies can be distinguished by their specific intention of empowering or improving the status of groups that have been historically excluded, marginalised or stigmatised, they are only ever progressive in relation to their context (Htun and Weldon, 2012). As not all policies will be transformative in every context, we need in-depth knowledge of the social, political, and economic contexts in which policies are executed. Analysing policy intervention's impact on women's lives, from the outset – that is without in-depth contextual knowledge – means running into

---

[2] In the organisation of labour, the division between work and care as well as between paid and unpaid labour are built on a gender hierarchy that places women in a secondary position. In the organisation of intimacy, the norms, values and institutions regulating sexuality, human reproduction and family life are based upon traditional concepts of masculinity and femininity resulting in unequal positions for men and women in private life. In the organisation of citizenship a persisting hierarchy exists between women and men as to the extent to which they can fully enjoy their main civil, political and social rights (See Verloo, 2005).

the risk of 'prescribing the process of empowerment and thereby violating its essence, which is to enhance women's capacity for self-determination' (Kabeer, 1999: 462). As a consequence, I propose to bring the model's two procedural criteria, empowerment of women's rights advocates and transformation with reference to the context, centre stage when analysing EU external policies. This implies mainstreaming these two process criteria throughout the model. I argue that, to allow for an in-depth analysis of EU external policy, these criteria need to be involved in the methodology itself and explicitly connected to all other quality criteria. I suggest to do this by involving the views of gender activists from the national context in the analysis and use their perspectives to assess the meaning of "quality".

This methodological approach thus follows Krizan and Lombardo's call for contextualisation and goes a step further as it aims to bridge the content and process dimensions of quality in its operationalisation by taking into account not only the perspectives of the EU programming officers in the EU delegation in Pretoria, but also the perspectives of major South African gender advocates to analyse EU development policy in South Africa. In other words, using this re-oriented methodological model I contrast the frames of South African gender advocates from autonomous feminist organisations with those of EU policy makers with regards the content and process criteria to analyse the quality of gender mainstreaming in EU external policy. I analyse the extent to which their frames relate to each other, as well as how both actors perceive and evaluate each other's role. Taking into account the perspectives of gender advocates allows for a contextual reflexivity which has the ability to unveil Eurocentric paternalist assumptions of policy-makers who claim that progressive "universalist" entitlements of human and women's rights are "Western" values inapplicable to "traditional" settings. Furthermore it allows to detect 'silences' (what is not said) in EU development discourse (Debusscher, 2011) which are helpful to gain a deeper understanding of the EU as a global gender actor.

In what follows I will turn to the case of EU development co-operation with South Africa from 2007 to 2013. First I give an overview of the integration of gender in EU-South African development co-operation based on policy document analysis and interviews at the EU delegation in Pretoria. Next I apply the proposed model to the case and use the perspectives of major South African gender advocates to analyse the quality of EU development policy in South Africa with regards its content and policy processes: genderdness, intersectionality, the structurally transformative focus of policies, the empowerment of women's rights advocates and the transformative potential with reference to the prevailing context.

3. THE CASE: EU-SOUTH AFRICAN DEVELOPMENT CO-OPERATION

EU development assistance with South Africa totalled 980 million Euro for the period 2007-2013 and was defined in a Joint Country Strategy Paper and a Multi-annual Indicative Programme. The Joint Country Strategy Paper defined the goal of development co-operation to be the reduction of poverty and inequality, in line with the South African government's policies and targets. It focused on three main areas: the promotion of pro-poor, sustainable economic growth; the improvement of the provision and quality of basic services to the poor; and the promotion of good governance.

The Multi-annual Indicative Programme outlined the budget and timing and had two main focus sectors: employment creation on the one hand and capacity development for service delivery and social cohesion on the other. In addition, there were three smaller "non-focal areas" including governance, regional and pan-African support, and the facilitation of the trade, development and co-operation agreement of 1999. Notably, the EU's development aid to South Africa was distributed through sectoral budget support programmes which encompass the transfer of financial resources from the EU directly to the South African government's National Treasury in support of a sector programme following the fulfilment of agreed conditions for payment. Next to the main sector budget support programmes, the EU Delegation in South Africa provided support to civil society organisations in the justice, health, youth, education, employment, research and human rights sectors. In what follows I give a brief overview of the practice of gender mainstreaming in the different areas of EU-South African co-operation.

3.1. EMPLOYMENT

The employment sector aimed to reduce unemployment and poverty levels and consisted of three parts. The first part, the "Employment Creation Support Programme", was a 100 million euro sector budget support programme which assisted South Africa's economic government departments to increase the number of quality jobs and create 'a better enabling environment for business and skills development and increased capacity in the productive sectors of the economy' (Delegation of the EU to the Republic of South Africa, 2014) One gender indicator on the employment of women in short-term community jobs was outlined (e.g. the 2013 target aimed at 27,648 women employed).

The second part consisted of a 'Local Economic Development Programme' and a 'Sustainable Rural Development Programme' in the Eastern Cape and aimed to significantly reduce the number of households living below the poverty line by setting up factories and creating employment in poor areas with a high unemployment level and a low level of service delivery. The programmes did not include gender equality indicators or objectives.

The third part, the 'Risk Capital Facility' (RCF), was a 50 million Euro programme aimed at providing job opportunities to 'historically disadvantaged persons' active within the small and medium enterprise sector. The programme invested in small and medium enterprises through a Development Co-operation Bank with the aim of facilitating employment creation. It provided finance to enterprises owned by historically disadvantaged persons, such as black businesses for whom it is often difficult to get a loan as they might lack the experience, the collateral, etc.

The RCF programme focused on seven result areas including improved access to development funding and increased empowerment of historically disadvantaged people through shareholding and (training) opportunities to hold managerial positions. One of the seven performance indicators was to generate 60,000 jobs of which a minimum of 30 per cent were reserved for women. Additionally, there were targets for the ownership and management of the companies, such as a minimum of 25 per cent black shareholders and a minimum of 30 per cent female managers and shareholders. Although these targets were strictly spoken not mandatory, companies were strongly encouraged to embark on changes as it greatly enhanced the chances of receiving the loan. The EU had a project steering meeting every quarter to monitor and discuss the results with the South African government, the European Investment Bank, the private sector partners of small and medium enterprises. Notably, the Women Development Bank, which aims to promote economic empowerment and social uplift of women in South Africa, was participating in the monthly steering meetings.[3]

3.2.CAPACITY DEVELOPMENT FOR SERVICE DELIVERY AND SOCIAL COHESION

The aim of the second sector 'Capacity Development for Service Delivery and Social Cohesion' was to deliver "better services to all South Africans", as this would 'unlock the scarce and necessary skills crucial for both economic growth and sustainable development' (European Commission, 2007a: 11). Again an economic framing of service delivery seems present. The two main programmes provided support for primary education (122 million Euro) and primary health care (126 million Euro).

The overall objective of the 'Primary Education Sector Policy Support Programme' was to improve learner performance in literacy and numeracy at primary school level. This was expected to lay the foundations for improved throughput to secondary and higher education, as well as to vocational training. Financial support was provided directly to the Government to expand the provision of quality early childhood development opportunities, effective curriculum implementation, and strengthen initial teacher education for the early grades. No gender indicators or objectives were outlined.

The health programme was better in this respect. The EU and the South African Department of Health jointly developed a 'Primary Health Care Sector Policy Support Programme', which aimed to improve the access to and quality of public health services. The programme provided financial and technical support to the Government in the form of sector budget support, and also provided funding to civil society organisations. Five result areas had been outlined, including improved maternal and child health, increased access to primary health care services, increased quality of primary health care services, improved capacity for the management of primary health care facilities and accelerated implementation of the national plans for HIV/AIDS and tuberculosis. The health sector also contained an 'Outreach Programme' encompassing mobile clinics – including midwives – travelling to areas that are difficult to reach. Lastly, the health sector included a 'School Health Programme' involving awareness raising in schools on topics such as sexual and reproductive health, protection against STDs, pre-

---

[3]   See http://wdbinvestments.co.za/.

gnancy, HIV/AIDS and gender power relations (e.g. on consensual sex or gender-based violence).

3.3. NON-FOCAL SECTORS

The areas 'Governance, Regional and Pan-African Support' and 'Support to the Trade, Development and Co-operation Agreement' were largely gender-blind. Although the EU-South African Multi-annual Indicative Programme had mentioned that gender would be mainstreamed in these sectors, in practice nothing happened. Only the governance sector contained one performance indicator measuring 'access to justice for vulnerable groups', which included women and children, among several other groups.

3.4. SUPPORT TO CIVIL SOCIETY

Under the EU-South Africa co-operation programme a significant amount was set aside for supporting civil society in the sectors of justice, health, youth, higher education, science and technology, employment, environmental actions and democracy and human rights. The most feasible areas for civil society organisations working on gender equality were access to justice and democracy and human rights, accounting for 5 million Euro and 2.4 million Euro respectively.

4. ANALYSING THE QUALITY OF GENDER POLICY IN EU-SOUTH AFRICAN DEVELOPMENT CO-OPERATION

In the next sections I will apply the quality model to the case and contrast the EU-South African development programmes with the views of South African gender advocates.

4.1. GENDEREDNESS

The main solutions to gender inequality – job creation for women and sexual and reproductive health – were predominantly framed within a Millennium Development Goals (MDGs) framework and focussed on achieving poverty reduction and full employment (see also Debusscher and van der Vleuten, 2012). Indeed, 'promoting the achievements of the MDGs in Africa' has been an important EU objective and supporting gender equality has been 'considered as [a] prerequisite ... for attaining these goals' (European Commission, 2007a: 18). Furthermore, EU aid to South Africa had a strong focus on "reduced poverty and inequality, mainly through economic growth" (European Commission 2007a: 21) and aimed to "create the right economic environment for achieving the MDGs" (European Commission, 2007b: 5). Solutions for gender inequality were thus frequently formulated in line with dominant (economic) development frameworks. Within these frameworks gender equality is interpreted in a limited way and often not seen as an aim in its own right. Although the more optimistic evaluations of the MGDs have stressed their contribution to 'en-gendering' the global development agenda', critics have commented on the MDG's limited agenda (Chant, 2007: 10, Subrahmanian, 2007; Mukhopadhyay, 2007). This agenda was too much focussed on what women can contribute to development, e.g. women's potential as human resources, while systemic political and gender power issues were being neglected. This criticism was shared by some key South African gender advocates. For instance, some advocates mentioned the often instrumental and limited framing of women's reproductive health, in isolation from gender power relations. As put by one advocate:

Maternal mortality has many causes, but women become reduced to women's bodies! To vessels! 'Infant mortality' they say is 'gender', but that doesn't get addressed! ... Also [concerning]' violence', what do you mean with violence? It is dangerous and scary how it gets depoliticized. It still is about power differences (Interview 2013a).

As regards the underlying vision of gender equality, a mixed picture came to the fore. In a number of programmes, a limited equal treatment approach seemed to underlie EU policy: men and women were considered to be *de facto* equal as they had equal rights to access health care. The EU Delegation thus seemed to conceptualise health – with the exception of school health and maternal health – as a gender-neutral area which they were 'not super-conscious about' as 'health automatically is about men and women' (Interview 2013b). Indeed, the EU's performance indicators on general access to health were not gender-disaggregated as equal access for men and women was already assumed by the EU Delegation.

    In contrast, a 'difference approach' could be found in some programmes, such as the programme on maternal and children's health which accommodated for women specifically, with respect to their role as mothers.

Arguably, the Risk Capital Facility Programme which had a 30 per cent quota for female employment, management and ownership could also be considered 'a difference approach' as it was argued that women have a specific situation and are 'historically disadvantaged' from men and need specific actions to tackle this disadvantage. In general however, gender advocates viewed this the programme positively, as being focussed on long-term changes and having the potential to structurally transform society. In this respect the underlying vision could be defined as 'transformation'.[4] Nevertheless, one advocate was still sceptical towards the transformative potential and pointed out that 'quotas can't work by themselves' (Interview 2013a) as a place on the table does not guarantee a voice due to a continuation of sexism at the workplace.

4.2. INTERSECTIONALITY

EU-South African co-operation included some indicators measuring different grounds of discrimination and exclusion, such as race or disability. However, as these indicators were not connected in a meaningful way, an intersectional approach seemed to be absent. For instance, the EU's Erasmus Mundus Programme for the mobility of students and higher education staff to EU countries, contained indicators on the recipient's gender, disability and race, however as these indicators were not coupled, some gender activists felt that the programme was just to push numbers and could not bring substantial change. The interviewed advocates felt that linking these indicators, would probably reveal significant distortions. In addition, some were concerned about the degree of intersectionality in the Risk Capital Facility Programme (reserving a 25 per cent quota for black people and 30 per cent quota for female employment, management and ownership) and questioned the extent to which black women were represented in the figures.

Also interesting in this respect was that some gender advocates mentioned an implicit racial discrimination in the way in which civil society funding was being distributed, as they felt it has been easier for organisations headed by white women to receive funding as they spoke 'the right

---

[4] Indeed, since its launch, the programme has achieved significant success. Historically disadvantaged female participation has exceeded the 30 per cent target at all levels – jobs created, management and shareholding. The results for 2012 were overwhelming with 35 per cent female employment, 49 per cent female ownership and 34 per cent female management.

language' – a language the predominantly white and/or European EU Delegation staff could relate with. As was put by a black gender advocate:

"It is largely influenced by the historical reality of the country. For example, the GBV field was mainly dominated by white women and this has continued. It is problematic in the way you would understand issues, life experiences... It's not difficult to write a proposal, but certain language is easier to use if you don't live in that reality. For example [major donor in South Africa] is very fond of a discourse of "poor women", "poverty"... But who is she? It's easy to picture a poor women or what a poor women looks like. For me it is hard to define and ... it speaks back to me. In certain ways ... I am poor myself. ... The donor community seems to understand that terminology." (Interview 2013c).

4.3. STRUCTURALLY TRANSFORMATIVE FOCUS OF POLICIES

Most gender advocates warmly welcomed the gender dimension in the Risk Capital Facility Programme as a structurally transformative approach and applauded the gender indicators for representation in management and ownership as it gave women 'a far greater choice' (Interview 2013d).

Likewise, gender advocates were positive about the 'School Health Programme' and generally encouraged programmes that included the education of children and young adults on gender power relations, sexual harassment, STDs and (unwanted) pregnancy. They felt that raising awareness on gender issues in schools early on can have a potentially transformative effect on society.

In contrast, gender advocates were very critical on certain employment programmes and claimed that they focussed mostly on practical 'instrumental' needs (such as short-term low-skilled employment). One programme connected to the South African Government's 'Community Works Programme' offered short time community jobs (such as cleaning gardens or making dolls or brooches) for maximum two days a week to provide poor people with an income (of maximum 800 rand which is approximately 60-70 Euro) and contained targets for the employment of youth and women. Another employment programme did not contain specific gender indicators although the export factories for garments and beadwork that have been set up have employed almost exclusively women and youth. Gender advocates were sceptical towards both programmes and stressed 'the importance of the quality of work' (Interview 2013e). They considered the employment programmes as typical conservative approaches that built on stereotypical assumptions about women and entrenched negative stereotypes in society. Advocates felt that such programmes could only serve as 'plasters' (Interview 2013f) that could not bring real change. Or, as was put by one advocate:

"It's good that people can get some money, but they don't need dolls. Also... what is the education? ... What does the community need? Maybe it is not making dolls. It is very stereotypical, it stereotypes women as cleaners, doll makers... It is ... more charity based. It's like giving the fish and not the rod." (Interview 2013f).

Some advocates where even more sceptical stating that such low income programmes created a backwards move as they were undermining 'women's self-worth' (Interview 2013c) and further entrenched stereotypes about the value of women's work in the economy. In general, advocates strongly felt that EU-South African development co-operation should be geared towards more long-term, strategic 'Gender and Development' goals instead of the more practical, short-term 'Women in Development' measures.

4.4. EMPOWERMENT OF WOMEN'S RIGHTS ADVOCATES

As regards EU support to civil society, all interviewed gender advocates were familiar with the EU funding programmes as their organisations had already participated in EU bids, some of them successfully. All advocates felt that such funding opportunities for civil society were absolutely necessary and felt grateful for its existence. However, several advocates also mentioned problematic issues regarding the specific funding modalities. Most local EU calls for projects had a short time frame, lasting two to three years and thus did not allow organisations to engage in longer-term planning or conduct more time-intensive projects as they seldom offer instantly measurable results. Also some felt that the EU is a quite technical donor geared towards 'ticking boxes' rather than bringing real change on the ground. Or, as was put by one respondent:

"Funding is a constant battle. We try to translate our work [to EU frames] and encourage them to think outside their box. Nevertheless proposals come with boxes that you have to fill, but sometimes it is just not possible to get our language into them. The EU has a top down approach to things, the expectations are quite clear. You have to fit into them." (Interview 2013a)

The EU's eligibility criteria were based on an organisation's legal status, work plan, budget formulation, short term deliverables, pre-acquired financial capacities and previous experience in international projects. The strict bureaucratic set-up has made it difficult for some non-state actors to fit their initiatives into a successful format and renders projects into aid industry products (Minoia, 2012). Also some advocates felt that the projects which were granted funding were too focused on "reactive measures as supposed to being preventive" (Interview 2013f) and that there were too little calls for proposals allowing civil society organisations to do their own research.

"[Research] is very important for our advocacy work. It has to be evidence based. It is so hard to get funding for research. It is geared to academic research. ... But the way academic research is framed, it does not always work so well. NGO type of research is different. You need to understand the state and governance well, how to engage,... It influences government and policies and it gives direction to our organization. We are able to pick up what are the gaps, but we need research to do this." (Interview 2013c).

Indeed, although the EU distributed 26.4 million Euro in funding for various research projects under the 'Science and Technology' sector, funding for research seemed to be geared towards South African higher education institutions and companies, mainly on the topics of health, environment, bio-economy and ICT. The support the EU was providing to South African women's rights advocates in civil society could thus be evaluated as mixed: while it enabled them to empower themselves and sustain their organisations, it also geared them towards certain agenda's and work methods, focusing on short-term deliverables and easily measurable results.

The empowerment of women's rights advocates in the policy process was further complicated by the use of sector budget support, which involves a transfer of funds directly to the government's national treasury to be used in pursuit of an agreed set of sector outputs and outcomes. Although there had been contact with gender advocates in the framework of the EU's support to civil society, there seemed to be a lack of civil society involvement with regards the main chunk of development aid which was distributed directly through budget support. From a gender perspective, general and sector-wide budget support are controversial as gender advocates worldwide fear it equals a de-prioritisation of gender equality 'given the lack of public accountability systems' and 'mechanisms for the implementation of national obligations to gender equality' (Karadenizli, 2007). In line with this reasoning, several of the interviewed gender advocates were critical of the EU's preference for budget support in South Africa as they pointed out it only trickled down to some extent and seldom got 'down to the grassroots' (Interview 2013f). Others stressed that policies should start from what is necessary at the local level and that – in the context of a gender-neutral EU sector budget support – strengthening civil society it became even more important to hold governments accountable for their commitments on gender equality. In addition, gender advocates pointed out that gender had been largely forgotten in the EU's dialogue with the Ministries of Health and Education and stressed the importance of strong women's movements to engage at the government level. Some advocates also questioned the accuracy of the government's gender data provided to the EU. They claimed for instance that the government's indicators on maternal mortality were biased as there was no correct data collection taking place at the local level.

4.5. TRANSFORMATION WITH REFERENCE TO THE PREVAILING CONTEXTUAL LEGACIES

Gender advocates mentioned several silences in EU-South African cooperation with regard to the country's specific contextual legacy. For one, South Africa is a relatively young democracy, challenged with transforming the legacy of its devastating apartheid ideology. One problematic inheritance in this respect constitutes the former 'homelands' where black South Africans were confined during apartheid. The former homelands' lack of economic opportunities have forced many to work as migrant labourers and the areas have been typically inhabited with women, children and older people (Outwater *et al.*, 2005). As the apartheid system, which institutionalised racial separation, was "founded upon and extended existing racial and gender hierarchies" (Britton, 2006a: 60), the demise of apartheid resulted in an explicit transformation of the South African socio-political environment in which racial and gender equality became pivotal factors in the building of the new democracy (Outwater *et al.*, 2005). Women of all walks of life have been actively involved in the process towards democracy and have made significant gains in the political arena (Britton, 2006b). Today, the South African Constitution is one of the most progressive in seeking to promote equality and redress past discrimination (Scribner and Lambert, 2010). Nevertheless, while the struggle for gender-equal democracy has a long history in South Africa, the progress made during the transition period has not automatically translated into gains for all women in all policy areas (Groenmeier, 2011). For instance, the country notoriously tops international rankings of occurrences of inter-personal violence and crime, including rape and sexual violence, exacerbated by the legacy of apartheid violence, patriarchal authority and the social consequences of migrant labour force (Britton, 2006b; Outwater *et al.*, 2005). The EU-South African co-operation in the Eastern Cape which has set up factories to create employment in poor areas with a high unemployment level, implicitly addressed one of these problematic legacies, as it typically involved the former 'homelands'. In practice however these policy interventions appeared to perpetuate the employment of black female labour in lowly-paid and labour-intensive industries. While well intended, the programmes in the new economic zones located in the former homelands did not significantly challenge existing racial and gender hierarchies resulting from previous ideological systems as there was little upwards mobility and training provided. The extent to which inequalities of class, gender and race have been lessened as a consequence of these interventions thus remain highly questionable.

Furthermore, several advocates mentioned the EU's seeming unawareness with regards to the recently enacted Women Empowerment and Gender Equality Bill ensuring the 50/50 participation of women in both public and private bodies. With respect to the 30 per cent female employees, managers and shareholders in the RCF, certain gender advocates were therefore critical. They viewed the indicators as "good minimum conditions" (Interview 2013d), but indicated that in the light of South Africa's contextual legacy as well as the upcoming bill stipulating "that gender equality should be everywhere", the targets should have been set at 50 per cent (Interview 2013g). South Africa's specific socio-political environment in which gender and racial equality have become fundamental principles of democracy seems to be neglected.

Another issue that was brought forward by gender activists was South Africa's specific historical context with regards to education. In the past, education used to reflect the fragmented society, it was based in and 'hardly created conscientious, critical citizens' (Msila, 2007: 1). In this respect gender advocates found it worrisome that a female empowerment dimension was not included in the EU's co-operation programme. It was however argued by the EU Delegation that there was no gender aspect in education, as the enrolment of girls was higher compared to boys in primary, secondary and tertiary education and that boys were even dropping out of school more often. The EU Delegation thus reasoned that 'gender should not be a priority' and so decided to focus on improving the quality of education as this was the most urgent problem in their view (Interview 2013h).

Gender activists warned, however, that gender equality in schools should not "be just about bums on seats" (Interview 2013f) and goes way beyond the numerical data. Activists pointed out the issue of gender-based violence in or on the way to school, differences in performance due to girls' care responsibilities and the lack of intersectional data which connects gender to race, class and/or disability. Also the concept of 'quality' was defined much broader. Gender activists stressed that, in the South African context, education should be used as a transformational tool to empower learners for effective citizenship rooted in the constitutional values of democracy, social justice, non-racism, equality and reconciliation. Quality education would thus enable students to question stereotypical gender norms and encourage male and female students to take up non-traditional study choices.

5. DISCUSSION AND CONCLUSION

This chapter has analysed the quality of EU development co-operation with South Africa, with the aim of gaining a deeper understanding of the EU as a global gender actor. The research has shown that the EU is framing its policies to promote gender equality in line with dominant (economic) development paradigms, such as the focus on women's inclusion in the labour market to reduce poverty. As regards the underlying perspective on gender equality, a mixed picture emerges. While I encountered a number of presumably gender neutral programmes in which women and men are considered to be *de facto* equal (equal treatment perspective), some programmes included a perspective of 'difference' and were geared towards women's role as mothers or took into account women's historically disadvantaged position compared to men. Notably, one programme, the RCF, encompassed an underlying vision of 'transformation'. It is likely that the more transformative perspective underlying this programme can be be attributed to the participation of external gender advocates in the policy process (Interview 2011i). This finding is in line with literature claiming a correlation between the inclusion of gender advocates in decision-making processes and high-quality gender policy (among others Htun and Weldon, 2012).

However, due to the particular set-up of EU decision-making processes and the specific modalities of its aid policies, the EU as a global actor is only sporadically including the voices of national gender actors in its external policy. For instance, the increased use of general and sector budget support as aid modalities in EU external policy seem to go hand in hand with the side-lining of gender advocates from public institutions and civil society in decision-making processes. From a feminist perspective, budget support is therefore controversial as it lacks mechanisms for the implementation of (inter)national gender equality obligations and raises questions about 'who owns?', 'who is accountable to whom?' and 'how gender power relations are at play in these process?'. The case has indeed shown that EU policy dialogues with the South African Ministries have not been directly conducive to high quality gender equality policies and are sometimes even reproducing inequalities. Furthermore, intersections of race, gender and disability, have been largely neglected in EU-South African programmes, while some of its employment interventions seem to perpetuate the employment of black women in low-paid labour-intensive industries and confine "poor women" in gender stereotypical roles with no upward mobility. An approach grounded in the lived realities of women and their organisations seems more appropriate and allows policy-makers to question their predetermined labels and solutions, as well as the implications they have. If the EU wants to stay relevant as an innovative and qualitative promotor of gender equality globally, it should find a way to meaningfully include the voices of national gender advocates from civil society and public bodies in its external policy processes. Lastly, as the EU is an international frontrunner on the use of budget support, the European Commission and its Delegations should make sure this aid modality explicitly includes a gender dimension and guarantees a female ownership. Such female ownership not only requires the condition that women are substantially represented in all stages of decision-making, but also calls for an increase in resources for local, national, regional and international women's organisations who, as evidence shows, have proven to be key actors in advancing women's rights by acting as policy watchdogs and norm catalysts in society.

APPENDIX

List of interviews referred to:
Interview 2013a: civil society representative, 17 January 2013, Pretoria.
Interview 2013b: EU Delegation, 17 January 2013, Pretoria.
Interview 2013c: civil society representative, 21 January 2013, Johannesburg.
Interview 2013d: civil society representative, 18 January 2013, Johannesburg.
Interview 2013e: civil society representative, 14 January 2013, Pretoria.
Interview 2013f: civil society representative, 21 January 2013, Johannesburg.
Interview 2013g: South African Government official, 21 January 2013, Pretoria.
Interview 2013h: EU Delegation, 15 January 2013, Pretoria.
Interview 2013i: EU Delegation, 15 January 2013, Pretoria.

REFERENCES

Britton, Hannah (2006a). *South Africa: Mainstreaming Gender in a New Democracy,* in: Bauer, Gretchen and Britton, Hannah (eds.) *Women in African Parliaments*, Lynne Rienner, 2006, 59–84.

Britton, Hannah (2006b). *Organising against Gender Violence in South Africa.* Journal of Southern African Studies, 32(1):145-163.

Chant, Sylvia (2007). *Gender, Cities, and the Millennium Development Goals in the Global South* (New Series Working Paper, Issue 21), London: LSE Gender Institute.

Debusscher, Petra (2011). *Mainstreaming Gender in European Commission Development Policy: Conservative Europeanness?* Women's Studies International Forum, 34(1): 39–49.

Debusscher, Petra and van der Vleuten, Anna (2012). *Mainstreaming Gender in EU Development Co-operation with Sub-Saharan Africa: Promising Numbers, Narrow Contents, Telling Silences*, International Development Planning Review, 34(3): 319-338.

Delegation of the EU to the Republic of South Africa (2014). *Employment Creation.* Available at http://eeas.europa.eu/delegations/south_africa/eu_south_africa/dev_coop/employment_creation/index_en.htm.

European Commission (2007a). Multiannual Indicative Programme 2007-2013 for South Africa.

European Commission (2007b). Joint Country Strategy Paper 2007-2013.

Groenmeyer, Sharon (2011). *Intersectionality in Apartheid and Post-apartheid South Africa: Unpacking the Narratives of Two Working Women.* Gender, Technology and Development, 15(2): 249-274.

Htun, Mala and Weldon, Laurel (2012). *The Civic Origins of Progressive Policy Change: Combating Violence against Women in Global Perspective, 1975–2005*. American Political Science Review, 106: 548-569.

Karadenizli, Maria (2007). *Who Decides? Gender Mapping the EU's Policy and Decision-making in the Areas of Development, External Relations and Trade*. Brussels: WIDE Network.

Krizsan, Andrea and Lombardo, Emanuela (2013). *The Quality of Gender Equality Policies: A Discursive Approach*. European Journal of Womens Studies 20(1): 77-92.

Minoia, Paola (2012) *Included or Excluded? Civil Society, Local Agency and the Support Given by the European Aid Programmes*. Fennia, 190 (2): 77-89.

Msila, Vuyisile (2007). *From Apartheid Education to the Revised National Curriculum Statement: Pedagogy for Identity Formation and Nation Building in South Africa*. Nordic Journal of African Studies, 16(2): 146–160.

Mukhopadhyay, Maitrayee (2007). *Mainstreaming Gender or "Streaming" Gender Away: Feminists Marooned in the Development Business*, in: Cornwall, Andrea, Harrison, Elizabeth and Whitehead, Ann (eds.), *Feminisms in Development: Contradictions, Contestations and Challenges* 112–21. London: ZED Books.

Outwater, Anne, Abrahams, Naeema and Campbell, Jacquelyn (2005). *Women in South Africa: Intentional Violence and HIV/AIDS: Intersections and Prevention*. Journal of Black Studies 35(4): 135-154.

Scribner, Druscilla and Lambert, Priscilla (2010). *Constitutionalizing Difference: A Case Study Analysis of Gender Provisions in Botswana and South Africa*. Politics & Gender, 6(1): 37-61.

Subrahmanian, Ramya (2007). *Making Sense of Gender in Shifting Institutional Contexts: Some Reflections on Gender Mainstreaming*, in: Cornwall, Andrea, Harrison, Elizabeth and Whitehead, Ann (eds.), *Feminisms in Development: Contradictions, Contestations and Challenges* 112–21. London: ZED Books.

Verloo, Mieke (2005). *Mainstreaming Gender Equality in Europe: A Critical Frame Analysis Approach*. The Greek Review of Social Research 117 (B): 11–34.

Verloo, Mieke *et al.* (2011). *Final QUING Report*. Vienna: Institute for Human Sciences.

CHAPTER 8:

GENDERING EU-LATIN AMERICA INTER-REGIONAL RELATIONS

Conny ROGGEBAND and Andrea RIBEIRO HOFFMANN

This chapter analyses to what extent and how gender has been addressed in EU-Latin America and Caribbean inter-regional relations in order to contribute to the discussion on the relevance of the (inter-)regional level in the dynamics of norm diffusion and norm travelling in a multi-level process of governance. More specifically, it tries to understand the processes that led to gender becoming a priority in the Declaration and Action Plan for the EU-CELAC Summit in 2013. It argues that, contrary to the expectation that the EU would be the main driver behind the inclusion of gender in the inter-regional agenda with CELAC in 2013, transnational advocacy networks and EUROLAT have been key actors channelling these processes. The fact that EU-CELAC relations do not include trade might have facilitated the prioritisation of gender to the extent that traditional opposition from business lobbies to gender mainstreaming in bi-regional agreements was not present.

1. INTRODUCTION

The Summit between the European Union (EU) and the Community of Latin American and Caribbean States (CELAC) in 2013 in Santiago de Chile had a remarkable outcome. The final Declaration and Action Plan (2013-2015) list gender as a priority in the bi-regional relations. The Santiago 2013 Declaration stated that the inclusion of a gender perspective within the EU-CELAC association "will strengthen gender equality, democracy and will foster fair and egalitarian societies" (Santiago Declaration, point 38). While gender concerns have been on the agenda in the bi-regional relationship between the EU and the Latin American (LA) region, it so far occupied a rather marginal space and lacked precise instruments of implementation. The 2013 Santiago Declaration refers to gender in three paragraphs. While paragraph 17 calls for a commitment towards gender equality in order to ensure peoples' quality of life, in a similar (broad) framing as previous declarations, paragraph 19 recognises for the first time a relation between gender and investment, and paragraph 38 creates a bi-regional dialogue on gender issues. The Santiago Action Plan for 2013-2015 includes gender as one of its eight priorities and establishes a number of precise objectives and a joint work programme which lists dialogue, co-operation activities, and expected results. The three focal points are: i) Political participation of women; ii) Elimination of all forms of violence against women and girls, including sexual violence; and iii) Economic empowerment of women and their participation in the world of work and in all decision-making processes.[1] This level of prioritisation and specification is exceptional in comparison with the previous commitments in EU-LAC bi-regional co-operation. The new prioritisation of gender is puzzling and calls for further scrutiny: How did this come about? What is the role of the different actors involved in the agenda-setting?

So far, remarkably little research has been done on gender in interregional relations in general, and the EU-Latin American relations in particular (but see Angulo and Freres, 2006; Debusscher, 2012; Ribeiro Hoffmann, 2014, van der Vleuten, van Eerdewijk and Roggeband, 2014). Gender and feminist theories point to a number of factors that influence the incorporation of gender in bi-regional co-operation, such as interests of regional organisations to show the commitment to comply to international norms, pressure from regional or trans-regional feminist groups, and the presence of women in top political positions, such as during the 1st EU-CELAC Summit. Some authors express their optimism about the role of regional organisations in promoting gender norms, since they create an extra layer of opportunity that may be more accessible for advocacy organisations. Also, regional organisations may provide more tailored monetary and informational resources to advocacy networks helping to mobilise effectively (Montoya, 2009). Yet, recent research indicates that the primary role of economic actors in regional economic integration constitutes a serious obstacle to gender equality norm diffusion (van der Vleuten, van Eerdewijk and Roggeband, 2014). Since the bi-regional relationship between EU and

---

[1]   Available   at   http://www.eeas.europa.eu/la/summits/docs/2013_santiago_summit_ eu-celac_action_plan_en.pdf.

CELAC does not include trade commitments this might make a (positive) difference in the gender commitments.

In this chapter we analyse to what extent and how gender has been addressed in EU-Latin America and Caribbean inter-regional relations in order to contribute to the discussion on the relevance of the (inter)regional level in the dynamics of norm diffusion and norm travelling in a multi-level process of governance. Given the EU's commitment to gender and its self-promotion as a normative power (van der Vleuten *et al.*, 2014), one would expect that the EU exports gender norms to Latin America in their bi-regional relations. Yet, in this chapter we argue that it is not necessarily the EU that actively promotes gender issues in its relations with Latin America. Gender is not a prominent issue in EU foreign policy and development policy towards Latin America. During the 2013 bi-regional summit where gender appeared as a prominent issue, it rather seemed to be Latin America that acted as norm promoter. Other factors such as the 'left' turn of governments in Latin America, and their prioritisation of gender issues are particularly relevant. Yet, more importantly we want to point to the mobilisation and lobbying of trans-regional advocacy networks (TRANs) who have been working for almost a decade to have gender issues included in the bi-regional agreements.

The structure of this chapter is as follows. First, we analyse the historical relationship between the two regions and how gender has been addressed. Second, we have a look at the different efforts in regional blocs to institutionalise the issue of gender. Third, we reconstruct the role of parliamentary, civil society actors and networks that try to push for the integration of gender issues in the agenda. Finally, we draw some conclusions about the actors and norms dynamics related to the inclusion of gender in the inter-regional relations between the EU and CELAC.

2. INTER-REGIONALISM AND RELATIONS BETWEEN EUROPE AND LATIN AMERICA

2.1. INTEGRATION OF GENDER-EQUALITY PRINCIPLES

2.1.1. OVERVIEW

The main institutionalised channel for the relations between Europe and Latin America has been the inter-regional dialogues and agreements between the European Communities (EC)/European Union (EU) and regional organisations in Latin America, such as the Southern Common Market (Mercosur), Andean Community (CAN), and more recently, the Community of Latin American and Caribbean Countries (CELAC). Inter-regional relations typically include three pillars: political dialogue, development co-operation and trade liberalisation. Often, parallel inter-parliamentary dialogues takes place (van der Vleuten and Ribeiro Hoffmann, 2010).

Already during the Cold War, the EC developed so-called dialogue partnerships with other regional groupings, creating a hub-and-spokes system gravitating around the EC. Hardacre and Smith (2009) argue that the EU has systematically supported regional integration and simultaneously promoted inter-regionalism as key components of its foreign policy strategy. The Commission acted as the main sponsor of regional integration and inter-regionalism in the world, using strategy papers and trade and development policies as key instruments. The Council has been less consistent in its support to inter-regionalism, and, especially since the crisis of 2008, has favoured an economic policy that promotes the conclusion of bilateral free trade agreements with key partners as a growth strategy. The Council's policy has therefore moved the EU away from inter-regionalism, promoting instead special partnerships with individual countries, viewed as instrumental in increasing exports. The role of the European Parliament (EP) is not easy to assess. Hardacre and Smith argue that the EP has not had a major influence over EU strategy vis-à-vis other regions, but other authors have shown that the role in inter-regional parliamentary dialogues is not to be dismissed (Costa and Dri, 2014). The EP and Latin American Parliamentary assemblies co-operate through the Euro-Latin American Parliamentary Assembly (EUROLAT) that was created in 2006. EUROLAT adopts and submits resolutions and recommendations to the various organisations, institutions and ministerial groups responsible for development of the bi-regional strategic level of relations.

The bi-regional relationship between the EU and Latin America was motivated by a number of factors. Despite the specificity of sub-regional organisations, these relations must be seen in the context of triangular relations with the US. For Latin American (sub)regional organisations such as Mercosur, balancing the US and the Free Trade Area of the Americas (FTAA) had been a main objective in the intensification of inter-regional relations with the EU in the 1990s. According to Roy (2012), one of the EU's main objectives for a strong bi-regional relationship with Latin America has historically been the expectation of spreading its model of integration as a base for economic and social progress and political reconciliation. The relation with Latin America is defined as a strategic partnership that traditionally deals with general themes and issues, such as trade and aid, but also new issues such as the environment, climate change and energy; science, research and technology; migration, employment and social affairs. In its Regional Strategy paper the EC defines the relation mainly in terms of economic and social development co-operation programmes. The EU is one of the largest donors in the region (3 billion euros between 2007-13).

Yet, more recently, the rather asymmetrical relationship with its emphasis on the EU's role in developing the region has started to change. This is due to a number of reasons. First, the EU's position has weakened, since it is facing a number of difficulties, like the Euro-crisis, its failed constitutional project, the 2004 enlargement, and one can add, the current economic crisis and waves of refugees, and the political polarisation between left and right extremism in most Member States. Second, the position of Latin America has strengthened because of economic growth in some Member States and a new self-awareness in many countries that drives new efforts of intra-regional co-operation such as Bolivarian Alliance for the Peoples of Our Americas (ALBA) and Union of South American Nations (UNASUR). Third, new partners, like China, have become important players in the region. CELAC therefore now situates itself differently in relation to the EU and according to some commentators this can be viewed both in the discourse and the results of the EU-CELAC Summit in Santiago in 2013 and the subsequent CELAC summit in Cuba in 2014. Yet, despite this new self-awareness CELAC has problems presenting itself as a solid bloc vis-à-vis the EU or the USA. There are strong and marked political and economic differences between the countries, and their approaches to foreign policy are varied (Roy, 2012).

2.1.2. GENDER ON THE BI-REGIONAL AGENDA

Before the creation of CELAC, the EU had since 1999 formal relations with LAC countries by means of the EU-LAC Summits. The meetings in this framework did not address gender in a systematic manner; we can only find some references to gender equality in the final declarations of the summits. But gender issues were not integrated in a consistent agenda.

As already mentioned, it was only with the Santiago Summit that gender became a relevant issue at the inter-regional agenda. The final Declaration and Action Plan (2013-2015) list gender as a priority in the bi-regional relations. The Santiago 2013 Declaration stated that the inclusion of a gender perspective within the EU-CELAC association "will strengthen gender equality, democracy and will foster fair and egalitarian societies" (Santiago Declaration, point 38). While gender concerns have been on the agenda in the bi-regional relationship between the EU and the Latin American and Carribean region, it so far occupied a rather marginal space and lacked precise instruments of implementation. The 2013 Santiago Declaration refers to gender in three paragraphs. While paragraph 17 calls for the commitment towards gender equality in order to ensure peoples' quality of life, in a similar (broad) framing as previous declarations, paragraph 19 recognises for the first time a relation between gender and investment, and paragraph 38 creates a bi-regional dialogue on gender issues. The Santiago Action Plan for 2013-2015 includes gender as one of its eight priorities and establishes a number of precise objectives and a joint work programme, which lists dialogue, co-operation activities, and expected results. The three focal points are i) political participation of women; ii) elimination of all forms of violence against women and girls, including sexual violence; and iii) economic empowerment of women and their participation in the world of work and in all decision-making processes.[2]

In order to understand why gender became a priority in the EU-LAC inter-regional relations, and to explore the role of different actors and dynamics in this agenda-setting we first look at the track record of gender equality norms and institutions in both the EU and Latin American regional organisations. The integration of gender equality issues has been both the result of national, regional and international strategies. The international level and the UN framework have been of particular relevance; in both regions the 1995 Beijing Summit resulted in the institutionalisation of a gender equality agenda. Despite the common UN level background, the in-

---

[2]   Available   at   http://www.eeas.europa.eu/la/summits/docs/2013_santiago_summit_
eu-celac_action_plan_en.pdf.

stitutionalisation process has evolved differently in both regions, as seen next.

2.2. GENDER IN THE EU AND LATIN AMERICAN REGIONAL ORGANISATIONS

2.2.1. THE EU AND GENDER

The EU gender regime includes both the formal legally binding norms, institutional actors, and expert networks as well as informal statements, declarations and practices reinforced by interactions at the numerous conferences and events organised by each presidency and by the major institutions of the EU (Woodward and van der Vleuten, 2013). The first thirty years of EU equality legislation was based on an agreement of the ILO on the principle of equal pay (van der Vleuten, 2007). It was only with the Treaty of Lisbon in 2007 that gender equality was incorporated among the core values of the EU (Article 2). As for the secondary law, directives are the strongest instruments as they may lead to sanctions by the European Court of Justice when Member States do not conform to EU law. In the domain of gender equality, however, directives have been used relatively sparsely and are all related to the labour market, with a particular focus on non-discrimination or equal treatment, addressing women as workers. It was only with the Treaty of Amsterdam (1997) that the EU gained powers to act on gender inequality beyond its connection to market integration as it widened the scope of EU anti-discrimination policy with Article 13, providing for "appropriate action to combat discrimination based on sex, racial or ethnic origin, religion or belief, disability, age or sexual orientation" (now TFEU Article 10) (Woodward and van der Vleuten, 2013).

According to Woodward and van der Vleuten (ibd.), gender equality issues are increasingly dealt with by soft law instruments such as recommendations and the Open Method of Coordination; this preference for soft measures is also reflected in the key policy document *The Strategy for Equality between Women and Men 2010-2015* (European Commission, 2010b), which includes the objective of making gender important in external actions. Still according to these authors, the EU also has a complex and sophisticated gender machinery, including specialised units, Advisory Committees and expert groups dedicated to gender topics in the various Commission services, the Committee on Women's Rights and Gender Equality

(FEMM) in the European Parliament, and the European Institute for Gender Equality (EIGE), established in 2007. At the informal level, the EU has developed connections with civil society, and since the mid-nineties transnational social actors such as the European Women's Lobby (EWL) have become key players. Woodward and van der Vleuten (ibd.) also call attention to the role of individuals who move among positions wearing the varying hats of feminist activist from the women's movement, elected official, civil servant and technocratic/academic experts. For example, Barbara Helfferich circulated from the EWL to the Commission carrying ideas and contacts from social movements with her (ibd.).

In 2010, the European Commission adopted a Women's Charter in which it presented its ambitions to export gender equality norms towards international partners, not only in development relations but also toward other regional organisations:

"Our ambition is not limited to the borders of the Union. Gender equality must be fully incorporated into our external policies too so as to foster the social and economic independence and advancement of women and men throughout the world... Reducing gender inequalities, tackling gender-based violence, and promoting women's rights are essential for developing sustainable democratic societies... We will promote and strengthen co-operation with international and regional organisations on advancing gender equality..." (European Commission, 2010a: 4-5).

Also, the European Commission claims that "Through all relevant policies under its external action, the EU can exercise significant influence in fostering gender equality and women's empowerment worldwide" (European Commission, 2010b: 28). Yet, studies on the role of the EU as an international normative leader in the diffusion of gender equality norms show that the EU does not promote a consistent set of norms, but it exports norms which may be mutually contradictory or promotes a norm which it undermines by its own behaviour (van der Vleuten and van Eerdewijk, 2014). Van der Vleuten and van Eerdewijk (ibid.) argue that the promotion of regional integration and market liberalisation norms might actually go against the promotion of gender justice and women's rights.

2.2.2. Latin American regionalism and gender

Historically, 'regionalism' in the Latin American context has two divergent meanings: one is intra-regional co-operation between countries in Central and South America and the Carribean and the other refers to inter-American or hemispheric co-operation involving the United States (Hurrell, 1992). Examples of the former are the Andean Pact/Community (CAN) (1969), the Latin American Integration Association (LAIA) (1980), Southern Common Market (Mercosur) (1991), Bolivarian Alliance for the Peoples of Our America (ALBA) (2004), UNASUR (2008) and CELAC. Inter-American co-operation has a longer tradition which commences with the Organisation of American States (OAS) (1948). The thirty-two countries that make up CELAC are also members of thirteen other systems of integration. Most of these regional constellations have paid little attention to gender since their main emphasis has been on international trade and economic co-operation. Out of the thirteen regional organisations, only six have created specialised organs to deal with gender topics (see table below).

Table 1: Gender equality institutions within (Latin) American regional organisations

ALBA	Committee of Female Ministers and Equal Opportunities
CAN	Andean Council of High Female Authorities and Equal Opportunities (CAAAMI)
CARICOM	Office for Women's Issues
MERCOSUR	Meeting of Female Ministers and Women's Highest Authorities (RMAAM)
OAS	Inter-American Women's Commission (CIM)
SICA	Council of Female Ministers of Central America and Dominican Republic (COMMCA)

Sources: de la Riva and Múnoz 2015

We discuss the work of the OAS and Mercosur in more detail next since these organisations have advanced further in the institutionalisation of gender. The other regional organisations, ALBA, CAN, CARICOM and SICA only established institutionalised spaces where national representatives on women and equal opportunities regularly meet. These bodies work to identify common issues and exchange information, but have not developed international norms so far.

2.2.3. OAS / CIM

The OAS has the longest history and strongest track record in relation to promoting gender equality issues. OAS is the oldest regional integration system in the world, successor of the old International Union of American Republics, created in 1890 and including all states on the American continent (de la Riva and Múnoz, 2015: 28). Within the OAS several units are particularly important for the promotion of women's rights: the human rights mechanisms and the Inter-American Commission of Women (Friedman, 2009). The Inter-American Commission on Human Rights (IACHR) and the Inter-American Court of Human Rights were established to supervise the actions of states and uphold the rights of individuals (ibid.). These judicial bodies have proven effective mechanisms to make states comply with international human rights treaties. The Inter-American Commission of Women of the OAS (Comisión Interamericana de Mujeres – CIM) is an autonomous organisation, made up of 33 delegates who are designated by the governments of the OAS Member States. It was established in 1928 in response to pressure from women's rights activists who sought to have the OAS's predecessor, the Pan American Conference, to promote women's suffrage. After its establishment in 1928 it played an important role in pressing national governments to extend female suffrage. The CIM meets every two years and provides technical and advisory support to the OAS Member States on the implementation of key conventions and other agreements regarding women's rights in the region. Despite its political nature, limited mandate and small staff, CIM has been able to set its own agenda and draft a number of Inter-American Conventions on women's rights (Meyer, 1999; Friedman, 2009). One of its major accomplishments has been the development of the most progressive international norm on violence. In 1994, the OAS General Assembly adopted the Inter-American Convention on the Prevention, Punishment, and Eradication of Violence Against Women that established an international obligation for states to prevent, investigate and punish violence against women. As different authors (Friedman, 2009; Hawkins and Hume, 2002; Keck and Sikkink, 1998) argue, this is all the more remarkable considering the institutional weakness of the OAS. National activists have successfully used the judicial bodies of the OAS to make their governments comply with the Convention (Friedman, 2009; Roggeband, 2014). Since 2000 CIM organises meetings between female ministers or other high level authorities responsible for the policies on women in Member States. Currently, the priority areas set by these meetings are: (1) women's rights and gender violence; (2) women's substantive citizenship within democracy and governance; (3) citizenship and economic security of women; (4) citizen security from a gender perspective; and (5) gender mainstreaming of the OAS work (De la Riva and Múnoz 2015).

2.2.4.MERCOSUR

In 1998 Mercosur created the *Reunion Especializada de la Mujer* (REM – Specialised Meeting of Women), the first body in Mercosur that directly addressed gender matters in a broader domain than employment (Espino, 2008, Orsino, 2009). The REM was composed of government delegations that could be advised by regional women's organisations. In 2011, the REM was replaced by the *Reunion de Ministras y Altas Autoridades del Mujer* (Meeting of Ministers and High Authorities – RMAAM) with REM's objectives and structures which implied an upgrade in the political level of the participants. The RMAAM consists of national delegations of government officials for women's affairs from each Mercosur (associated) Member State,[3] and its main functions are to assist and propose measures, policies and actions in gender matters. According to RMAAM internal regulations from 2005 (Title 7 of civil society participation, Article 8), regional civil society organisations which promote the defence of women's rights can participate as observers.[4] Its meetings take place at least twice a year, and its Pro-Tempore Presidency follows Mercosur's rotating Presidency. The preparation for the meetings is organised in *Mesas Tecnicas* (Technical Tables). Currently, there are two such 'Tables', one on gender-based violence (dealing with domestic violence and sexual exploitation), and the other on gender, labour and economic integration. REM / RMAAM can issue (non-mandatory) declarations and submit proposals for recommendations and decisions to the Common Market Council (CMC) via the Common Market Group (CMG). The CMC is Mercosur's main legislative body and composed of the national Ministers of Foreign Affairs and Eco-

---

[3] Some countries have a Minister or State-Secretary for Women's Affairs. Also, the top level of national women's policy machineries participates in RMAAM. For a list of participants at the II RMAAM, see http://www.mercosurmujeres.org/userfiles/file/rmaam_2012_2/IIRMAAM_ANEXO1_LISTA_PARTICIPANTES.pdf.

[4] The organisations which have been accredited so far are *Foro de Mujeres del Mercosur*, *Articulación Feminista Marcosur*, Comité de América Latina y el Caribe para la Defensa de los Derechos de la Mujer (CLADEM), *Comisión de Mujeres de la Coordinadora de Centrales Sindicales del Cono Sur* and *Red Internacional de Género y Comercio* (see http://www.mercosurmujeres.org/es/sociedadcivil-li7).

nomy; it issues mandatory decisions and non-mandatory recommendations. The CMG is an executive organ, composed of officials from the Ministries of Foreign Affairs and Economy and the Central Bank, and issues mandatory resolutions (Ribeiro Hoffmann, 2014).

Mercosur has gradually started to adopt gender norms in the late 1990s, and there has been an increase in norm development since 2006. A number of resolutions were approved in 2000, in line with the Beijing Platform for Action; Resolution 79 calls upon Member States to conduct studies and approve special laws on domestic violence, and Resolution 84 requires Mercosur institutions to incorporate a gender perspective in all its activities which is a breakthrough achievement (Ribeiro Hoffmann 2014). Decision 14 from 2012 required RMAAM to elaborate a policy of gender equality, including a gender perspective in the agenda of the different bodies of Mercosur institutional structure. Several recommendations dealt with topics such as the participation of women in the economy, participation of women in politics, family agriculture, violence and peacekeeping operations, showing how the concern with gender evolved from its initially narrow labour related approach. Gender violence, in particular, has become a key new gender issue for Mercosur in the last years. Mercosur has also become a pro-active organisation trying to act as a norm entrepreneur as evidenced by the Recommendation 10 from 2012 which proposed to gender mainstream all Mercosur agreements with third parties (Ribeiro Hoffmann, 2014). In 2013 the MERCOSUR Council has approved the Directive of the Policies for Gender Equality in MERCOSUR, designed by RMAAM, which seeks to promote the "design, creation, implementation, monitoring and evaluation of the policies, regulations, strategies, programmes, action plans as well as resource management and budget design" for the gender mainstreaming in two distinct dimensions: the institutional and the regional policy dimension"[5] (de la Riva and Múnoz, 2015: 29).

As for CELAC, it does not have any specialised organ to deal with gender matters. CELAC is in general slim on permanent institutions when compared with other regional institutions in the Americas. It was created in 2011 with the main objective of advancing political dialogue among Latin American and the Caribbean countries, excluding the US and Canada. It has

---

[5]   Available   at: http://www.mercosurmujeres.org/userfiles/file/files/RMAAM_2013_2/
Documento\%20Directrices\%20Aprobado\%20VI\%20RMAAM_ES.pdf.

actually been often promoted as an alternative to the OAS. CELAC incorporated the legacy of the Rio Group, an institution created in 1986 which does not have permanent bodies either, but which has played an important role in promoting multilateral co-operation in Latin America.[6] During the Summits joint objectives are issued in the form of Declarations and Plans of Action, co-operation relies mainly on co-ordination of policies among Member States. Before the EU-CELAC summit in 2013, gender equality or women's issues were not relevant to the organisation. During the II CELAC Summit held in Havana, Cuba, January of 2014, a Special Declaration on the Promotion of Equality and Empowerment of Women in the New Post-2015 Development Agenda was formulated.[7] An emphasis was made on the need for continuous work on the three working areas of the SAP and the importance of gender perspectives as a universal element in all actions.

2.2.5. CONCLUSIONS

This overview of the integration of gender equality principles in the different regional organisation in Europe and Latin America shows that there are many differences in the institutionalisation of gender equality issues in both regions. The EU has the most elaborate gender regime, whereas in Latin America the level of institutionalisation is diverse and uneven. Some regional organisations like the OAS and Mercosur have created mechanisms to promote gender issues and developed some strong norms on gender equality as well.

This leads to the important question of norm promotion and to what extent the EU or Latin American organisations are better situated to act as norm promoters. In its relations with Latin America and Carribean countries and regional organisations, the EU is the materially and institutionally dominant power. Also, in contrast to the Latin American regional organisations the EU explicitly aims to promote gender equality in its external relations (although Mercosur has also included norms in this regard more recently). Does that give it an automatic position as powerful norm pro-

---

6   The Rio Group was itself created after the successful experience of the Contadora Group which presented an alternative solution from the US to the crisis in Central America during the Cold War. The Rio Group also had bi-regional relations with the EC at the time (Saraiva, 1996).

7   Special Declaration on the Promotion of Equality and Empowerment of Women, available at http://ECLAC.cubaminrex.cu/sites/default/files/ficheros/doc_3_7_declaracion_esp__sobre_genero_espanol.pdf.

moter? Existing studies show that the track record of the EU in exporting gender equality to Latin America is weak. The EU has not acted as an active norm promoter in its development co-operation policies (Debusscher, 2012) nor in its trade policies (Ribeiro Hoffman, 2014) with Latin America. At the inter-regional level, the EU is not an active promoter of gender-equality norms in a transformative way, beyond some discursive norm promotion (van der Vleuten *et al.*, 2014). It is therefore hard to conceive of the EU as a normative power on gender equality.

If neither EU nor CELAC can be clearly identified as gender equality norm promotors, which actors or factors may account for the formulation of a joint gender agenda at the Santiago summit? In the next section, we have a look at the role of agenda-setters within the framework of bi-regional relations. We point to the important agenda-setting role of inter-regional networks consisting of civil society actors and parliamentary actors (regional parliaments and EUROLAT).

3.SPACES FOR AGENDA-SETTING: CIVIL SOCIETY FORA AND EUROLAT

3.1.BACKGROUND

Rather than regional organisations we argue that trans-regional advocacy networks (TRANs) are important promoters of gender equality issues in the bi-regional agenda. Such networks may emerge to address issues that are important for both regions. Transnational networks play a central role both in processes of international agenda-setting and the promotion of new norms (Finnemore, 1996; Keck and Sikkink, 1998). Transnational actors act as norm entrepreneurs or brokers that actively propagate their ideas and promote norm change. TRANs are networks consisting of differently situated actors with overlapping national, (sub)regional and cross-regional positions that through changing patterns of coalition building seek the benefits of multilevel governance. The flexible, multilevel character of such networks affects their composition and shape. TRANs build new links among actors in civil societies, states, and regional organisations, and by doing so they multiply the channels of access to influence the bi-regional agenda and agreements. NGOs and civil society organisations play a key role in such networks, often acting as initiators and key promotors.

The emergence of TRANs in bi-regional relation between the EU and CELAC can be explained by the limited access and position that civil society organisations have had in bi-regional co-operation. Formal channels to get access to bi-regional negotiations are lacking. The EU claims to envision an important role for civil society in inter-regional relations and has been promoting a "European social model, which combines free market aspects with social dialogue and public participation through civil society, and [should be] of a more ambitious scope than simple trade agreements" (Economic and Social Council, 2002). Yet, in practice the access and involvement of civil society actors in inter-regional negotiations has been uneven (Grugel, 2002: 618). Business groups and development NGOs that deliver European aid get far more access to negotiations compared to other civil society organisations (ibid.). Since 2000, regular civil society consultations are organised by the European Economic and Social Committee.[8] Grugel (2002: 619) notes, however, that these meetings were "more ceremonial than substantive" and it is not clear where the recommendations of the Civil Society Forum go and what status they have (ibid.).

Latin America regional institutions do not have a better track record of including civil society and are mostly lacking formal mechanisms of representation and inclusion. The second CELAC summit in Cuba did not include any interaction with civil society. The EU- CELAC Summit in Santiago according to civil society actors marked a historic step forwards. For the first time, representatives of civil society networks[9] were received by foreign ministers and senior officials from Latin America and the Caribbean and Europe to present the conclusions and recommendations of the VI Euro-Latin Caribbean civil society Forum "For a change of course" that was held in September 2012.[10] Yet, civil society networks indicated that

---

[8] 7th Meeting of European Union-Latin American civil society organisation was held in Santiago de Chile, 4-6 December 2012.

[9] MESA, the coalition of national NGO associations and regional networks in Latin America and the Caribbean, and the European NGO Confederation, Concord, were represented at the Summit by Laura Becerra of the Association of Mexican Civil organisations ADOC, Miguel Santibanez, president of the Chilean NGOs Association ACCION, and Carlos Cabo of Concord Europe.

[10] Declaration of Civil society organisations, available at http://www.ong-ngo.org/en/ declaration-vi-european-latin-american-caribbean-forum-of-civil-society-organisation s-2012-santiago/. Recommendation 3.6 was to "take integrated measures in a plan of action to ensure women's empowerment, gender equality and the eradication of all

after the summit "regressive steps were perceived due to the minimal insti-
tutionalized and unpredictable space for open dialogue with civil society".[11]

To increase their leverage, civil society organisations have targeted
the parliamentary arenas in both regions. The establishment of the inter-
parliamentary body EUROLAT in 2006[12] provided civil society organisations with an important new ally to influence the agenda of bi-regional co-
operation between the EU and Latin America. EUROLAT was set up as a
body of parliamentary consultation, supervision and monitoring of the Strategic Partnership between the two regions.[13] Stavidris and Ajenjo (2010: 12)
point to an important paradox concerning EUROLAT:

"The EU [...] develops its relations with Latin America mainly through the executive domain, leaving a very limited decision making role to its parliamentary
dimension, [...] while the presidential regimes in Latin America have taken a parliamentary bias in their respective regional and sub-regional integration efforts".

Also, the status of EUROLAT as a representative body is dubious. EURO-
LAT has 75 members from both regions, yet does not take into account
the different parliamentary structures that exist in Latin America, i.e. whether representatives are directly elected or appointed.[14] This, according to
Stavidris and Ajenjo, creates a clear deficit for the citizens involved in the
process (ibid.). The EUROLAT mandate is limited. It only enjoys advisory and consultation status. Despite these limited powers, Roy claims that

---

forms of violence against women, including femicide. This must comply strictly with
the Convention on the Elimination of All Forms of Discrimination against Women
(CEDAW), the Convention on the Prevention, Punishment and Eradication of Violence
against Women (Convention of Belem do Para) and the European Convention for
Prevention and Combating of Violence against Women".

11   See www.oidhaco.org/uploaded/content/article/1808734488.pdf.
12   Yet, prior to setting up EUROLAT there were 17 biannual inter-parliamentary conferences between the EP and the PARLATINO, the PARLANDINO, the PARLACEN,
and the then PARLASUR parliamentary committee (Stavidris and Ajenjo, 2010: 11).
13   According to Stavidris and Ajenjo (2010: 17), the creation of EUROLAT is representative of a "growing parliamentarization of international relations".
14   The 75 European members are all MEP, and thus all directly elected, whereas the 75
Latin American members are members of the Parlacen (elected), Mercosur (directly
elected since 2011) Parlandino, Parlatino (appointed), plus two Committees for the two
countries – Chile and Mexico – that do not currently belong to any of those Latin American regional processes.

EUROLAT is quite successful in its effort to develop an agenda for the EU-Latin American relations and that its resolutions (2012: 6). The limited formal access and role of civil society and parliamentary actors in the bi-regional co-operation provides an explanation for the emergence of co-operation between both arenas and the development of TRANs. As we will elaborate below, we found evidence of that, by joining forces, civil society actors and members of EUROLAT have successfully created vehicles of informal power to advance gender equality issues in the bi-regional space. In the next paragraph we describe the emergence and work of two TRANs focusing on gender issues that emerged within the framework of EU-LAC relations. The first has been the single-issue network around the issue of feminicide that started in 2006 and was initiated and led by European NGOs[15] in co-operation with the Greens/EFA group within the European Parliament. A second network is called the Euro-Latin American Forum for Women. This is a hybrid network consisting of civil society actors, academics, politicians, and members of the European Parliament and Latin American parliamentary assemblies. These two advocacy networks followed parallel paths, with little coordination and co-operation between them. We will examine how the two initiatives contributed to the 2013 success and point to some "critical junctures" that led up to political success.

3.2. THE FEMINICIDE NETWORK

The feminicide campaign was initiated and led by European NGOs and the European Parliament, although it tried to engage and recognise the work of Latin American activists that had mobilised on the issue long before. In 2006, the Heinrich Böll Foundation, an in dependent German NGO affiliated with the Green Party in Germany, started a campaign to make the problem of feminicide visible and to lobby for better international legislation and policies. Between 2006 and 2014, the network organised seven inter-

---

[15]   Mostly European NGOs led by the Heinrich Böll Foundation, and co-promoted by Copenhagen Initiative for Central America (CIFCA), Grupo Sur, the Asociación Latinoamericana de Organizaciones de Promoción al Desarrollo (ALOP) have been essential in this work. Other organisations that co-hosted or co-organised the meetings of the networks were the Latin–American organisations CLADEM, CEFEMINA, LIMPAL, Corporación Humanas, Red Chilena contra la violencia contra mujeres, Oficina Internacional de los Derechos Humanos Acción Colombia (OIDHACO), Amnesty International, Fédération internationale des ligues des droits de l'homme (FIDH) and IACHR.

national conferences on feminicide in the capitals where the EU-(CE)LAC Summits were taking place. These meetings served as a transnational space to bring together women rights activists, civil society representatives, academics and politicians from Europa and Latin America. Also, other activities such as publications, strategy meetings, debates and other advocacy activities were organised on a regular basis. In 2006, the network managed to get some attention for the issue of feminicide during the 4th Summit of EU-ALC Heads of State in Vienna. Andrea Medina Rosas, representative of the Latin American and Caribbean Committee for the Defense of Women's Human Rights (CLADEM) in Mexico, gave her report at the summit's civil society forum and talked to the the the hosting Austrian Minister of Foreign Affairs, Ursula Plassnik.[16] Within the EP a left-wing coalition started to lobby for a Resolution. MEP Romeva drafted a report for a Resolution on feminicide that proposed to make the issue of violence against women and in particular feminicide a priority on the bi-laterial and bi-regional agenda with Latin America. The report is the first official EU document using the concept of feminicide, which is framed as a social phenomenon happening especially in the Latin American context – in particular Mexico and Central America. Also, it positions the EU as a norm promotor and problem solver. In October 2007, the EP adopted a Resolution on feminicide. A next step for the transnational feminicide network was to take the issue to the Euro-Latin American Parliamentary Assembly (EUROLAT). During the EURO-LAT meeting in Lima (2008) the issue was integrated in the 2008 resolution on Poverty and Social Exclusion that contains a specific paragraph on feminicide (nr. 18) that:

"Calls upon the governments of the European Union, Latin America and the Caribbean to firmly condemn violence against women and feminicide as an extreme expression of discrimination against women and in the context of their strategic partnership to support (with adequate financial and technical resources) preventive and protective policies relating to violence against women, such as the establishment or the enhancement of training and awareness programmes concerned with gender issues; to increase the budget of the bodies responsible for investigating the murders, to establish effective systems for protecting witnesses, victims and their families, and to make judicial bodies, security units and public prosecutors better able to pursue and punish the culprits; also calls for the promotion of greater coordination amongst institutions in these areas at all levels of government".

---

[16]   See www.gwi-boell.de/en/2011/02/24/feminicide.

The final declaration of the EU-Latin America and Caribbean (LAC) Summit held in Madrid in May 2010 for the first time mentioned the issue of violence against women and condemned "all kind of gender-based violence and recognise the need to take every necessary measure to prevent and eradicate it." The almost simultaneous statement of High Representative for Foreign Affairs and Security Policy Catherine Ashton suggests that she acted as a key promotor of this issue within the bi-regional agreement. In her declaration Ashton expressed the EU's concern about the "increasing number of homicides against women and girls that take place in some contexts of mass violence and structural discrimination". Yet, despite this support, the issue of gender-based violence was not integrated into the EU-LAC Action Plan 2010 – 2012 and therefore no action was taken during the period. During subsequent EUROLAT meetings, the network lobbied for a EUROLAT resolution on feminicide. The meeting held in Montevideo from the 17th to the 19th of May 2011 was crucial for civil society networks in both Europe and Latin America, since it opened room for exchange. The civil society networks and organisations made a series of recommendations on how to improve civil society participation. In particular, they stressed the importance of the presence of EUROLAT members in sessions with the civil society and the implementation of an inclusive monitoring mechanism of the dialogue and initiatives arising therefrom. The establishment of a permanent contact group of civil society organisations from both regions was also recommended. Subsequently, during the fourth meeting with the commissions in Brussels (21-23 November 2011), the importance of institutionalising the participation of civil society was highlighted. In 2012, at the EUROLAT Assembly held in Cadiz, representatives of the civil society were able to intervene during the meetings of the commissions and raise the issue of feminicide. As a result of this statement the Social Affairs Committee expressed its support for a resolution on feminicide. The EUROLAT meeting held in July 2012 in Vilnius, Lithuania was then used to continue this lobby for a EUROLAT resolution of feminicide.

Yet, before EUROLAT made its decision to adopt a resolution, things started to move at a higher level. During the EU – CELAC Summit held in Chile in January 2013, Argentina[17] successfully pushed for the inclusion of a strong gender paragraph the EU-CELAC Action Plan 2013 – 2015.

---

[17]   See www.mrecic.gov.ar/es/secretar\%C3\%Ada-de-relaciones-exteriores-1.

This chapter has created a bi-regional dialogue on the elimination of all forms of violence against women as one of its three focal points. In order to achieve this goal, the Action Plan proposes to "Promote actions to combat and eliminate all forms of violence against women and girls, through activities such as publishing gender educational programmes and manuals and standardising protocols of investigation to prosecute and punish the perpetrators, among other actions". As expected results the Action Plan mentions the organisation of a "Bi-regional seminar for the exchange of experiences on gender-based violence, to share best practices and the most effective measures to prevent and combat it." And to "Promote concrete measures for the investigation of gender based killing". The Action Plan states that "There should also be created a bi-regional intergovernmental working group to define shared objectives about the three gender-related focal points." Based on these recommendations, two members of the Euro-Latin American Parliamentary Assembly (EUROLAT), Gloria Flores, an Andean Parliamentarian and MEP Raül Romeva i Rueda started the process for the elaboration of the Resolution on feminicide in the EU and Latin America which was approved by parliamentarians during the EUROLAT session held in Athens in March 2014. This reconstruction shows that the long-term lobbying effort of the trans-regional feminicide network made incremental progress to get the issue of violence against women on the bi-regional agenda.

3.3. The Euro-Latin American Forum for Women

Another transnational identity-based advocacy network emerged in 2011. The Euro-Latin American Forum for Women (from here referred to as the Women's Forum), like the feminicide network, also uses the EUROLAT as its central platform. The Women's Forum was initiated in 2010 by an Italian NGO called Cefial. While the Women's Forum neither gained an official status nor receives any structural funding, it managed to get the status of an informal caucus within EUROLAT and is co-presided by EUROLAT members. Since the presentation of the Forum by initiator Isabel Recavarren,[18] during a EUROLAT assembly held in Seville (2010), the Forum managed to be integrated on a structural basis in the agenda of the bi-annual EU-

---

[18]   Recavarren is a Peruvian scholar directing the Milan-based CEFIAL. CEFIAL is a study center that presents itself as specialist in bi-regional relations between the EU and Latin America.

ROLAT plenary gatherings.[19] The Women's Forum was declared an extra-parliamentary mechanism of the EUROLATs Social Committee during the EUROLAT gathering in Hamburg in May 2012. This points to a strong sponsorship of the initiative within EUROLAT. While EUROLAT is its cen-tral focus, the Women's Forum also organises sessions outside this frame-work to stimulate co-operation and exchange between Latin American and European politicians, gender experts and civil society actors. The Forum mainly brings together Latin American women and MEPs from countries that have strong relationships with Latin America due to historical reasons or because of large migration from Latin Americans to those countries. Its focus and agenda concentrates on issues of political and economic partici-pation and migration issues.

When Recaverren presented the idea of a Forum during the meeting of the Committee of Social Affairs at the EUROLAT meeting in Seville in May 2010, her initiative was applauded and adopted by PARLACEN member Xanthis Suarez who explained that a women's caucus (bloque de mujeres parliamentarias) had just been established within PARLACEN and that within the Central American region many other similar political and economic women's networks were doing successful advocacy work. According to her, in many existing political processes, including the EURO-LAT meetings, men continued to be "the kings of the party" (los reyes de la fiesta) and therefore a women's initiative was urgently needed.[20] Another supporter of the initiative was Edite Estrella, Socialist member of the EP, who had organised the intervention of Recavarren. After this presentation in Milan, the initiative rapidly developed and a directing committee was formed that consisted of members of the European and Latin American parliaments, women working in different ministries in both continents and women representing civil society organisations. During the bi-annual EUROLAT meetings the Forum as an extra-parliamnetary mechanism managed to channel and voice civil society demands to EUROLAT.

The Women's Forum successfully influenced the agendas and resolutions of EUROLAT. During its first participation in Montevideo in May 2011, EUROLAT adopted a resolution on the economic participation of women.

---

[19] EUROLAT gathers twice a year one meeting in Europe and one in Latin America.
[20] The presentation and discussion afterwards can be found at www.facebook.com/video/ video.php?v=126904503998329\&ref=mf.

During subsequent EUROLAT meetings it pushed issues of political participation, female entrepreneurship, the feminization of migration and violence against women. The recognition of the Forum as extra-parliamentary mechanism of the EUROLAT Social Committee makes clear that the Forum rapidly gained a voice as agenda-setter for the EUROLAT. The overlapping political positions of the Forum's Latin American members who are not only a member of the bi-regional parliamentary assembly, but also hold influential positions at the national level, gives the Forum extra possibilities to influence the agenda through multilevel lobbying efforts.

While the trajectory of the Forum is too short to make a good evaluation of its work and success, it is important to note that it managed to mobilise highly positioned professional women with a clear interest in women's issues. Also it effectively channelled demands and agenda points to EUROLAT and gained leverage in both the interparliamentary and extraparliamentary arena. As it intersects with and builds upon other cross-party collaborations between women's representatives (in national and (sub) regional caucuses) it has a high potential for doing multi-level lobbying.

3.4. COMPARING THE TWO NETWORKS AND THE WAY AHEAD

The table below compares some central features of the networks. First, there is an important difference in its central focus: whereas the feminicide campaign lobbied on a single issue, the Women's Forum sought to engender the agenda of the bi-regional relations and is still developing its agenda which is potentially open to new input of actors that connect to the Forum. Yet this agenda-setting process is not at all clear due to the hybrid and non-formalised structure of the Forum.

The comparison makes clear that the Women's Forum is better equipped and positioned to potentially influence the bi-regional agenda, in particular in view that it seeks to connect to and integrate women in powerful political and economic positions. Also, it is a multi-issue network that has extended agenda considerably in its short period of existence. Yet, the initiative is still too recent to properly assess its effectiveness. "Feminicide" has been a single issue campaign that has been successful to get the issue on the bi-regional agenda, but that may resolve in the near future if no new issues appear on the agenda. The inclusion of the issue of feminicide and the gender paragraph in the EU-CELAC action plan 2013-2015 are an important breakthrough for both advocacy networks. Even if no strong measures have been taken, symbolically, the recognition of gender as a central issue on the bi-regional agenda creates an important stepping stone for furthering the agenda.

Table 2: Networks active in EU-CELAC relations in comparison

Feminide Campaign	Foro Euro-Latinoamericano de la Mujer
Single issue network	Multi-issue
Principal Actors: NGOs and MEPs (initial connection: Heinrich Böll-EP Greens)	Hybrid model: civil society, academics, politicians, members of EP and Latin American Parliaments
Principal platform of mobilisation: EP and more recent EUROLAT)	Structural position at EUROLAT meetings
Mainly EU oriented	Bi-regional
Main strategy: pushing from EU	Main strategy: multi-level pushing (from below and above)

Source: Elaborated by the authors

4. CONCLUSION

This chapter tried to understand the processes that led to gender becoming a priority in the Declaration and Action Plan for the EU-CELAC Summit in 2013. It investigated the role of actors as advanced in theories about international co-operation, norm diffusion, social movements and feminist approaches, namely, interests of these regional organisations, presence of women in top positions of Member States, and pressure from civil society and transnational advocacy networks. We found evidence pointing to the relevance of the latter, although further empirical analysis could be pursued in order to trace these processes in more detail.

By looking at the gender agenda and the institutionalisation of gender in the EU and CELAC we found that these organisations did not act as norm promoters. The EU has a strong gender regime, and given its desire to promote its own norms abroad, it would be expected to play a major role. However, this was not the case; based on secondary literature, we showed that the EU has not promoted gender norms in its external relations with Latin America. CELAC has a very weak gender regime; its Member States belong to other regional organisations in Latin America which contain a gender agenda but except for the OAS and Mercosur, not too much was done in this area. Mercosur has increased its gender regime, and issued norms showing its willingness to mainstream gender in its trade agreements with third parties, but these are only some of the CELAC Member States. The OAS has a strong human rights regime, including gender matters such as the Inter-American Convention on the Prevention, Punishment and Eradication of Violence Against Women from 1994, but does not have a direct role in the EU-CELAC relations. Actually, CELAC has been created partially as an alternative to the OAS.

The agenda of EU inter-regional relations, including CELAC, is traditionally designed by the EU Commission, but we found evidence that in the case of gender issues the Euro-Latin American Parliamentary Assembly (EUROLAT), established in 2006, has been particularly active. It has both acted directly in favour of the inclusion of gender in the inter-regional agenda, and indirectly, by offering a space for transnational civil society actors and transnational advocacy networks to interact. Two strong trans-regional advocacy networks focusing on gender issues emerged linking EUROLAT members, civil society organisations and national politicians. One of these TRANs was established on the issue of feminicide. While initiated and dominated by European activists and politicians, it has used the bi-regional space to successfully advance this issue. It has been highly successful to push for Resolutions. Both the European Parliament and EUROLAT adopted a resolution on feminicide. The issue was also adopted as part of the 2013 Santiago Action Plan. Since the network successfully managed to include the issue in the bi-regional agenda, we expect this TRAN to demobilise and decline. Another network that emerged more recently is the Euro-Latin American Women's Forum, which has a wider scope and managed to establish a broad women's network that integrates actors active in civil society, national and international politics, business and academia. It allows women to co-operate across geographical and party lines, making it a potentially strong force. It managed to gain a structural, albeit informal inclusion in the EUROLAT meetings and to unfold a broad agenda. We therefore expect this network to have a continuing presence and influence in the bi-regional negotiations and agreements. Both networks used EUROLAT as a key platform to achieve concrete results at the bi-regional summits.

Our preliminary findings thus suggest that contrary to the expectation that the EU would be the main driver behind the inclusion of gender in the inter-regional agenda with CELAC in 2013, transnational advocacy networks have been key agents in channelling demands and agenda points to EUROLAT, and finally to the final Declaration and Action Plan approved in Santiago. Further research would be necessary to explore other factors and actors in depth, but we have not found strong evidence for alternative explanations. The fact that EU-CELAC relations do not include trade might have facilitated the prioritisation of gender to the extent that traditional opposition from business lobbies to gender mainstreaming in bi-regional agreements was not present.

REFERENCES

Alvarez, Sonia (2000). *Translating the Global Effects of Transnational Organizing on Local Feminist Discourses and Practices in Latin America*. Meridians 1: 1, 29-67.

Angulo, Gloria and Freres, Christian (2006). *Gender Equality and EU Development Policy towards Latin America, in: Lister, Majorie and Carbone, Maurizio (eds.), New Pathways in International Development: Gender and Civil Society in EU Policy*, Aldershot: Ashgate, 45-58.

Costa, Olivier and Dri, Clarissa (2014). *How does the European Parliament Contribute to the Construction of the EU's Inter-regional Dialogue?* in: Baert, Francis, Scaramagli, Tiziana and Söderbaum, Fredrik (eds.) *Intersecting Interregionalism*. Springer.

Dahlerup, Drude and Freidenvall, Lenita (2011). *Electoral Gender Quota Systems and their Implementation in Europe.* Brussel: European Parliament.

De la Riva, Marta Carbalo and Múnoz, Enara E. (2015). *The Issue of Gender Relations between the EU and LAC: State of the Art and Opportunities for Biregional Co-operation*. EU-LAC Foundation.

Debusscher, Petra (2012). *Gender Mainstreaming in European Union Development Policy toward Latin America: Transforming Gender Relations or Confirming Hierarchies?* in: Latin American Perspectives, 39: 6, 181-197.

Espino, Alma (2008). *Impacting Mercosur's Gender Policies: Experiences, Lessons Learned and Ongoing Work of Civil Society in Latin America*, Paper presented at the Montreal International Forum 2008.

Finnemore, Martha (1996). *National Interests in International Society*. Ithaca: Cornell University Press.

Finnemore, Martha and Sikkink, Katherine (1998). *International Norm Dynamics and Political Change*, International organisation, 52: 4, 887-917.

Friedman, Elisabeth J. (2009). *Re(gion)alizing Women's Human Rights in Latin America*. Politics & Gender, 5: 349-375.

Hardacre, Alan and Smith, Michael (2009). *The EU and the Diplomacy of Complex Inter-regionalism* in: The Hague Journal of Diplomacy, Vol. 4, p. 167-188.

Htun, Mala (2015). *Inclusion without Representation: Gender Quotas and Ethnic Reservations in Latin America*. Cambridge University Press.

Hurrell, Andrew (1992). *Latin America in the New World Order: A Regional Bloc of the Americas?*, International Affairs, 68: 1, 121-139.

Keck, Margaret E. and Sikkink, Kathryn (1998). *Activists beyond Borders: Advocacy Networks in International Politics*. Ithaca: Cornell University Press.

Krook, Mona Lena (2004). *Gender Quotas as a Global Phenomenon: Actors and Strategies in Quota Adoption*, European Political Science, 3(3), 59-65.

Locher, Birgit (2012). *Gendering the EU Policy Process and Constructing the Gender Acquis*, in: Abels, Gabriele and Mushaben, Joyce Marie (eds.) (2012) *Gendering the European Union. New Approaches to Old Democratic Deficits*, Basingstoke: Palgrave Macmillan.

Macrae, Heather (2010). *The EU as a Gender Equal Polity: Myths and Realities*, Journal of Common Market Studies, 48(1), 155-174.

Meyer, Mary K. (1999). *Negotiating International Norms: The Inter-American Commission of Women and the Convention on Violence against Women*, in:Meyer, Mary K. and Prügl, E. (eds.), *Gender Politics in Global Governance*, New York: Rowman & Littlefield, 58–71.

Moghadam, Valentine M. (2005). *Globalizing Women: Transnational Feminist Networks*, Baltimore: John Hopkins University Press.

Montoya, Celeste (2009). *International Initiative and Domestic Reforms: European Union Efforts to Combat Violence against Women*. Politics & Gender, 5(03), 325-348.

Orsino, Susana (2009). Los Procesos de Institucionalización de los Mecanismos Regionales para la Equidad de Género: Reunión Especializada de la Mujer del Mercosur (REM), available at http://www.mercosurmujeres.org/userfiles/file/Orsino.pdf.

Ribeiro Hoffmann, Andrea (2014). *Gender in EU-Mercosur Relations*, in: van der Vleuten, Anna, van Eerdewijk, Anouka and Roggeband, Conny (eds.), *Gender Equality Norms in Regional Governance Transnational Dynamics in Europe, South America and Southern Africa*. Palgrave.

Risse, Thomas, Ropp, Stephen and Sikkink, Katherine (eds.) (1999). *The Power of Human Rights: International Norms and Domestic Change*, Cambridge: Cambridge University Press.

Roggeband, Conny (2014). *Latin American Advocacy on Violence Against Women and the OAS Convention*, in: van der Vleuten, Anna, van Eerdewijk, Anouka and Roggeband, Conny (eds.) *Gender Equality Norms in Regional Governance*

Transnational Dynamics in Europe, South America and Southern Africa. Palgrave.

Roy, Joaquin (2012). *European Union-Latin American Relations in a Turbulent Era*. Jean Monnet Robert/Schuman Paper Series. Vol 12.

Saraiva, Miriam (1996). *Politica Externa Europea: el caso de los Dialogos Grupo a Grupo com America Latina de 1984 a 1992*. Grupo Editor Latinoamericano.

Stavidris, Stelios and Ajenjo, Natalia (2010). EU-Latin American Parliamentary Relations: Some Preliminary Comments on the EUROLAT. Jean Monnet/Robert Schuman Paper Series. Vol 10:3.

van der Vleuten, Anna (2012). *Gendering the Institutions and Actors of the EU*, in: Abels, G. and Mushaben J. (eds.) (2012) *Gendering the European Union. New Approaches to Old Democratic Deficits*, Basingstoke: Palgrave Macmillan.

van der Vleuten, Anna and Ribeiro Hoffmann, Andrea (2013). *The Politics of Inter-regionalism: Relations between International Regional Organisations*, in: Reinalda B. (ed.) *Handbook of International Organisations*, Routledge.

van der Vleuten, Anna, van Eerdewijk, Anouka and Roggeband, Conny (eds.) (2014). *Gender Equality Norms in Regional Governance Transnational Dynamics in Europe, South America and Southern Africa*. Palgrave.

Woodward, Alison (2012). *From Equal Treatment to Gender Mainstreaming and Diversity Management*, in: Abels, G. and Mushaben, J. (eds.) (2012). *Gendering the European Union. New Approaches to Old Democratic Deficits*, Basingstoke: Palgrave Macmillan.

INDEX OF AUTHORS

Marina Blagojević Hughson, PhD, Research Professor at the Institute for Criminological and Sociological Research (IKSI) at the University of Belgrade, Serbia. She is a sociologist, social demographer, as well as gender scholar and international gender expert and activist.

Petra Debusscher Dr., postdoctoral fellow at the Research Group Citizenship, Equality & Diversity at the University of Antwerp's Department of Political Science. Her research and teaching intersects at the crossing point of European Union Studies, International Relations and Gender Studies.

Nikolina Kenig, Professor of psychology at "Ss. Cyril and Methodius University" in Skopje, Macedonia. Her teaching area includes methodology, psychometrics and gender-based violence and her research is focused mainly on ethnic and gender identity, violence prevention and multiculturalism.

Aida Orgocka, Research Associate and Course Director at York University, Toronto, Canada. She has worked in applied and academic settings in programme design, management and evaluation of initiatives that focus on education, gender, civil society, aid and migration in countries in Eastern Europe, Eastern Africa, South Asia.

Andrea Ribeiro Hoffmann, Professor of International Relations at the Catholic University of Rio de Janeiro. She has published in the areas of regional integration, comparative regionalism in Europe and Latin America, inter-regionalism, democracy and legitimacy at the global level.

Karolina Ristova-Aasterud, Associate Professor at the Faculty of Law "Iustinianus Primus," UKIM, in Skopje, Macedonia. Her teaching/research/publishing focus is in jurisprudence, political theory, feminism, EU enlargement, and EU's parliamentary dimension.

Conny Roggeband, Assistant Professor at the Department of Political Science, University of Amsterdam. She has written on the politicisation of gender mainstreaming and equality policies, social movements and transnational feminist networking based on research conducted in Europe and Latin America.

Anna van der Vleuten, Professor of Contesting Europeanization at the Institute for Management Research, Radboud University, the Netherlands. Her research interests include supranational policymaking in the field of gender equality, LGBT rights, comparative regionalism and inter-regionalism (EU, SADC, Mercosur).

Sam Wong, Assistant Professor at University College Roosevelt, the Netherlands. His research interests lie in gender, development and inequality. He has worked in South Asia (Bangladesh and India) and Sub-Saharan Africa (Ghana, Uganda and Nigeria).

Gender-Diskussion

Hella Ehlers; Claudia Kalisch; Gabriele Linke; Nadja Milewski; Beate Rudlof;
Heike Trappe (Hg.)
Migration – Geschlecht – Lebenswege
Sozial- und geisteswissenschaftliche Beiträge
Bd. 27, 2016, 280 S., 29,90 €, br., ISBN 978-3-643-13139-3

Thomas Kruessmann (Ed.)
Gender in Modern Central Asia
vol. 26, 2017, ca. 182 pp., ca. 29,90 €, br., ISBN-CH 978-3-643-90676-2

Susanne Kranz
Between Rhetoric and Activism
Marxism and Feminism in the Indian Women's Movements
Bd. 25, 2015, 360 S., 39,90 €, br., ISBN 978-3-643-90648-9

Małgorzata Jarecka-Żyluk; Oliver Holz (Eds.)
Gender and Education from Different Angles
Bd. 22, 2014, 280 S., 34,90 €, br., ISBN 978-3-643-90519-2

Elektra Paschali
Masculinities in Politics
On Gender Constructions within Political Youth Organizations in Greece
Bd. 21, 2014, 200 S., 29,90 €, br., ISBN 978-3-643-90460-7

Gottfried Lorenz
Töv, di schiet ik an
Beiträge zur Hamburger Schwulengeschichte
Bd. 20, 2013, 560 S., 49,90 €, br., ISBN 978-3-643-12173-8

Hella Ehlers; Gabriele Linke; Nadja Milewski; Beate Rudlof; Heike Trappe (Hg.)
Körper – Geschlecht – Wahrnehmung
Sozial- und geisteswissenschaftliche Beiträge zur Genderforschung
Bd. 19, 2013, 272 S., 29,90 €, br., ISBN 978-3-643-12154-7

René Levy; Eric D. Widmer
Gendered Life Courses Between Standardization and Individualization
A European approach applied to Switzerland
vol. 18, 2013, 400 pp., 31,90 €, br., ISBN-CH 978-3-643-80143-2

Kathleen Starck (Hg.)
Von Hexen, Politik und schönen Männern
Geschlecht in Wissenschaft, Kultur und Alltag. Landauer Vorlesungsreihe *Gender*
Bd. 17, 2013, 120 S., 19,90 €, br., ISBN 978-3-643-11942-1

Constance Gunderson
Human Trafficking
The Trafficking of Women in Northern Germany for the Purpose of Sexual Exploitation.
Systemic Overview of Community Based Responses and Challenges
Bd. 15, 2012, 280 S., 34,90 €, br., ISBN 978-3-643-90263-4

Gesa C. Teichert
Mode. Macht. Männer
Kulturwissenschaftliche Überlegungen zur bürgerlichen Herrenmode des 19. Jahrhunderts
Bd. 14, 2013, 296 S., 24,90 €, br., ISBN 978-3-643-11427-3

LIT Verlag Berlin – Münster – Wien – Zürich – London
Auslieferung Deutschland / Österreich / Schweiz: siehe Impressumsseite

Michael Groneberg; Christian Funke (Eds.)
Combatting Homophobia
Experiences and Analyses Pertinent to Education
Bd. 13, 2011, 272 S., 24,90 €, br., ISBN 978-3-643-11146-3

Hella Ehlers; Gabriele Linke; Beate Rudlof; Heike Trappe (Hg.)
Geschlecht – Generation – Alter(n)
Geistes- und sozialwissenschaftliche Perspektiven. Unter Mitarbeit von Marieke Bohne,
Jacqueline Hoffmann und Andrea Ressel
Bd. 12, 2011, 264 S., 19,90 €, br., ISBN 978-3-643-11072-5

Quirin J. Bauer
Potenzialentwicklung durch Gender Mainstreaming in der Organisation Hochschule
Zur Implementierung erfolgreicher Gender Mainstreaming Maßnahmen und Strategien
Bd. 11, 2010, 256 S., 29,90 €, br., ISBN 978-3-643-10614-8

Birol Mertol
Männlichkeitsbilder von Jungen mit türkischem Migrationshintergrund
Ansätze interkultureller Jugendarbeit
Bd. 9, 2008, 224 S., 24,90 €, br., ISBN 978-3-8258-1723-7

Hella Ehlers; Heike Kahlert; Gabriele Linke; Dorit Raffel; Beate Rudlof;
Heike Trappe (Hg.)
Geschlechterdifferenz – und kein Ende?
Sozial- und geisteswissenschaftliche Beiträge zur Genderforschung
Bd. 8, 2009, 296 S., 19,90 €, br., ISBN 978-3-8258-1647-6

Maria Buchmayr
Technologiefolgen – Nachhaltigkeit – Geschlechtergerechtigkeit?
Bd. 7, 2017, 208 S., 19,90 €, br., ISBN 978-3-8258-1632-2

Claudia Derichs; Susanne Kreitz-Sandberg (eds.)
Gender Dynamics and Globalisation
Perspectives on Japan within Asia
Bd. 6, 2007, 200 S., 29,90 €, br., ISBN 978-3-8258-9761-1

Maria Buchmayr; Julia Neissl (Hg.)
work-life-balance & Wissenschaft – ein Widerspruch?
Bd. 5, 2006, 152 S., 14,90 €, br., ISBN 3-8258-9525-4

Christine Künzel; Gaby Temme (Hg.)
Täterinnen und/oder Opfer?
Frauen in Gewaltstrukturen
Bd. 4, 2007, 272 S., 24,90 €, br., ISBN 3-8258-8968-8

R. Johanna Regnath; Mascha Riepl-Schmidt; Ute Scherb (Hg.)
Eroberung der Geschichte
Frauen und Tradition
Bd. 3, 2006, 304 S., 24,90 €, br., ISBN 3-8258-8953-x

Elisabeth Tuider (Hg.)
QuerVerbindungen
Interdisziplinäre Annäherungen an Geschlecht, Sexualität, Ethnizität
Bd. 2, 2008, 256 S., 17,90 €, br., ISBN 978-3-8258-8879-4

Marianne Heimbach-Steins; Bärbel Kerkhoff-Hader; Eleonore Ploil; Ines Weinrich (Hg.)
Strukturierung von Wissen und die symbolische Ordnung der Geschlechter
Gender-Tagung Bamberg 2003
Bd. 1, 2004, 200 S., 15,90 €, br., ISBN 3-8258-7251-3

LIT Verlag Berlin – Münster – Wien – Zürich – London
Auslieferung Deutschland / Österreich / Schweiz: siehe Impressumsseite